# Moving in Circles:
# Willa Muir's Writings

## Aileen Christianson

**WP**
BOOKS

First published by Word Power Books, 2007.
Word Power Books
43-45 West Nicolson Street,
Edinburgh, EH8 9DB.
Tel 0131 662 9112
www.word-power.co.uk

Designed by Leela Sooben.
Printed and bound in Scotland by Thomson Litho Ltd.

ISBN 978-0-9549185-5-2
British Library Cataloguing in Publication Data.
A catalogue record for this book is available from the British Library.

The publisher acknowledges subsidy from the Scottish Arts Council
towards the publication of this volume.

# Contents

# Acknowledgments

My grateful thanks are due to Carol Anderson, Esther Breitenbach, Ian Campbell, Katy Gordon, Catherine Kerrigan, Alison Lumsden, A. J. MacLean, Margery Palmer McCulloch, Lynne Stark and Liz Sutherland for their help in various indispensable ways; to Ron Turnbull, previously of *Edinburgh Review*, for originally commissioning the book; to Julie Lawson and the Scottish National Portrait Gallery; to the National Library of Scotland, Robin Smith and all the staff of the Issue Desk and the North Reading Room; to the University of St. Andrews Library Special Collections staff and Norman H. Reid; to the British Library; to the heads of department of English Literature, Sarah Carpenter, Cairns Craig and Randall Stevenson; to the English Literature Research Committee and the School of Literatures, Languages and Cultures, the University of Edinburgh, for teaching relief time and sabbatical leave to permit me to begin and complete writing the book; to the students in my Scottish Women's Fiction (20th century) course over the last nine years who have seen my ideas on Willa Muir develop and have contributed to them with their discussions; and to Elaine Henry and Word Power Books for publishing the book and to Leela Sooben for typesetting the book into its final form.

Finally, particular and very grateful thanks are due to Mrs Ethel Ross, for early permission to use Willa Muir material for the *Oxford Dictionary of National Biography* (ODNB) entries on Willa Muir and Edwin Muir, and for her kind letters about her memories of Willa and Edwin; and to her son Kenneth Ross for permission to publish material from Willa Muir's works, published and unpublished, in this book. My thanks are also due to Isobel Murray who began the process that led to this book by asking me to write the *ODNB* entry for Willa Muir in 1996; to Sue Innes whose work on *Women: An Inquiry* underpins my approach to that work in 'Polemics'; and, lastly and with particular gratitude, to Glenda Norquay who read early drafts of several of the chapters and Kathy Chamberlain who read late versions of all the chapters; both of them improved the book immeasurably with their suggestions.

# Illustrations

# CHAPMAN

## Scotland's Quality Literary Magazine

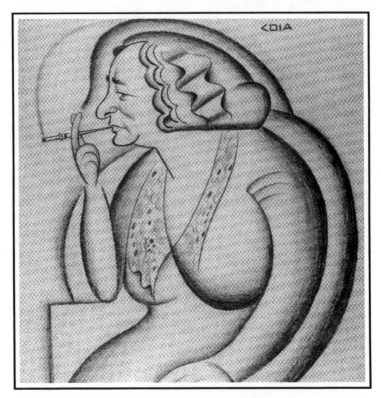

*Peerie Willa Muir*

**Robin Jenkins – Mairi NicGumaraid – John Dixon**

**Scotland's Music, Art, Poetry, Prose in review**

**No 71**                                    **Winter 1992–93**

Emilio Coia, *'Peerie Willa Muir'*.

# Introduction

Willa Muir places a critique of society's gender relations near the centre of all her writings; this critique caused much of the delighted response to her novels when they were rediscovered in the nineteen eighties and nineteen nineties. The two published novels were *Imagined Corners* and *Mrs Ritchie*; she also published some short non-fiction pieces, many translations (both with and without Edwin Muir), *Living with Ballads* (in fulfilment of a contract of Edwin's), and her memoir of Edwin, *Belonging*. Her work shows that bright young women of the early twentieth century had the same response to gender injustices as women in later decades, grounded as it is in a kind of female universal. Equally, of course, her feminism proved problematic during her life, particularly for those of her friends or acquaintances that felt overly challenged by her attitudes.

Often regarded as putting her own career on hold to support Edwin Muir as the writer / poet of the family with her own reputation sidelined by his pre-eminence, the dates of Muir's published work (mainly in the nineteen twenties and thirties and then the nineteen sixties after Edwin's death) seem to confirm this view. Yet she gives a clearly feminist analysis in *Belonging* of their respective household positions in relation to their writing space and she wrote all the time even when not publishing her own work: journals and letters, two further novels, an analysis of women's position, doggerel verse, poetry and short stories.[1] What her extensive unpublished papers show is the extent to which her whole adult life was spent in writing and how narrow the gap between her life and her 'imaginative' life is. Traces of this life recur in her published non-fiction writing, her early polemical essays, *Women: An Inquiry* (1925), and *Mrs Grundy in Scotland* (1936), and the later study, *Living with Ballads* (1965). Equally, strands of her preoccupations explored in these works also appear in her published fiction, *Imagined Corners* (1931) and *Mrs Ritchie* (1933). It is clear that she constantly recycles her own life. This study considers the complex inter-relationship between autobiography, fiction and non-fiction in all of Muir's work, published and unpublished, in the context of her own feminist analysis of her life. It explores her unpublished writing, taking them as a hidden constant behind her published works.

To an extent Muir's work can be (and is here) discussed chronologically. But the links between her works are so strong that it can also be discussed thematically, with aspects of her works from all points of her chronological life being subsumed into the discussion, as though all her times happened simultaneously. All of her works seem underpinned by a deep-seated scepticism about 'rationalism', 'enlightenment' (*Living with Ballads* 148) and Calvinism, as well as by an equal belief in feminism and the unconscious. It seems that the strength of these intellectual and emotional beliefs is such that, once formulated, she consistently re-explores them in whatever kind of work she is writing and whether intended for publication or not. The boundaries between genres seem porous, with all of the work consistently sustained by her discourses on feminism, Freudianism and anti-Calvinism.

This book on Willa Muir is a critical study of her work but it has also become both a biographical study and a cultural history of one woman's response to her surroundings. Johanna Alberti comments, when discussing the work and life relationship of Ray Strachey that, as a reader, she wants 'to be given a context for the reading of texts, however difficult I recognize the boundary between text and context is to maintain' (74). Difficulties of boundaries between text and context, work and life, can be seen throughout Muir's work, published and unpublished, fiction and non-fiction. Therefore, in this assessment and discussion of Willa Muir's work, I consider both the representative nature of her writing and its individuality. Placing Muir within the context of her fellow women writers, as well as within modernist and renaissancist contexts, ensures that she is not read as 'unique' in that overly Romantic response to the figure of the 'writer'. The following chapters cross-reference the incidence of repeated and overarching preoccupations that occur between her texts. All of them contextualize her work but also contain detailed text-based discussion.

The first chapter gives an overview of Muir's biographical details as well as her intellectual and friendship connections. The chapter on modernism and renaissancism, briefly referencing many of the participants in these movements, provides the essential cultural and literary context (Scottish and wider) for my exploration of Muir's works. The following chapters concentrate on Muir's specific works. *Women: An Inquiry* (1925) and *Mrs Grundy in Scotland* (1936), published eleven years apart, are considered together as part of the output of polemical pamphlets produced in that inter-war period. Muir's two published novels, *Imagined Corners* (1931) and *Mrs Ritchie* (1935), are each discussed in individual chapters; these chapters concentrate on specific literary analyses of each novel, although their intellectual and literary contexts are also referenced. Her publishing life stretches from *Women: An Inquiry* in 1925 to *Belonging* in 1968 and *Laconics Jingles & other Verses* in 1969. Much of her output was translation work, mainly sharing title page credit with Edwin Muir. These translations were essential in financing the Muirs' writing lives and also introduced writers such as Hermann Broch and Franz Kafka to the English speaking world. I consider this work in the chapter 'Translating for a living' which also assesses Muir's responsibility for the translation.

Muir also wrote two further novels, *Mrs Muttoe and the Top Storey* (1938-40) and *The Usurpers* (1950-52) which remain unpublished. These two novels exist in typescript form (in St Andrews University Library Special Collections) and I consider them in the chapter 'Fragments of a writing life'. Muir's personal writing in letters and journals provides a valuable indication of her attitudes and gives information about her life, and I use them as such throughout this study. But they are also a characteristic part of her writing output so a consideration of them is also given in the 'Fragments' chapter, along with a brief look at her late analysis of ageism and gender, 'This Lop-sided World'. *Laconics Jingles & other Verses* (1969), privately published in a limited edition, is strictly Muir's last published work, including poems from throughout her life. But I include a brief consideration of her poetry as part of 'Fragments' as her poetry was more intermittent (and more rarely published) than her prose works. Her two final published prose works were *Living with Ballads* (1965), written in fulfilment of a commission of Edwin's, and *Belonging*, her memoir of Edwin. Their close connections to Edwin's and to her own life places my discussion of them together in the last chapter as late examples of her creative achievement. Finally, I include four appendices to give easy access to some of Muir's work that is discussed in this study: one of her early and two of her late letters and Marion Lochhead's 1933 article 'Willa Muir and her work. Translator, novelist and poet'; the 1934 short story,

'Clock-a-doodle-doo'; the concluding nightmare of *Mrs Muttoe and the Top Storey*; and a selection of her poetry.

In some of her writing, Muir acknowledges but does not explore her Shetland roots. However prevalent her sense of being in a Shetland household in the Montrose of her childhood (with her father, mother and paternal grandmother all born in Unst), Muir's preoccupation is more with being a woman in Scotland. But her family background must have given her an early sense of tragedy: her paternal grandfather drowned at sea and her paternal uncle, the Shetland poet Basil Ramsay Anderson, died young (before she was born). The family's origins may have contributed to Muir's sense of herself as an outsider in mainland Scotland, and their tragedies to her sense of imbalance and a need for personal 'Belonging', but her uncle's existence as a poet must also have suggested the possibility of pursuing a writing life.

The *Glasgow Herald* obituary of Willa Muir, 27 May 1970, acknowledges her as a 'Scottish woman writer and translator . . . widow of Edwin Muir and herself a writer of distinction' and writes of her life, 'equal partner in many ways', with Edwin. But Peter Butter, Edwin's biographer, feels able to say in 1990 that her 'greatest work, I think she would gladly agree, was to make possible the production of his poetry' although he does go on to 'give her credit for what she, in spite of difficulties, achieved as a writer' (Butter, 1990 59). However the reprinting of *Imagined Corners* (1987, 1996) and *Mrs Ritchie* along with some of her non-fiction (1996) have enabled a reassessment of Willa Muir as a writer in a way that she could not achieve in her lifetime.

Muir's article 'Moving in Circles' explores her sense of being a 'circular-minded woman' (*Listener*, 22 Sept. 1938 603); it charts her movement from regarding this as 'a dreadful weakness' (602) to her final assertion of the importance of 'circular-mindedness' (603) over the limitations of a 'straight-line' approach. Its argument in favour of what she defined as the female characteristic of 'moving in circles' is emblematic of the way that she circles and returns to the same beliefs and ideas all her life and for that reason I have chosen to take it as the title to this study of her writing. The intention of this first full length study of Willa Muir is to assert her literary achievement and her position in the canons of Scottish and women's writing, neither fully acknowledged in her lifetime. It also intends to provide a guide to her times and her works. But it must also contain the reminder that works can disappear again, moving in a different kind of circle. Those of her published works that were republished between 1985 and 1996 are once more out of print. Marginal positions for writers (whether of gender, class or nation) always carry within them the possibility for re-disappearance from the canon.

Note

1. Short references will be given to sources for quotations from Willa Muir's journals, correspondence and unpublished novels after each quotation. Most of her manuscripts and typescripts are to be found in St Andrews University Library and the National Library of Scotland with some letters in the Schiff papers, British Library; the reference numbers are listed in Willa Muir Bibliography along with her published works (including her translations) and contemporary reviews of her works. References for manuscript letters by others than Muir are listed after the quotations. All other sources, including criticism of Muir, will be given in a shortened form after the reference or quotation and then listed in Bibliography of other sources.

Wilhemina Anderson, St Andrews, 1910.

# Life and contexts

Willa Muir is a writer who continuously mines her life in her narratives; she revisits her opinions and experiences and re-approaches the ideas that preoccupy her throughout her life. The minutiae of dates and places of so peripatetic a life, with details about the who, the what and the when, provide a useful guide through her life events. Despite Roland Barthes' concept of the death of the author, new criticism's concentration on text and text alone and a new historicist emphasis on text and context, all ensuring that previous ideas of an author's life being an intrinsic and necessary part of the understanding of an author's work are challenged, this is a traditional chapter on the details of her life. It is a longer version of the entry that I contributed to the *Oxford Dictionary of National Biography*, with additional material, discussion and opinions. The following chapters also include many references to Muir's life in her journals, letters and *Belonging*; these I use as commentary and criticism but also take them as part of her life-writing and, therefore, as part of her life's work.

Willa Muir was born Wilhelmina Johnston Anderson.[1] Known as Minnie as a child and at university, she called herself Willa as an adult. She uses Willa with her married surname of Muir for most of her works although she published a few translations under the name Agnes Neill Scott. I shall use Minnie to refer to her during her childhood and student period and Willa to identify her in adulthood in this chapter on her life, while Muir is used where references are made to her writing; Willa Muir or Muir are used in the discussion in following chapters. Edwin Muir is referred to as either Edwin or Edwin Muir to ensure clarity. Some of Muir's retrospective comments from her journals and *Belonging* are inserted in counterpoint and commentary at the appropriate points in this chapter. The facts and dates of her life are those that exist outside of interpretation, but her commentary and memories explored retrospectively must be read with an awareness of the writer's bias and interpretation; Willa Muir's 'I' remains a constructed 'I' and her point of view is not identical with objective truth; in her non-fiction writing she remains a witness to her own life and as such is as subject to the tendency to reorganise (consciously or unconsciously) her 'truths' as any other writer.

Minnie Anderson, born 13 March 1890, at 14 Chapel Place, Montrose, Forfarshire, was the oldest of the four children of Peter Anderson (1864-99) and Elizabeth (Betty) Gray Anderson (1866-1930). Peter was a draper and ran his own business at 180 High Street from 1889; Betty was a dressmaker; first cousins, they had married 22 February 1889. Both originally from Unst, Shetland, Muir traced her restlessness to her parents' status as emigrants from Shetland to Montrose: 'All emigrants are Displaced Persons. My parents were D.P's [sic] in Angus. So I grew up not fitting into Angus tradition and therefore critical, resentful, unsure' (n.d.; journal; 1947-Jan. 1848). Minnie's brothers were Basil Ramsay (1892-1960) and William John (1894-1930); their sister Elizabeth Ramsay Gray was born and died in 1899. Minnie went to Miss Davnie's small private school, 32 Bridge Street from age three. The family moved to 81 High Street in 1896. With a contraction of the family's means in 1899 on Peter Anderson's death, Minnie and Basil were moved to the Townhead Elementary Board School. She later wrote that she spoke Shetland at home, a kind of English at the private school, and Montrose in the street and at the Board School, and that this flexibility in dialect led to her facility in languages (*Belonging* 20). She won a scholarship to Montrose Academy, and began there in August 1902. She learned Latin and Greek from John Yorsten, principal teacher of classics and later the Rector. Her Higher passes, 1906-7, were in French, Latin, Mathematics and Science, with honours in English and Greek, and she won medals for English, Latin and Greek, coming fourth in the University of St Andrews Bursary competition.

In *Belonging,* Muir described a feeling of belonging to the universe that she first experienced when she was two and a half:

> My first awareness of it came at the age of two, when I was being pushed
> high in a swing, a small wooden chair slung from the branch of a tree. At
> the top of my swing I looked up and saw a pattern of green leaves against
> the blue sky. Boundless delight floated me for one moment up into that
> sky beside the green leaves, a moment which I have never forgotten.

Muir adds authenticity and specificity to this epiphany by grounding it in her mother's identification of the moment as occurring during a church outing to Glenesk, near Edzell.

> This 'floating' experience recurred at odd times, always with an uprush of
> joyousness . . . . [O]ne evening when I was sixteen . . . . I was sitting in
> a boat beached at the back of the island in the throat of the tidal lagoon,
> called the Basin, behind Montrose; the sun was setting before me and
> the Basin was full. Except for the distant curlew's call there was no living

sound. The 'feeling' came upon me like a cloud floating me out and up into the wide greening sky — into the Universe, I told myself. That was the secret name I gave it: Belonging to the Universe. (*Belonging* 14)

Muir describes this feeling of 'Belonging', found during her small town, semi-rural childhood, early in *Belonging* because it relates to her first reading of Edwin Muir's early work, *We Moderns*, published under the pseudonym of Edward Moore. She scorned much of it as she read, but when he wrote of a 'sense of overflowing feeling' she recalls wondering if it was 'essentially the same' as her feeling of 'Belonging' (*Belonging* 14-15). It is the first point of connection between them; written into her narrative of their relationship, it becomes central to her interpretation of their relationship in *Belonging*, her memoir of Edwin.

A less romantic, more troubled view of her life as a child in Montrose surfaced in a dream in early 1948 when she was living in a Prague which was full of political uncertainty and danger:

Last night I dreamed that in 81 High St Basil, aged about 15 or 16, was lying dead and naked on the bamboo hat stand in the lobby. Granny picked him up & carried him down to the dustbin in the close, round the corner by the old washhouse. And that was that! It woke me up in a sweat of horror; I lay thinking about Montrose, & Basil, & my mother, who was in many ways such a simple woman with simple ideas & conventions. And about Willie. And I realised how much I feared and loathed that house by this time; too many dead people have been carried out of it. My father, my baby sister, Grannie, mother and Willie. The me that felt all that is still somewhere within my body. (13 Feb. 1948; journal; Jan.-May 1948)

Muir's description of her dream is in line with her own acceptance of the importance of dreams and the unconscious. But the immediacy of recording it along with her feelings the next day gives it a more unmediated status than *Belonging*, while also giving a sense of some specifics of 81 High Street, bamboo hat stand and the route to the dustbin in the close by the washhouse. Her acknowledgment of heightened feelings of grief and death associated with her childhood home and her awareness that the 'me' was still within her are characteristic of her approach to the dreams she regularly records in her journals.

Minnie began at St Andrews University, age 17, October 1907, lodging with her friend Emily Stobo, age 18, in Grantown House, South St., St Andrews. Emily's signature follows Minnie's in the list of first year students for the winter session, 1907-8; she and Minnie are on the composite of photographs of the 'bejants' (first year students at St Andrews) that appears in the student magazine, *College Echoes* (1907-8 op. 340; Emily is row three, fourth from left and Minnie next to her, fifth from left; see 84). What is interesting (and perhaps surprising) is the number of women that attended St Andrews; there are 28 in the photograph, with 42 men. (The numbers of female to male students in the following years that Muir attended university are similar.) Attendance at summer term classes were optional, so, to save money, Minnie attended only the autumn and spring terms. She studied Latin and Greek, 1907-10 (with Mathematics, Logic and Ancient History as her respective outside subjects each year), and English and Modern History in 1910-11. She graduated, July 1911, with first class honours in classics and was awarded the Berry Scholarship of £80 which enabled her to study English Literature, 1911-12. Minnie took part in the Women's Debating Society (where she successfully defended the motion 'that strong principles conduce to narrow-mindedness' on 5 November 1909), and the Women's Suffrage Society. She became President and Vice President respectively, as well as being a member of the Students' Representative Council. She was also on the editing committee of *College Echoes*, 1910-11 (see opposite) and 1911-12.

Wilhelmina Anderson and friend, St Andrews.

She fell in love with Cecil Wilmot Morrison (originally from New Zealand and later of South Africa), a St Andrews medical student with a protracted University career, begun 1803-6, resumed 1910-11; he finally qualified in 1916 and became a Captain in the Royal Army Medical Corps. He had played rugby for New Zealand and for the university first eleven and is on the rugby first eleven photograph for 1910-11 (published in *College Echoes*).

*College Echoes* Editing Commitee, 1910-11.

with them in St Andrews in 1938 before emigrating to the United States) and Kafka, accomplished with interest and pleasure. Willa had learned Czech and was fluent in German, and was later to maintain in her journal, 20 August 1953, that most of the translation work was hers: 'I am a better translator than he is'; she thought she should have shouted aloud 'Most of this translation, especially Kafka, has been done by ME. Edwin only helped'. But she had told Marion Lochhead in 1933:

> [W]hen we translate a book, we divide it in two: after we have finished, Edwin goes over my half ruthlessly, and I go over his half ruthlessly, and the combined effort is put together. We have no hesitation in cutting each other's versions to pieces in the interests of the final product. (3 March 1933; NLS; see Appendix I)

She also told Catriona Soukup in Edinburgh during the war that they divided Kafka in two, translated their own half and then exchanged them for further work (C. Soukup 24). Between 1925 and 1938 they translated works by Sholem Asch, Hermann Broch, Carl Burckhardt, Lion Feuchtwanger, Ernst Glasser, Zsolt de Harsanyi, Gerhart Hauptmann, Kurt Heuser, Franz Kafka, Ernst Lothar, Heinrich Mann, Robert Neumann, E. A. Reinhart, Ludwig Renn, and others. The majority of the title pages credit Willa Muir before Edwin Muir (see Willa Muir Bibliography). Willa also translated Hans Carossa and Christa Winsloe as Agnes Neill Scott, and, under her own name, *5 Songs from the Auvergnat* (into Scots).

When Neill's school was disbanded and moved to Summerhill in England, Willa and Edwin also returned to Britain, arriving in Montrose, July 1924. Edwin wrote to Schiff shortly after their arrival that Scotland was 'a sad disappointment to us after all the longing we had for it, so shut in, unresponsive, acridly resolved not to open out and live. For our own sake we shall not live here for long' (2 Aug. 1924; Schiff papers; Butter, 1974 41). Willa added a postscript to both Violet and Sydney:

> Don't imagine that our depression is something *in* ourselves: we are merely facing the fact that we are out of touch with the environment we used to fight against. It is in itself an excellent symptom: we have grown away from past entanglements. (Schiff papers; BL)

The Muirs stayed in Montrose until Christmas, getting to know Christopher Grieve (Hugh MacDiarmid), then editor of the *Montrose Review*, and his first wife Peggy. Willa began work on *Women: An Inquiry* (published 1925). She corresponded with Sydney and Violet Schiff about her essay and possible publishers between November 1924 and February 1925. Leonard Woolf then accepted it as a Hogarth essay. When they heard this, Edwin wrote that they were overjoyed while Willa added the postscript: 'I have been making such awful noises round the house that Edwin begged me to desist — again, pure joy' (4 March 1925; Schiff papers; BL). At this time, they were living in a house in Penn, Buckinghamshire which the Schiffs had found for them, but they then returned to Montrose where Willa had a miscarriage in December 1925. She wrote about it to F. Marian McNeill:

> I had no idea that I was pregnant (I thought I had just got a chill, & when I was sick I thought it was caused by lumbago) and then we were worried by a debt which suddenly cropped up — very worried — and then I had the miscarriage, to my own shock & surprise. No wonder I was brooding over the bearing of children! (26 Jan. 1926; NLS)

In February 1926, they were able to move to St Tropez until October after being commissioned to translate Feuchtwanger's *Jew Süss* which they worked on there (*Belonging* 121-22). In 1922, in Dresden, Willa had been discouraged by Edwin from completing her verse drama of a contemporary Noah (*Belonging* 71-72; 20 Aug. 1953; journal; Jan. 1951-Sept. 1953). She now began her first novel, *Imagined Corners*, in St Tropez. They moved to Menton near the Italian border until May 1927. Not published until 1931, her work on the novel was interrupted by continuing translation work and the birth of their son, Gavin. Willa recorded later of that she threw herself into characters, living in them as much as possible so 'they are bound to be versions of myself' ([late Jan.] 1948; journal; Jan.-May 1948, 'The Putsch, and after'). When she reread it in 1948, it appeared 'better than I thought it was. Complete absorption in personal values, plus God or Nature: no apparent knowledge of social fabric *effects*. Quite pre-Marxian! But a good picture of the world I grew up in' (18 March 1948; journal; Jan.-May 1948). Her final judgement was that it contained enough material for two novels (*Belonging* 163). Despite her reservations, the intense engagement with the interlocking stories of the Shand and Murray families in 'Calderwick' makes a powerful novel with its portrait of inner and outer feelings and of the society of the town. A contemporary review in the *Glasgow Herald* described it as 'a memorable contribution to the cartography of the soul of Scotland' (2 July 1931).

The Muirs' only child Gavin was conceived during the Menton carnival; Willa wrote later, perhaps with an awareness of his troubled history, 'he could not have had a more carefree origin' (*Belonging* 134). So that he could be born in Britain, they returned to England, May 1927, and settled in the White House, Dormansland, Surrey, where Gavin Anderson Cormack Muir duly appeared after 'about 65 hours' of labour pains, 29 October 1927 (Butter, 1974 65). Willa kept the Marmaduke journal, observing his progress from six weeks, including his breast-feeding ('[t]he comfort-complex attached to sucking makes him suck (and noisily) at his fingers') and his bowel movements: 'A beezer of a motion — 5 nappies gone west, & a frock & a petticoat. Good looking stuff — not much curd — orange colour & smells like narcissi!' By 24 January 1928, he had had 'one or two erections: but apparently pays no attention to them at all'. Her habit of observation was applied to Gavin and linked analytically to ideas of child development:

> A queer thing that life at his age should be so intense & yet leave no traces in memory. He has a conscious — a personality — and an individual un-conscious (he makes habits of sleep & rest & food, recognises times & people & things) he remembers his milk & yet that is all wiped out — even the milk, the most important event of all to him. What is it which is not yet awake? Probably the faculty of fixing things in a definite & rec-ognisable shape — i.e, language. A kind of blood memory he has already, but not a systematic memory, not thought'. ([16 Feb. 1928]; Marmaduke journal)

Later, in 1948, she applied the same kind of analytic observation to Gavin's asthma attacks which she saw as symptoms of separation anxiety from his parents:

> First asthma as a child of 5 while we went to P.E.N. in Budapest: (1932) second when we thought of sending him to Canada in 1940: third, now, when he feels division from us again. Soothed, encouraged, cossetted him: he is now all right: sense of division, I think, smoothed out. (10 Jan. 1948; journal; 1947-Jan 1948)

Willa's brother, Willie, died of tuberculosis, 31 January 1929, and her mother, Betty, already ill from cancer and a heart attack in December 1928, died in February 1929, two of those deaths that haunted her 1948 dream about 81 High Street, Montrose. From March 1929 until October 1932, the Muirs were based at the Nook, Crowborough, Sussex (*Belonging* 148-49). In August 1931, Willa had three weeks in hospital to repair internal damage caused by Gavin's birth.

In May 1932, Edwin and Willa went as the Scottish delegation to the PEN in-ternational congress in Budapest, Hungary; they found the political atmosphere frightening. They had been instructed to insist on the separateness of the Scottish delegation from the English: 'we had to assert ourselves continuously as being at least on the same independent footing as the delegates from Esthonia'; they gave a Congress invitation 'in the name of *Scotland*' for 1934. In a rare assertion of na-tionalism, Willa concluded: 'Of course, we cannot eat our cake and have it: as an independent Scotland we must rank with the smaller nations, and cannot have the prestige of England or France or Germany. But it will be our own prestige, and we must establish it' (Helen Cruickshank; 26 May 1932; see also 'Conclusion').[3] The Muirs went from there to Vienna to visit Broch whose *The Sleepwalkers* they were translating. Broch could not reassure them after their first experience in Hungary of 'political fear'. It was 'more faceless and more like a chill, penetrating fog than any other fear in the world . . . . From his tall height Broch looked down on us compassionately as on a pair of children who had just been learning the facts of European Life' (*Belonging* 157).

On their return to England, they moved from Crowborough to 7 Downshire Hill, Hampstead, in early October, financed by some money left Willa by her mother. It cost £120 a year and was near Catherine and Donald Carswell. Willa planned a Hogmanay celebration there: 'I am asking the Carswells & Mary Litchfield and the two young Glaswegians called Coia (artists)[4] and one or two other Scots: my avowed intention is just to have a spree, and I think there will be no intellectual fireworks but plenty of nonsense' (WM to Taylor; 23 Dec. 1932; NLS). It was while they were in Hampstead that Christopher Grieve visited them full of his plans to liberate the Stone of Scone from Westminster Abbey, telling all his Scottish friends in London about it 'confidentially': 'His yellow hair fizzed up; he was radiant with sheer daftness' (*Belonging* 165). It was also in this Hampstead house that Edwin had a bare study in the attic and Willa's study was on the ground floor 'intruded upon at all hours' (*Belonging* 162). She used to work at night, as when she was a student, to try and get translations finished and proofs corrected. She had begun her second novel *Mrs Ritchie* in June 1932 (WM to Broch, 2 June 1932; cited Allen 247) and finished it in Hampstead in the press of other work; 'it does not surprise me that I lost control of it in the second half, although the first half is quite good' (*Belonging* 163). Published in July 1933, like *Imagined Corners* it was also set in 'Calderwick', but it concentrated on the damage one woman inflicts on her family, herself already damaged by Calvinism and by the limitation of possibilities for women. Darker in tone than *Imagined Corners*, it has a powerful and negative sweep with an overly analytic narrator, 'the result is nearer to science than to art' (*TLS* 13 July 1933). It was while Muir was writing *Mrs Ritchie* that she wrote a summary of her life so far to Marion Lochhead; Lochhead's article on Muir in her intermittent series 'Scottish Women Writers of To-day' appeared in *The Bulletin and Scots Pictorial*, 29 March 1933. Lochhead, picking up on Muir's education and intellect, wrote about the 'creative work' of 'many of our women writers of to-day' being 'solidly based on an intellectual heritage'; Muir's 'full force of . . . intelligence is not yet felt, for even her best work . . . hardly does her justice' and concluded that Muir's 'rich background of culture and her own immense vitality' made her 'one of the most fascinating women writers of to-day' (for Muir's letter and Lochhead's article, see Appendix I; for the photograph of Muir illustrating the article, see frontispiece).

Gavin was run over and his leg badly broken in July 1933; they took him to Orkney for a month to recuperate away from traffic. Willa later dates Gavin's troubles as stemming from this time, believing that his 'confidence in the world and in us

[A] very earnest, rather melancholy freckled little being — whose dossier is that, come into civilization from amid the gillies and haggises of Goy or Arran, living in poverty, he fell in with that massive, elderly scottish lady next to him — that is his wife. She opened her jaws and swallowed him comfortably. There he was once more inside a woman, as it were — tucked up in her old tummy. In no way embarrassed with this slight additional burden (the object of all her wishes, of masculine gender — but otherwise little more than a sexless foetus) she started off upon the *grand tour*. And there in the remoter capitals of Europe the happy pair remained for some time, in erotic-maternal trance no doubt. (Lewis, *Apes* 300).

Lewis continues his spiteful picture of Edwin and Willa Muir and Sydney Schiff:

*All* his history, circumstances (with special attention to financial details) — age of his wife, climacteric approaching, what residue of breeding years (circumstances of old-better half with special attention to financial details) — marital relations . . . early upbringing of *Unknown Idiot*, in the highland-home — fingers in the porridge pot, tending of the shadowy, mist-wrapt kine (excellent training for subsequent attendance upon Lionel — boredom-proof is to be assumed!): juvenile 'complexes,' little hopes and fears and infant vanities, hatred of vermicelli, imperfect acquaintance with classical idioms, french, shorthand — gallantry exhibited in early struggles brought to conclusion by the arrival of God's messenger, pawky Peggy. (Lewis, *Apes* 302)

The large elderly Mrs. Keith is representative of a view of the university-educated Willa Muir as swallowing up Edwin, the autodidact from Orkney. Edwin was three years older than Willa, but that did not interfere with Lewis's enjoyment in analysing their relationship in Freudian terms. Muir records that Schiff 'engineered a meeting between us and Wyndham Lewis, for at that time Sydney was a partisan of Lewis's' (*Belonging* 120); this was probably in early 1926; Willa also records impressions of Lewis which, although written long after the meeting and the publication of Lewis's *Apes of God* in 1930, probably represent accurately her analysis of Lewis at the time as 'one of those Englishmen who do not have the habit of talking to women. My invisible antennae conveyed to me that he resented my being there at all, that in his opinion a wife was out of place and that Edwin was a coward for having brought me as protective cover' (*Belonging* 120-21). Her feminism ensured that she was always suspicious of English public school educated men (as Lewis was), believing them to represent a particular kind of male stereotype, hostile to or afraid of women who did not conform to their assumptions of what norms of female behaviour should be.

But it was not only English men who were challenged by Willa. A visual version of Lewis's 1930 assault on the Muir relationship appeared in the second number of MacDiarmid's *Voice of Scotland. A Quarterly Magazine of Scottish Arts and Affairs* (Sept.-Nov. 1938 1:10). It was listed in the contents as 'Willa and Edwin Muir (Caricature)'. Alan Bold notes that Barbara Niven's caricature of Edwin as a small fawn at the side of a large headless Willa in a bathing costume is based on 'Wyndham Lewis's satirical masterpiece' as well as 'Valda's memory of Willa holding forth on the beach at St Andrews in 1935' (Bold, 1988 373). The sketch was apparently Valda Grieve's idea, and justified by her on the grounds that she 'had heard reliable reports of Willa's malicious gossip: how she was in the habit of denouncing MacDiarmid as a charlatan' (Bold, 1988 374).[6] An unrepentant MacDiarmid was criticised by Helen Cruickshank and the Communist Party for publishing it (see Bold, 1984 125).

Yet for all these satirical responses to Willa Muir's apparent dominance over Edwin by Lewis and MacDiarmid (respectively representative of English high modernism and Scottish renaissancism), the Muirs' individual writing and life trajectories still conform to and confirm the norm of female and male expectations, the man: poet, critic, and translator, taken seriously, and the woman: intermittent, 'miscellaneous' writer, sidelined in critical memory. This is the interpretation that Muir felt herself circumscribed by, although she contributed to it by the way she lived her life and recorded her own critical and self-denigratory analyses of her work in her journals and *Belonging*. It is reaffirmed in the recent chapter on her in William Knox's *Lives of Scottish Women*, entitled 'Willa Muir: Living with Genius (2)' with its implication that her importance rests with Edwin. But recently it has been Willa Muir who is studied in Scottish literature courses at universities and Edwin Muir who has lost his previously central place in the study of Scottish literature. This has partly been caused by the reprinting of Muir's novels, and the contemporaneous move towards introducing women's writing into the hitherto overly male centred Scottish literary canon. When she was pregnant, she recalled thinking as she looked at her ungainly shape '[b]ut I am still me' (*Belonging* 143). The following detailed chapters on all of Willa Muir's work provide evidence of the intrinsic importance and interest of her writing. The chapters also establish the extent to which she was always 'still me' in all that she wrote.

## Notes

1. Willa Anderson's birth certificate, Montrose, 22 March 1890, lists her as Wilhelmina Johnston Anderson. Her death certificate, Dunoon, 22 May 1970, lists her as Willa Johnstone Muir. She was clearly named for her maternal grandmother Williamina Johnston (b. 1836), married 1862 in Unst to William John Anderson (b. 1834). Her parents' common grandparents were Jerome William Anderson (b. ca. 1795), of East Yell, and Janet Margaret Robertson (b. 1799), of Mid Yell. Her paternal grandfather was Peter Anderson (1829-66); her paternal grandmother, Elizabeth Ramsay (1831-1909), lived with the Andersons in Montrose during Willa's childhood. Her paternal uncle was Basil Ramsay Anderson (1861-88), poet, born in Unst and died in Edinburgh. His work was published in *Broken Lights: Poems and Reminiscences of Basil R. Anderson* (Edinburgh, 1888). I am grateful to Robert Alan Jamieson for drawing my attention to these Shetland connections.

2. Muir is using a conventionally negative interpretation of bohemian; for a wider exploration of what 'bohemian' meant and who the bohemians were, see Nicholson, *Amongst the Bohemians*.

3. For the rest of Muir's long letter about the PEN conference to Helen Cruickshank, secretary of Scottish PEN, 26 May [1932], see Butter, 1974 72-76.

4. Emilio Coia (1911-97), who became best known for his many published caricatures, had met Marie Neale (1907-78) at Glasgow Art School; because of his parents' disapproval, they had eloped to London and married in November 1932.

5. Gavin Muir's death certificate records that he had been a college lecturer in Aberdeen, retired at the time of his death (from carcinoma of the liver) in Edinburgh in 1991. Ethel Ross noted in 1999: 'We lost touch with Gavin when his mother died but did visit him during his last years in a Residential Home for I think Cancer patients in Edinburgh. He was so quiet and patient. I think happy enough' (letter to Aileen Christianson).

6. Bold gives some background to the social group in St Andrews, 1935-36, before Edwin Muir and MacDiarmid fell out so bitterly: 'Muir, contemplating *Scott and Scotland*, was unhappy in St Andrews and had become disenchanted with MacDiarmid's Communism as he himself was moving towards a wholly Christian commitment . . . . Willa, who had been educated at St Andrews University, was

in her element, making herself the centre of attention. Valda had an unpleasant memory of a day on the beach in St Andrews on account of Willa's insensitivity to MacDiarmid's illness [i.e., his breakdown]. Some years later she recalled "Willa sprawling on the beach in one of those modern bathing costumes — four sizes too small — just oozing with grossness & holding forth unnecessarily on her favourite topic — phallic symbolism" [to Helen Cruikshank; n.d., prob. Sept. 1938; Edinburgh University Library]. Willa was then writing, for the "Meanings for [Voice of] Scotland" series, her book on sex and Scotland, *Mrs Grundy in Scotland* (Bold, 1988 333). I include this because it gives external corroboration from an unsympathetic witness of the way that Willa's psychoanalytic tendencies were endemic in her behaviour and attitudes. Valda Grieve was Christopher Grieve's second wife, and Willa had been friendly with his first wife Peggy in Montrose in 1926 (see *Belonging* 116-18). George Mackay Brown, another younger poet, met and liked Willa at Newbattle during his first stay there, 1951-53. He wrote about a social occasion when the Edinburgh poet Norman MacCaig was criticising everyone with 'blistering scorn': 'Willa Muir of course laughed her head off all the time' (Fergusson 109). But Maggie Fergusson also records in her biography of Mackay Brown that Bernard Bergonzi (also a Newbattle student) thought Willa 'the most malicious woman' he had ever 'encountered' (Fergusson 113) and G. N. Scott acknowledges in his short memoir of Muir in 1980 that her 'sense of humour was onesided and her wit at times verging on the unkind' (Scott 42). Ethel Ross, Edwin and Willa's niece, noted in 1999 that Willa was 'humorous and helpful (with my Latin studies) yet belittling on occasions' (letter to AC). Muir wrote in *Mrs Grundy in Scotland* that 'there is no human being who has not suffered at some time or another from a sense of inferiority' (*Mrs Grundy* 3); she clearly disguised her own insecurity with surface noise and directness, confusing the people who found her apparent confidence threatening.

*The Modern Scot*, cover, April 1931.

# Modernism and Renaissancism

Before looking at Willa Muir's pre-world war two work in the following chapters, this chapter begins with a discussion of modernism, that generalised term for both period (roughly between 1910 and 1939) and work produced in the 'Anglo'-American world of the first decades of the twentieth century. The writers T. S. Eliot, Ezra Pound, James Joyce and Virginia Woolf are still largely taken as representative of the central canon. Their work makes a virtue of foregrounding the new, the disrupted, the fragmentary, both rejecting and challenging the 'norms' of the preceding Victorian and Edwardian eras. They delight in the cultural relativism which could find roots of their work in those who had been responsible for breaking down the religious and political certainties of the nineteenth century, Charles Darwin, Karl Marx and Friedrich Nietzsche, followed closely by Sigmund Freud, Albert Einstein, and J. G. Frazer. The increasing uncertainties of a capitalist world collapsing into a long and brutish (mainly) European war, 1914-1918, served only to increase for the writers their sense of past reference points being disrupted or rejected. Michael Levenson, in the *Cambridge Companion to Modernism* (1999), writes of the twentieth century discovering early that it 'would be the epoch of crisis':

> The catastrophe of the First World War, and before that, the labor struggles, the emergence of feminism, the race for empire, these inescapable forces of turbulent social modernization were not simply looming on the outside as the destabilizing context of cultural Modernism; they penetrated the interior of artistic invention. They gave subjects to writers and painters, and they also gave forms, forms suggested by industrial machinery, or by the chuffing of cars, or even, most horribly, the bodies broken by war. // If the social cataclysms left traces on modernist art, so did that art inform and to an extent form the conception of social life within historical crisis. (Levenson 4)

This accurately places the way the movement was both influence on and influenced by its historical and contemporary context. The concept of the Modern was much used at the time (for example, Edwin Muir's *We Moderns* (1919)), but the term 'modernism' itself was one applied retrospectively. The early use of the term was for architecture and painting, not for writing. The *Oxford English Dictionary* lists the earliest use of 'modernism' in 1929, by H. R. Hitchcock in *Modern Architecture: Romanticism and Reintegration* (New York): 'A city whose "modernism" consists in copying in the poorest French models of the New Tradition' (OED; Hitchcock 205). The OED finds 'modernist' in 1927 in relation to painting in F. J. Mather, *A History of Modern Painting from Goya to Picasso* (London: Stanley Paul & Co., [1927]): 'Modernist pictures are becoming discreet, almost cautiously monotonous in color' (*OED*; Mather 372). Mather also names his last chapter 'Modernist Movements in the Twentieth Century', dating their beginning from 'about the year of Cezanne's death, 1907' (Mather 353). By 1934, Reginald Blomfield in *Modernismus* (London: MacMillan) refers to 'Modernism' as perhaps ending 'in the bankruptcy of Literature and the Arts' (v) but is also more concerned with architecture; he finds that 'Modernism . . . has invaded this country like an epidemic' (v); he is still more concerned with architecture and sculpture than literature: 'I have already called attention to the disastrous effect of Modernism on architecture, painting, and sculpture . . . . I find the same insidious and repulsive influence at work in a good deal of contemporary music' (OED; Blomfield 145). The 1932 publication, *Oxford Companion to English Literature*,[1] has no definition for modernism, although it does have entries for Einstein, Frazer (with a separate entry for *The Golden Bough*), Freud, Eliot and Woolf, but not for Pound. Indicating the retrospective nature of 'modernist' or 'modernism' as terms for art, architecture, literature or the times in the first half of the twentieth century, an entry for modernism does not appear in any of Harvey's subsequent editions, second (1937), third (1946) or fourth (1967), but there is an extensive entry in Margaret Drabble's fifth edition (1985).

Many of the ways in which we might now 'read' modernism can be seen already in comments on the pre-world war one movements such as Futurism or Vorticism (in, for example, *Blast: the Review of the Great English Vortex*, founded June 1914 and edited by Wyndham Lewis). A review of a futurist exhibition in the *Pall Mall Gazette* in March 1912 describes the paintings in terms of breakdown: 'The majority of them strike one as the pictorial rendering of confused nightmares in which all objects are not only in motion, but in dissolution under the impulse of violent forces'. It concludes, using terms which encapsulate the sense of sharp change and rejection that the pre-world war one movements in art were assumed to represent:

We have seen many new movements in recent years. We have had our eyes trained to see nature in a new way. We have had spectral analysis introduced into art. We have seen many a violent break in the continuity of tradition, and many an arbitrary return to an earlier and more archaic tradition; we have even seen the Cubists turn the human body into geometrical figures. But the Futurists . . . not only break the continuity of artistic evolution, but they declare war upon all art of the past and the present'.

('The Italian Futurists. Nightmare Exhibition at the Sackville Gallery', *PMG*, 1 March 1912 5)

This is further evidence that the roots of much of the initial modernist criticism was in art. But 'Anglo'-American modernism encompasses not just art but also fiction and poetry, cultural commentary and critical writing. It was the most self-aware and self-reflexive of movements. The cultural and critical essays of Eliot or Woolf were as influential as their poetry or fiction. Indeed, Woolf's critical work in 1942, the year following her suicide, is at times valued more highly than her fiction; Martin Turnell, writing in *Horizon*, asserts that, while it was 'usually taken for granted' that she was 'a distinguished novelist who happened to write a few volumes of what she modestly described as "unprofessional criticism"', to him she was 'essentially a literary critic who wrote novels'; her criticism 'displayed a far greater range of imaginative sympathy', and in it she was 'not content to rely on the shabby conceptions derived from the Liberal agnosticism of the nineteenth-century thinkers which are the stock-in-trade of her novels and account for their poverty of outlook' (*Horizon* 6:31 (July 1942) 44). Turnell also dismisses her later more experimental novels but writes that her second (realist) novel, *Night and Day* (1919), 'made a genuine attempt to express the strange and scarcely articulate feelings that were fermenting beneath the surface of a crumbling civilization', while her later novels were to be criticised because 'her interest in method . . . distracted her attention from the very real discoveries that she had made' (Turnell 48). Of course, it is precisely with Woolf's later novels that her reputation as one of the central modernist authors lies. But Turnell's phrase, 'the strange and scarcely articulate feelings that were fermenting beneath the surface of a crumbling civilization' itself articulates one of the central tenets of modernism, akin to 'we seem to move on a thin crust which may at any moment be rent by the subterranean forces slumbering below' (Frazer, 1922 58); this is from Frazer's anthropological work, *The Golden Bough: A Study in Magic and Religion* (1890-1915), his intellectually and imaginatively influential comparative study of beliefs and myths, magic, superstition. Evelyn Waugh uses the same imagery, explicitly referring to the subconscious, in a review of *The Collected Poems* of the archetypal breaker of taboos, D. H. Lawrence, in the October 1928 *Vogue*: 'He writes upon volcanic crust; underneath, and liable at any moment to burst through, is the whole subconscious field so rarely accessible to civilised man' (*Vogue*, Oct. 1928 86). A metaphor that Muir also uses in relation to Elizabeth's feelings in *Imagined Corners* (*IC* 115), it is emblematic of the inter-war years' sense of fragility with a scarcely contained violence (actual or subconscious) shifting threateningly beneath the surface.

Woolf is not the only woman critic of the time; journals and newspapers played their part in the production of the new literature by reviewing new works, with many of their reviewers women. There were also critical works published in the nineteen twenties which take account of the new ideas' presence in fiction in interesting ways. In *The Modern Novel: Some Aspects of Contemporary Fiction* (1926), the Anglo-American poet, critic and author, Elizabeth A. Drew[2] incorporates (not uncritically) extensive discussion of the 'new' assumptions and techniques. She identifies the reaction and rejection of Victorian values that underlay so much of the modernist impulse, that 'shock of disenchantment' that led 'the present generation of intelligentsia' to 'dismiss all "Victorian" beliefs as necessarily untrue', but she feels that they had rushed to the 'no less dishonest position of the opposite extreme' where their 'almost conscientious pessimism is the cause of a certain heavy air of self-consciousness which hangs over a good deal of the fiction by young writers' (Drew 138).

Drew discusses a wide range of American and British fiction, including D.H. Lawrence, May Sinclair, Rebecca West (her 'distinction of style cannot prevent the sex psychology at the conclusion of *The Judge* from becoming almost comic in its failure to carry any artistic or human conviction' (Drew 61)), Michael Arlen, Willa Cather, Edith Wharton, Rose Macaulay, Scott Fitzgerald and Virginia Woolf, in the context of chapters such as 'The Novel and the Age', 'Sex Simplexes and Complexes', 'The New Psychology', 'Is there a "Feminine" Fiction?', 'Yokel Colour', 'The American Scene', as well as four individual chapters on John Galsworthy, H.G. Wells, Arnold Bennett and Joseph Conrad. She concludes that 'the craftsmanship of these novels embodies to perfection all the sharp, shifting sense of the disconnection, the irrelevance in the facts and experience of life, in the emotions and thoughts of man's heart and mind, and the uncontrolled impulses of his unconscious being on which there is so obvious an emphasis today' (262); this sentence incorporates many of the tendencies of both 'Modernism' and modernist fiction.

Agnes Mure Mackenzie is a Scottish example of a professional writer of the time; she writes *The Process of Literature: An Essay Towards Some Reconsiderations* (1929) as an attempt to theorise the production of literature in the new age, rather than a critical book; Mackenzie was to become known more as a Scottish historian, but here turns her hand to a study of the 'process' of literature:

> Only a few weeks ago, an eminent physicist summed up the recent changes in our outlook on the material world by saying that the objects which we had been used to consider as *things*, now appear to us as a series of *events*. . . . [T]he modern psychologist thinks no longer in states or conditions of the mind, but of processes . . . . If, instead, we realise that an art is a sequence of dramatic process, and that its material productions (statues, pictures, books) are merely outward expression of a stage — and not the final stage — in the process, a great many classical difficulties disappear. . . . This point of view, the habit of regarding an art as a process of human activity rather than as a series of objects produced by that activity, has been foreshadowed here and there already . . . . I have tried in this book to study . . . literature, in these newer terms, and to describe the chains of process it involves, from the stimulus of the writer by his experience of life to the reader's reaction to what has been created as the result of that stimulus; and further, to relate this special sequence of processes to the general system that is human life at large. (Mackenzie 9-10)

The interconnectedness of her 'process' seems symptomatic of the 'newer terms' of modernism, though her mentions of Bergson, Freud and Jung later in the book are dismissive, making her analysis seem resistant to, rather than simply critical of, some aspects of the time. But Mackenzie's book is an early example of someone discussing theoretical concerns in relation to the production of literature. Having received a negative reader's report, she sent it for a pre-publication reaction to her friend Nan Shepherd who gives this reaction:

> And when I did get begun, I was reluctant to put it down till I was done, which is all the answer I deign to the gentleman who found it unreadable. Though of course on his behalf it must be said that its argument . . . was all the same immediately comprehensible to me because I had found its truth already and was therefore not hampered in my reading by unfamiliar idea[s]: against which must be said that though I have the ordinary educated person's knowledge of psychological vocabulary . . . I am nevertheless not a trained psychologist . . . . No, it's not unreadable . . . . An admirable piece of work — I am all the more impatient to see it in print for having already read it. Deil tak the ignorant Sassenachs that canna see a fine fat salmon when you play it under their noses! . . . Yet it ought to have a fair

public. Think of all the practitioners of the art of fiction alone. They all
ought to read it. (9 July 1928; MS: NLS 9221.68)

What is of interest in Shepherd's reply to Mackenzie, apart from her kind and
humorous attempts to reassure Mackenzie of the book's value and practical
use, is her mention of Mackenzie's incorporation of psychology into the discussion of the processes of literature; clearly its presence had been problematic to
the publisher's reader. Shepherd's reference to 'the ordinary educated person's
knowledge of psychological vocabulary' might be debatable as a description of
herself, graduate of Aberdeen University, 1915, and then a lecturer at the teachers' training college in Aberdeen. But it confirms the extent to which Shepherd
sees 'psychological vocabulary' as part of the common currency of the 'ordinary
educated person' of the late nineteen twenties. At this time, Shepherd was
working on her own second novel, *The Weatherhouse* (1930), which dealt with
the impact of world war one on an Aberdeenshire rural community in a way
that incorporates many modernist preoccupations. It is in this novel that we
find one of the most expressive summaries of the meaning of the recent changes
in the modern world of the early twentieth century:

> The world and its modes passed by and [Ellen] ignored them . . . . She saw
> — as who could have helped seeing — the external changes that marked
> life during the thirty years she had lived at the Weatherhouse: motor cars,
> the shortening skirt, the vacuum cleaner; but of the profounder revolu-
> tions, the change in temper of a generation, the altered point of balance
> of the world's knowledge, the press of passions other than individual and
> domestic, she was completely unaware. (Shepherd, 1930; 1996 10-11)

Shepherd's acknowledgment of the material effects of the mechanical in the life
of Ellen, a middle-aged woman, and Ellen's failure (even refusal) to notice the
'profounder revolutions' underlying the mechanical changes, is emblematic both
of the way that the world had changed and the way that 'ordinary' women could
live on the surface of these changes. But the phrase 'altered point of balance of
the world's knowledge' also provides a resonant phrase that expresses all those
intellectual and other changes underlying the discourses of modernism.

Houston A. Baker's 1987 study, *Modernism and the Harlem Renaissance*, problematises the 'Anglo'-American-centrism of the interpretation of modernism; he
writes a passage both descriptive and critical of what modernism is assumed to
be. I am going to quote this at length as it provides both a clear summary of the
general assumptions from which modernism is formed and an articulation of the
extent that 'modernism' is a self-conscious construction, not simply some cultural
phenomenon observed retrospectively:

The names and techniques of the 'modern' that are generally set forth constitute a descriptive catalog resembling a natural philosopher's curiosity cabinet. In such cabinets disparate and seemingly discontinuous objects share space because that is the very function of the cabinet — to house or give order to varied things in what appears a rational, scientific manner. Picasso and Pound, Joyce and Kandinsky, Stravinsky and Klee, Brancusi and H. D. are made to form a series. Collage, primitivism, montage, allusion, 'dehumanisation', and leitmotivs are forced into the same field. Nietzsche and Marx, Freud and Frazier [sic], Jung and Bergson become dissimilar bedfellows. Such naming rituals have the force of creative works like *Ulysses* and *The Waste Land*. They substitute a myth of unified purpose and intention for definitional certainty. Before succumbing to the myth, however, perhaps we should examine the 'change' that according to Woolf's calendar occurred on or about December 1910.

Baker, having placed his 'naming ritual' of people and 'isms in the encompassing 'myth' of modernism, then considers that 'change' which is seen to be at the root of so much post-world war one work and summarises the way it stems from the pre-world war one cultural world:

Surely that change is most accurately defined as an acknowledgment of radical uncertainty. Where precisely anyone or anything was located could no longer be charted on old maps of 'civilization', nor could even the most microscopic observation tell the exact time and space of day. The very conceptual possibilities of both time and space had been dramatically refigured in the mathematics of Einstein and the physics of Heisenberg. A war of barbaric immensity combined with imperialism, capitalism, and totalitarianism to produce a reaction to human possibilities quite different from Walt Whitman's joyous welcoming of the modern . . . . Regardless of their strategies for confronting it, though, it was *change* — a profound shift in what could be taken as unquestionable assumptions about the meaning of human life — that moved those artists whom we call 'moderns'. And it was only a rare one among them who did not have some formula — some 'ism' — for checking a precipitous toppling of man and his towers [cf. Eliot's 'Falling towers' in 'The Waste Land']. Futurism, imagism, impressionism, vorticism, expressionism, cubism — all offered explicit programs for the arts *and* the salvation of humanity. Each in its turn yielded to other formulations of the role of the writer and the task of the artist in a changed and always, ever more rapidly changing world. (Baker 3, 5)

Baker here provides a more explicit and detailed way of describing Shepherd's 'profounder revolutions, the change in temper of a generation, the altered point of balance of the world's knowledge' (Shepherd, 1930; 1996 11). After Baker's name checking of the perceived sources and meanings of modernism, he moves to his own difficulty, as an African-American critic, 'unconceived in the philosophies of Anglo-American, British, and Irish moderns', in finding 'intimacy either in the moderns' hostility to *civilization* or in their fawning reliance on an array of images and assumptions bequeathed by a *civilization* that, in its prototypical form, is exclusively Western, preeminently bourgeois, and optically white' (Baker 6). The 'specifically Afro-American modernism' (Baker 8) that became know as the Harlem renaissance, 'an outpouring of writing, music, and social criticism that included some of the earliest attempts by Afro-American artists and intellectuals to define themselves in "modern" terms' (Baker 9), is generally dated in the nineteen twenties. Baker dates a 'change' that marked the start of '"renaissancism" in Afro-American expressive culture' as early as 1895 (Baker 8), and then discusses the Afro-American minstrel mask and minstrelsy and its use in Booker T. Washington's 1901 autobiography, *Up From Slavery* (Baker 15-36). What Baker is doing is asserting a longer modernism period, as opposed to the high modernism of Pound, Eliot and Woolf. He places the Harlem renaissance, often defined as consisting of 'failed' writing by the standards of 'Anglo'-American modernism, in a wider cultural context that takes account of marginalisation by race, class and history. A longer modernism gives a greater flexibility of timeframe, allowing the incorporation of intellectual currents (from Nietzsche, Freud, Frazer, and so on) that both provide the climate necessary for modernism while themselves also being part of it, the works of these intellectuals becoming not just the cause but also an intrinsic part of modernism.

My interest here is the way that Baker's assessment of the Harlem renaissance intersects with the different but contemporary space of the Scottish renaissance. I use Baker's term and concept of 'renaissancism' as accompaniment and equivalent to 'modernism', with many of the same currents, preoccupations and styles of modernism, and as a concept that is both culturally useful and significant in the non-'metropolitan' spaces of Harlem, Scotland and Ireland. The Scottish literary renaissance follows the Irish literary renaissance. Luke Gibbons argues:

> Irish society did not have to await the twentieth century to undergo the
> shock of modernity: disintegration and fragmentation were already part of
> its history so that, in a crucial but not always welcome sense, Irish culture
> experienced modernity before its time. (Gibbons 6)

The Irish literary renaissance or Irish revival therefore occurs in the last part of the nineteenth century into the twentieth century, 'disintegration and fragmentation' so much part of Irish national history that they are an intrinsic part of the emerging new literature, from W. B. Yeats' drama and early poetry to James Joyce's stream of consciousness in *Ulysses* (1918 and 1922) and *Finnegan's Wake* (1939) that sweep all before them with the highest of 'modernist bravado' (Boone 5). The term Scottish literary renaissance was used by C.M. Grieve (Hugh MacDiarmid) in 'Causerie: a Theory of Scots Letters', *Scottish Chapbook* (February 1923):

> We base our belief in the possibility of a great Scottish Literary
> Renaissance, deriving its strength from the resources that lie latent and
> almost unsuspected in the Vernacular . . . . We have been enormously
> struck by the resemblance—the moral resemblance—between Jamieson's
> Etymological Dictionary of the Scottish language and James Joyce's *Ulysses*
> . . . . [I]ts potential uprising would be no less prodigious, uncontrollable,
> and utterly at variance with conventional morality than was Joyce's tremen-
> dous outpouring. (McCulloch, 2004 26-27)

The *Glasgow Herald*, 29 December 1923, heads a letter from Hugh Quigley in Manchester with 'The Scottish Literary Renaissance'. Quigley complains about the 'gradual submersion of everything we hold dear in our Scottish culture and thought in the wave of blasé eclecticism emanating from Cambridge and London' and advocates 'a closer regional cultivation of the genuine things of life':

> This search must leave London and Cambridge and Oxford aside and con-
> centrate on ground more familiar and more real. In Scotland it should lead
> to a Scottish Renaissance, in Ireland to an Irish Renaissance. In Scotland
> the indications of such a Renaissance have been multiplying during the last
> three years . . . . The ideal to be followed is clear — adherence to the real
> traditions of Scottish life and thought. (*Glasgow Herald*, 29 Dec. 1923 5)

The *Glasgow Herald*, in its first leader, 31 December 1923, 'A Scottish Literary Renaissance', continues with a reference to the Irish literary renaissance as past its peak:

> The Irish literary renaissance has apparently reached or passed its height.
> Its progress has been followed with something of envy by young Scottish
> writers who felt that Scotland, with her far stronger equipment in the
> way of national history, literature, and character, was capable of making a
> far more distinctive and more influential contribution to current English
> literature than Ireland . . . . [S]omething infinitely ahead of the 'Whistle
> Binkie' order of things is represented by the very large group of contem-
> porary Scottish writers headed by Neil Munro, John Buchan, Alexander
> Gray, Violet Jacob, C. M. Grieve, Edwin Muir, Hugh M'Diarmid, and

John Ferguson—to mention only a few of the more prominent names . . . .
That a genuine Scottish literary renaissance is in progress is to be deduced,
not so much from the fine work achieved by the leaders of the movement
as from the quality and inspiration of the work of the various rank and file.
(*Glasgow Herald*, 31 Dec. 1923 6)

The '"Whistle Binkie" order of things' is based on *Whistle-binkie . . . being a
Collection of Songs for the Social Circle*, a series of collections of sentimental
songs and poems published between 1832 and 1890, here used as a pejorative
representative of the supposed sentimentality of nineteenth century Scottish
writing. Leaving aside Munro and Buchan (both now known as novelists rather
than poets) who might neither normally be identified as 'modernist' writers, the
*Glasgow Herald* leader sets up two of the characteristics of the coming Scottish
literary renaissance as it was to be moulded by MacDiarmid: the centrality of
poets and the double presence of Grieve / MacDiarmid.[3] Although Jacob was
also a novelist, it was for her poetry that MacDiarmid expresses admiration. All
the writers listed (including Edwin Muir) had been published by Grieve in his
poetry anthologies, *Northern Numbers, First Series* (1920), *Second Series* (1921),
and *Third Series* (1922). I will return later to the positioning of women writers
(particularly the novelists) but what is of interest here is the evidence that this
Scottish renaissance, like 'Anglo'-American modernism, the Irish renaissance
and the Harlem renaissance, is seen as an essentially cultural movement, not just
literary, with an agenda for change (of both culture and politics), partly pursued
by rejecting its literary forebears.

In the case of both the Harlem and Scottish renaissances, there is a concentration
on language; writing in standard English is seen as problematic for those attempting the nurturing and recognition of a culture which was new but also had its
roots in their African past, however distorted by the so recently abolished slavery,
and for those who were invoking (in part) a Scottish golden literary age. Cairns
Craig sees the 'particular character' of the renaissance in Scotland as coming from
a 'conjunction of international "modernism" with vernacular revival' (Craig, 1987
4:6). Robert Crawford argues that a 'cursory account of Modernism stresses its
cosmopolitanism and internationalism, presenting it as a facet of "high" metropolitan culture. But there is another, equally important, side of Modernism that
is demotic and crucially "provincial"' (Crawford 218-19). It is Crawford's demotic
'equally important' side that MacDiarmid mainly emphasises in his contemporary
writing on the Scottish literary renaissance. But Craig's 'conjunction' is broadly
more useful. Though not part of '"high" metropolitan culture', the Scottish literary renaissance was neither disconnected from its proponents (for example,
Eliot, Pound, Woolf) nor devoid of 'cosmopolitanism and internationalism'. The

international reach of the phrase 'Scottish literary renaissance' seems confirmed when Denis Saurat publishes his article 'Le Groupe de "la Renaissance Écossaise"' in *Revue Anglo-Americaine* ((April 1924) 1-13; part published in McCulloch, 2004 53-54); Saurat had taught French at Glasgow University but was now at the University of Bordeaux. The peripatetic life of Edwin and Willa Muir (taking place actually and intellectually in European as well as London and Scottish contexts) and MacDiarmid's raiding of contemporary European writers for his poetry provide further examples of the interactions between these supposedly separate kinds of modernism and renaissancism. Another link is provided by Leonard and Virginia Woolf's Hogarth Press, founded in 1917, to publish new (with some experimental) work. They were to publish translations, and also pamphlets (in The Hogarth Essays) on politics, psychoanalysis, aesthetics, and feminism, including, in the first series, Virginia Woolf's *Mr. Bennett and Mrs. Brown* (1924), Roger Fry's *The Artist and Psycho-analysis* (1924), John Maynard Keynes's *A Short View of Russia* (1925), Willa Muir's *Women: An Inquiry* (1925) and Edith Sitwell's *Poetry and Criticism* (1925).

Both 'international' and 'national' modernisms and renaissancisms deal in discontinuities and continuities with their literary and cultural past. The 'shock of disenchantment' (Drew 138) in the Scottish renaissance's case is not just with the Victorians as a whole, but specifically with the Kailyard (part of the *Glasgow Herald's* 'Whistle Binkies'), that late Scottish Victorian movement of nostalgic poetry, drama and fiction which, for the renaissancists, conjures up the worst of images of a rural Scotland (full of 'lads o' pairts', ministers, patronised lower classes) that no longer, if it ever had, existed. C. M. Grieve writes, in an essay on Neil Munro, of 'the imminence — and vital necessity — of a very deep cleavage between us and all our predecessors'; he specifies George Douglas Brown's *The House with the Green Shutters* (1901) as 'a book of indubitable genius' which made a 'timely, desirable, effective, and irreversible contribution to Scottish letters' (Grieve, 1931 21, 23). It might be that the true start, in publishing terms, of the Scottish literary renaissance is the publication of Brown's enraged *The House with the Green Shutters*, the novel marking the essential turning point in the rupture with the nineteenth century for Scottish renaissancism and modernism. Brown's novel contains great sentimental moments like the death of the pony, illuminated in the loose-box by a 'shaft of golden light, aswarm with motes, slanted in the quietness' (Brown, 1901; 1985 136), equivalent to the deaths in Kailyard novels of students returning from the University with college prizes (see, for example, Ian MacLaren's *Beside the Bonnie Briar Bush*, cited Campbell 69-70). Brown's certainties of narrative style and control might also not seem 'modernist'. But the novel's absolute rebellion against and rejection of the recent Scottish writing of the Kailyard, its 'almost terrifying dissatisfaction' with the Scotland Brown had known (Speirs 161), provide the essential break with the past, Grieve's 'very deep cleavage', which allows for no return. Both of Willa Muir's published novels, Nan Shepherd's three novels (*The Quarry Wood* (1928), *The Weatherhouse* (1930) and *A Pass in the Grampians* (1933)[4]) and the first two novels (*Sunset Song* (1932) and *Cloud Howe* (1933)) of Lewis Grassic Gibbon's trilogy, *The Scots Quair*, all contain strong elements of Brown's anti-Kailyardism and exemplify intersections of anti-Kailyardism with modernism and renaissancism.

## Scottish women fiction writers of the Scottish literary renaissance

MacDiarmid, the driving force of the articulation of the Scottish literary renaissance, is primarily interested in poetry; his mapping of the renaissance in poetry (particularly his own), later taken as indicative of its true identity, led to a peripheralisation of prose fiction. This in turn allows the work of the women novelists of the renaissance to be discounted. Neil Gunn, from his Highland position, and Gibbon are acknowledged as exceptions to the poetic rule (their prose itself seen as at least partly poetic in language and style). But the novels by writers such as Lorna Moon, Catherine Carswell, Willa Muir, Nan Shepherd, Nancy Brysson Morrison (all publishing in the nineteen twenties and nineteen thirties) disappeared after their first publication until their republication as part of the search for both women and Scottish writers in the nineteen eighties and nineties' republications of Canongate Classics. Of Scottish women novelists of the literary renaissance, only Naomi Mitchison continued to have a literary reputation, partly because of her output as a historical novelist, and perhaps also through her links with 'metropolitan' modernism, for example her collaboration with Wyndham Lewis in *Beyond This Limit* (1935), an extraordinary tale of a nightmare journey in contemporary Paris and London, each section spurred on by (and interspersed with) Lewis's ultra-modernist illustrations. Of the five, only Mitchison is mentioned in Kurt Wittig's *The Scottish Tradition in Literature* (1978); he briefly refers to *The Bull Calves* (1947), giving it its place in his Scottish tradition as 'a serious attempt to recreate history as the people must then have seen it; the ultimate object . . . to determine the common denominator of Scotland's two national traditions, the Lowland and the Highland' (Wittig 324). Carswell's reputation, until the republication by Virago of *Open the Door!* in 1986 and *The Camomile* in 1987, rested more with her friendship with D. H. Lawrence and her biography of him, *The Savage Pilgrimage* (1932), and her *Robert Burns* (1933). She was one of the many journeywomen writers, earning her living by journalism, reviews, and commissions, but struggling during the Depression; she wrote in a 1931 letter to Florence Marian McNeill (another Scottish writer struggling to make a living, later known for *The Scots Kitchen*) about her financial situation:

> Yes, it is beastly never being able to get new clothes one chooses oneself
> and how tiresome all the shifts of poverty to oneself, and alas to others . .
> . . We must all hang on a bit longer. I get encouraging news from U.S.A.
> and more good reviews (no publishers' statements for a while yet) and
> I have a ticket and a half for the Irish Sweep, which is being run on my
> birthday. We may turn up trumps yet! (23 March 1931; Carswell, 1997 215)

A few days later, Gunn wrote to McNeill as well, commenting on Carswell's failure to publish more novels:

> I read Catherine Carswell's *Open the Door!* It's a splendid piece of work in
> every way. First class stuff in it. Why that woman did not go on writing
> novels, seeing she has taken writing as her job, heaven alone knows. One
> is almost tempted to wonder as to failure of inspiration or imagination or
> whatever it's called. Otherwise she is an ass. For it obviously is not laziness.
> Her energy, in detail, is remarkable. She has, however, two besetting sins:
> honesty and sincerity. (Gunn 12)

This comment applies not just to Carswell but to Muir (whom Gunn also knew), also always scraping for money, with her two published novels and a continuous working life connected with writing of various kinds. Gunn sees himself as having 'a certain second view from the non-literary angle. For I am not really a literary man . . . . I play a little at it, but I laugh a little too' (15 April 1931; Gunn 13); he writes this a few days after his comment on Carswell, to Nan Shepherd, that other writer who earned her living in another profession, Gunn in the Customs and Excise Office in the Highlands, and Shepherd in the Teachers' Training College in Aberdeen.[5] Both letters are reminders of the links in friendship that existed between all the Scottish renaissance writers, men and women, commenting on each others' work in letters and (in MacDiarmid and Lewis Grassic Gibbon's case) commissioning essays or pamphlets from each other. Catherine and Donald Carswell include both MacDiarmid's and Edwin Muir's poetry in their anthology, *The Scots Week-End and Caledonian Vade-Mecum for Host, Guest and Wayfarer* (1936), as well as work by other less well known contemporary Scottish poets such as Helen Cruickshank and William Soutar. The much more prolific Nancy Brysson Morrison was also known to

Muir;[6] her first novel, *Breakers* (1930), is historical, as is *The Gowk Storm* (1933; republished 1988) on which her reputation now lies. Her other works are biographical;[7] she also wrote, under the name of Christine Strathern, twenty-eight romance novels (1942-59) and presumably earned her living from her writing although only *The Gowk Storm* has been republished. Shepherd published only three novels, *The Quarry Wood* (1928; republished 1988), *The Weatherhouse* (1930; republished 1989), *A Pass in the Grampians* (1933; republished 1996), her collection of poetry, *In the Cairngorms* (1934), and her non-fiction exploration, *The Living Mountains* (1977; republished 1996); otherwise her literary work was mainly confined to her editing of *Aberdeen University Review*, 1957-64. But all these Scottish women writers, whether earning their living from their writing or by other means, write in their modernist fiction (that is, those works published within the modernist period of the nineteen twenties and nineteen thirties) about the position of women in Scotland; they all, in Rachel Blau DuPlessis's words, examine in various ways 'how social practices surrounding gender have entered narrative' and they all use 'narrative to make critical statements about the psychosexual and sociocultural construction of women' (DuPlessis 4), providing a very different view of Scotland than is to be found in their male counterparts' writing.

The extent to which Willa Muir devotes all her writings (life-writing included) to exploring DuPlessis's 'psychosexual and sociocultural construction of women' is considered in the following chapters. But 'Clock-a-doodle-doo', a short story that she contributes to *The Modern Scot* in 1934 (for the full text, see Appendix I; page references below are to the original publication), is her piece of work that fits most neatly into this discussion of modernism and renaissancism, providing a commentary and conclusion to this chapter. *The Modern Scot*, published by James Whyte in St Andrews, 1930-36, was an organ for the discussion of Scottish culture and politics from the perspective of the Scottish literary renaissance; it published critical and polemical discussions on culture, literature and art, reviews of current works, translations, original poems and short stories; its contributors include MacDiarmid, both Muirs, Catherine Carswell, and many others. Its second volume carries a review of Edwin Muir's novel, *The Three Brothers*, by Rebecca West (April 1931 85-87). Its early covers are fine examples of modernist art deco design with a Scottish slant (for the design for the April 1931 issue by Edward Calligan, Dundee School of Art, see 32)[8]. Evidence of the strong presence of art deco design in Scotland of the nineteen thirties can be seen in the advertisements that the Dundee firm, Thomas Justice and sons, placed regularly in its pages (for examples, see 102); perhaps Muir would have disliked this kind of 'good' modern furniture as G. N. Scott recalls 'her abhorrence of a word like "lounge"' (Scott 42). Whyte himself had his house in North St., St Andrews 'built in the then avant garde Bauhaus style' (Scott 38; see 48). Of Willa Muir's work, *The Modern Scot* published two pieces translated from Broch and one from Kafka, a review of A. S. Neill's *The Problem Parent*, and a chapter each from *Mrs Ritchie* and *Mrs Grundy in Scotland* (see Muir's bibliography for details). 'Clock-a-doodle-doo' is the piece of fiction that Muir wrote specifically for publication in volume 5 of *The Modern Scot*, apparently the only short story (as opposed to chapter from a novel) that she published, although other short stories exist among her archives (for example, 'The Fur Coat' (St Andrews)). Its importance lies in its context as well as its content, embedded as it is in what was in many ways the house journal of Scottish renaissancism in the nineteen thirties. It is a satire on modernist and renaissancist concerns and on ideas of time that opposes 'the great cosmic rhythm of Time' (5:47) to the world of a room of clocks; it is also a satire on the maleness of the Scottish literary renaissance.

The story's four and a half pages concern a group of clocks, 'of every conceivable size and shape' (5:47), which cover the three walls of a room; the fourth wall is 'clear glass as if it were an enormous show-case' (5:46), setting up the idea of an outside monitoring gaze. Both the rays of the sun and of the moon sweep the room. The only human being is 'a Woman' who comes in every day to wind up the clocks, a 'mere servant of the cog-wheels' (5:48), 'the servant of my will' (5:50), according to the 'Clever Clock'; she is the keeper of the display who 'handled the weights lovingly' (5:46) but is otherwise uninterested in the mechanisms of the clocks, puzzling them by her indifference. They resent her for this and for their fear, for if the mechanism of a clock fails in the night it is as if its reality is annihilated. An opposition between natural and clock time is established, with the 'Clever Clock' convinced that time runs according to the powerful, if erratic, 'super-clock' of the moon (5:46-47), while the room's one 'very grandfatherly clock' tries 'in vain to discourage . . . the heresy of revering the moon', insisting that they all 'belong to the great cosmic rhythm of Time' through the sun's daily movements (5:47). The old and wise clock's sounds are made inaudible by the impatient clacking of the younger clocks. Muir presents the old clock as a representative of wisdom and good sense who understands the rhythms of the natural world where everything moves in relationship to the cycle of the sun, the moon 'merely the sun's pendulum' (5:47). The story then moves from its opposition between nature and the mechanical into a satire on modernism itself. For the Clever Clock the whole point of the unreadable numbers on the moon's face (with which the young clocks identify) is that they are 'illegible, because its meaning lies hidden in its private cog-wheels, because it is an intricate and baffling piece of mechanism, unlike your hum-drum, bourgeois sun' (5:47). This is modernist art, the more intricate and baffling, the more successful it is, precisely because of its incomprehensibility. The readable is humdrum and bourgeois (like the Victorian and Edwardian novel or pre-Cubist art).

J. H. Whyte's house in St Andrews.

A critical review of a Futurist exhibition in 1912 describes, in terms the Clever Clock would approve, the kind of art produced specifically with the intention of asserting a split with the supposedly stultified past of Victorian and Edwardian values and artistic habits: 'You represent all the different planes in the flat, and then you disturb all their relations to each other, as if you had given them a jolt; your object being to express the sensation produced by the changes of swift and complex movement'. The reviewer sees Futurist art as being made to 'a recipe . . . which the dullest student could practise if he chose' (*Times*, 1 March 1912 11). But this description of the break up of the planes and disturbance of their relation to each other expresses what the modernist writers also attempt in their exploration of Shepherd's 'altered point of balance of the world's knowledge' (Shepherd, 1930; 1996 11). Drew explicitly connects writing and painting when she writes in 1926 about 'a literary parallel to those painters who attempt to suggest energy by breaking up figures and projecting their parts on to different planes so as to give an impression of movement' (Drew 260-61). Shepherd satirically connects the oddities of modern art and writing in *A Pass in the Grampians* (1933):

> 'There's a funny shy boy painting up above Balbriggie', said Jenny. 'You know, the kind of picture that you don't know what it is. It's all right in Paris and places like that, but rather odd when you know it's the Grassie Burn and Craig Clach, don't you think?'
> 'Like a manuscript that came in last month . . . . I couldn't make head nor tail of what it meant. The words were all in the wrong places. But the author thanked me for the beautiful typing, so I suppose he meant them like that'. (Shepherd, 1933; 1996 29-30)

These exchanges in *A Pass* are part of the larger battle between city and country for the heart of young Jenny, the battle that is an enactment of 'the dichotomy [Jenny] faces between a love of her home region and recognition that she must escape it' and part of 'a wider debate upon the role of the regional' (Lumsden 103). The modern is represented by the city which ultimately wins Jenny away from the Grampians. The effect of these passages, whether satirical or critical in intention, is to give an articulation of the jangling shock of the new that modernism and renaissancism relies on to make clear its break with the rejected past. And Muir's 'Clock-a-doodle-doo', while satirising the 'intricate and the baffling', is grounded thoroughly in this movement.

Elsewhere Muir expresses her dislike for the side of Scotland that wallows in sentimental piety, particularly in *Mrs Grundy in Scotland* and the much later *Living with Ballads*, connecting that piety with the repressive effects of Calvinism and presbyterianism. But in this story, written shortly before *Mrs Grundy*, it is only an insult thrown at the wise old clock by the Clever Clock. In the opposition between young and old, the Clever Clock accuses the old clock of simply trying to 'foist . . . face-values wrapped up in pious sentimentality' onto the young clocks (5:47). Muir's mischievous enjoyment here is in satirising the young, too-clever-by-half, Clever Clock. The title itself indicates that it is maleness that is being satirised, with the strutting of the cock, or the Clever Clock, shown against the background of 'the Woman' keeping the world to rights. It surely satirises MacDiarmid, the impassioned instigator of the Scottish literary renaissance for the previous ten years, intent on rejecting and casting off the cultural Father of Victorian Scotland. Always something of an *enfant terrible* and a clever clogs (in the colloquial sense of showing off his own knowledge and cleverness), politically both Marxist and nationalist, and swinging wildly between the two at times, MacDiarmid seems pointedly represented by the Clever Clock's joyful embracing of illegibility: 'I am I. I am my cog-wheels . . . . We must free our terminology from the materialism of content, if we are to discover the laws of Pure Horological Thought' (5:48-49). The Clever Clock might also represent metropolitan modernists such as Wyndham Lewis, both artist and writer, founder of the modernist statement *Blast*, and satirist in a particularly ageist way of Muir and her relationship to Edwin in *The Apes of God* (1930) (see 'Life and Context'). Of course, Lewis (born 1882) was older than Muir, and MacDiarmid only two years younger, but it is the impulse of rebellious youth assumed by male modernists, rather than actual youth, that is satirised in 'Clock-a-doodle-doo'.

The Clever Clock, not realising that 'there was a tiny screw loose' (5:49) which prevented his little wooden figures from moving, exasperated by 'marking Time' (5:49), dislodges the final balancing weight from his pendulum: 'Now I am Really Unique . . . . Now I can swing from one extreme to the other as much as I like! There is no other clock like me in the whole universe . . . . This is — clackety-clack — this is the Horological Renaissance!' (5:50). The Woman, finding a little pile of discarded numbers and the pendulum balance on the floor the next day, carries the self-destructed clock away: '"Now I move from the wall as I promised you. This Woman is the servant of my will"' (5:50). The woman carries him out, closing the door on a false renaissance based on individual male pride. It provides a sharp end to Muir's piece. Her only published piece of direct satire, it appears in *The Modern Scot* in June 1934, and cannot have endeared her to MacDiarmid who must have been able to interpret the obvious satirical strokes against the Scottish literary renaissance. However, any literalist interpretation seeking identities is entertaining but, in the end, unnecessary. The story is a successful joke or jeux d'esprit, detonating itself in the Scottish literary renaissance's current house journal. It remains a fresh and funny satire, light-heartedly targeting male presumptions as well as modernist and renaissancist preoccupations.

## Notes

1. Sir Paul Harvey (ed.); first published in November and reprinted December 1932, and then again with corrections in January and March 1933, and January 1934, it was intended as a 'useful companion to ordinary everyday readers of English literature' (v). The bookplate on my 1934 copy seems to confirm the breadth of intended readership; it is for the Institution of Railway Signal Engineers Incorporated, and the volume was presented as first prize, session 1934, to B. S. Finley Simpson for his essay on 'Protection of Level Crossings'.

2. Elizabeth A. Drew (1887-1965); Drew's works include *Discovering Poetry* (London: OUP, 1933), *The Enjoyment of Literature* (New York: Norton, 1935), *Discovering Drama* (London: Cape, 1937, and New York: Norton, 1937), *T. S. Eliot, the Design of His Poetry* (New York: Scribner's & Son, 1949, and London: Eyre & Spottiswoode, 1950), and a novel, *Six Hearts* (London: Cape, 1930).

3. Where Grieve publishes under his original name, Grieve is cited; where he publishes under his pseudonym, MacDiarmid is cited. 'Grieve' predates 'MacDiarmid', but in the end it was as MacDiarmid that he became most known, his poetic signature overshadowing his real name.

4. Grassic Gibbon arguably took much from Shepherd's *The Quarry Wood* (1928) to form his picture of Chris Guthrie's growing up in *Sunset Song* (1932). But he clearly found Shepherd's last novel unconvincing and irritating: 'Miss Nan Shepherd writes about farm life in Kincardineshire, a farmer's pretty granddaughter, a prima donna who disturbs the peace, and God alone knows who . . . . This is a Scots religion and Scots people at three removes —gutted, castrated, and genteelly vulgarised' ('Scots Novels of the Half-Year', *Free Man* 2:21 (24 June 1933) 7; McCulloch, 2004 97). Gibbon's assumption of superiority over his fellow north east writer may have a class root, an assumption that his rural Aberdeenshire background had been more deprived than Shepherd's, or may perhaps come from

the supposed superiority of one who leaves Scotland over one who stays. *A Pass in the Grampians* certainly contains hints of Kailyardism, particularly in the early descriptions of the grandfather and his three brothers, but Gibbon's criticism probably equally stems from his incapacity to understand the subtlety of Shepherd's approach in her short novel to the battles between the city and the country, the modern and the old.

5. Neil Gunn later wrote to J. B. Pick a letter that both illustrates the links between these writers and the financial realities and precariousness of their lives: 'The only writing I have done recently was to the Lord Advocate who wanted my appreciation of the national significance of the work of Marian McNeill (*The Scots Kitchen*) so that he could submit it to Downing Street. Result: Marian has got her Civil List pension. I have recently been moving towards a similar end in the case of Edwin and Willa Muir. But plenty of time for that, for Edwin is still using the cash an American University has given him for work on the Scottish ballads. That is the good and proper end for all true literary ladies and gents. But for the casuals or casualties of the literary fringe like you and me, it's the commercial world and never say die' (nd, late nineteen fifties; Hart and Pick 261).

6. Muir wrote one of her 'Ephemeridae' for Edwin to Nancy Brysson Morrison (see 165 and Appendix IV).

7. One of Morrison's biographies was *True Minds: The Marriage of Thomas and Jane Welsh Carlyle* (1974); Elizabeth A. Drew had earlier written *Jane Welsh and Jane Carlyle* (1928). Virginia Woolf also wrote on Jane Welsh Carlyle, famously describing her 'genius' as 'positive, direct, and practical,' and the 'incomparable brilliancy' of her letters as due to 'the hawk-like swoop and descent of her mind upon facts' (Woolf 1932 198). Presumably their interest in Welsh Carlyle was as a woman who wrote all her life but never published, as well as in her cultural role as storyteller and wife of Thomas Carlyle, himself representative of a metropolitan centre of Victorian and Scottish letters and of the Victorian patriarchy. In the 1924 pamphlet '*Mr. Bennett and Mrs. Brown*', Woolf expressed an explicit view of the damaging effect for both of traditional gender relations: 'consider the married life of the Carlyles, and bewail the waste, the futility, for him and for her, of the horrible domestic tradition which made it seemly for a woman of genius

to spend her time chasing beetles, scouring saucepans, instead of writing books'
(Woolf, 1924 5)

8. For more on James H. Whyte and *The Modern Scot*, see Normand 36-64.

# MRS. GRUNDY
# IN SCOTLAND

*by*

## WILLA MUIR

*in*

## THE VOICE OF SCOTLAND
### A Series of Ten Books

*Mrs Grundy in Scotland* dust cover.

# Polemics

Muir's pamphlet *Women: An Inquiry* (1925) and her short book *Mrs Grundy in Scotland* (1936) were written in the between-war period of the nineteen twenties and thirties when British society (in common with mainland Europe and elsewhere) was coming to terms with post-war capitalism and the changing position of women. Some of the intellectual and literary shifts have already been considered in the previous chapter. This chapter looks particularly at the vigorous discussions of women's roles and position that were taking place in these two works by Muir and in works by other feminists. The energy and intellectual passion shown by Muir in her two early non-fiction works lead to calling the chapter 'Polemics', using the word in a positive, not negative, way. Discussions of women's roles can be found from the point of view of the older feminists who had campaigned for the suffrage before the war and also by the newer, younger feminists. What they all have in common is the assumption that women's position and society had changed (and was still changing).

There is some evidence of feminist impact at the beginning of the war in Wyndham Lewis's *Blast*, that foundational text for British modernism; it contains a story by the feminist Rebecca West, 'Indissoluble Matrimony' (no. 1 (20 June 1914) 98-117); in the same issue, suffragettes are addressed (in large block capitals): 'A Word of Advice. / In destruction, as in other things, / stick to what you understand. / We make you a present of our votes. / Only leave works of art alone. / You might some day destroy a / good picture by accident'. Dekoven points out that, in its 'characteristically ironic' tone, it admires the 'energy' of the suffragettes. 'You and artists are the only things (you don't mind being called things?) left in England with a little life in them' (*Blast*, no. 1 151; Dekoven 177). This presence in *Blast*'s first issue of both ironic and straightforward references to feminism neatly confirms the early presence of women and their concerns in modernism.

Most of the suffragettes famously put aside their campaign for suffrage for women for the duration of the war. But works concerned with women's position and issues continues to be published. Dorothy Richardson's 'The Reality of Feminism' was a review of three books, *Towards a Sane Feminism, Women in the Apostolic Church* and *Woman's Effort* (*Ploughshare* n. s. 2:8 [Sept. 1917] 241-46; cited Vanacker 192-93). After 1918, the end of war, and the partial granting of the vote to women, concentration on the one issue campaign passes and there is a broader recognition of changing roles for women and the continuing need for discussion of these roles. Millicent Fawcett, perhaps the leading suffragist, publishes *The Woman's Victory — and After* in 1920; the suffragette Cicely Hamilton writes in *Time and Tide* in 1922 of 'The Backwash of Feminism':

> To-day in feminism, as in many other 'isms, is the day of disillusion and something like perceptible retreat; of the backwash, the natural reaction that follows on every advance. With the granting of enfranchisement the suffragist achieved her objective; but . . . found the fruits of victory not easy to grasp and, even when grasped, less substantial than they looked from a distance. (*Time and Tide* (1922) 2:853)

Despite the 'backwash', suffrage was extended to all women over 21 in 1928, just at that point where the world was about to descend into economic depression. It was clear that if women's position in society was to improve, it was dependent on more than full suffrage. Naomi Mitchison writes in 1928 to Elizabeth Haldane (her Suffragist aunt) about the feelings of younger feminists:

> You have still a balance to your life: all that incredible pre-war period when things seemed in the main settled, just moving solidly and calmly like a glacier towards all sorts of progress. But we have had the bottom of things knocked out completely, we have been sent reeling into chaos and it seems to us that none of your standards are either fixed or necessarily good because in the end they resulted in this smash-up. We have to learn to try and make a world for ourselves, basing it as far as possible on love and awareness, mental and bodily, because it seems to us that all the repressions and formulae, all the cutting off of part of experience, which perhaps looked sensible and even right in those calm years, have not worked. (NLS MS 6033.295; cited Alberti, 1989 222)

Muir, although seven years older than Mitchison and an adult by the start of world war one, seems also to be part of the post-war world that Mitchison describes, reaching for the incorporation of all parts of experience as a way of making sense of that society which has 'been sent reeling into chaos'. Part of that making sense was to analyse female / male relationships in terms current at the time. Muir's *Women: An Inquiry*, written three years before Mitchison's letter, must be read in relation to this 'time of political and theoretical turmoil for feminism' as one of the 'new accounts of the relative position and social contributions of women and men' (Innes

119). It can also be read as a narrative of Muir's struggle with what being a creative woman in a patriarchal world meant with Muir's insecurities about her first small book characteristically expressed in her letters to Sydney and Violet Schiff at the time.

Ray Strachey, another feminist, writes *The Cause. A Short History of the Women's Movement in Great Britain* to celebrate this point of gaining full suffrage. Its final chapter discusses the increasing freedom of women after world war one: 'In the ten years between the first instalment of Women's Suffrage and the granting of full political equality the Women's Cause moved fast' (Strachey, 1928 386). Strachey summarises her optimism for girls: 'In work as much as in play, in study as much as in games, there is now little divergence, and scholarship, athletics, travel, tobacco, and even latch-keys and cheque-books are no longer the sole prerogatives of men' (Strachey, 1928 387). She points out that the 'widening of the physical world for women which these changed conditions involve did not really begin before 1890' and goes on to discuss the bicycle as an 'emancipating agent' (Strachey, 1928 387). That her starting date, 1890, for this 'widening of the physical world for women' is also Willa Muir's birth date is not a suprise. It indicates that the young Wilhelmina Anderson grew up with the widening possibilities for women's equality and greater freedom beckoning from beyond the boundaries of Montrose.

The political and social movements for the equality of women, feminism (the word itself first used in 1895), suffragism and the more radical suffragette movement, were all on the move as Anderson grew up and then went to St Andrews to study in 1907. Strachey herself was a near contemporary of Anderson's; born Ray Costelloe in 1887, she studied mathematics at Newnham College, Cambridge, but spent so much time on suffrage campaigns between 1905 and 1909 that she was 280th out of 286 candidates in her Tripos, in contrast to Anderson's first class degree at St Andrews in 1911. Costelloe married Oliver (Lytton Strachey's brother) in 1911, and went on to a career as an activist, editor, journalist and writer, before dying in 1940 (Barbara Strachey 3-4). Her life trajectory, as part of an English political and cultural intelligentsia that was more privileged and certainly more metropolitan than was Anderson's upbringing and education, nonetheless carries parallels. She was more politically active, more of a historian with her concern to record the history of the women's movement from the perspective of the suffragists, working on it at much the same time as Willa Muir was writing her more philosophical pamphlet on women's position, *Women: An Inquiry*. Strachey provides another reminder that Anderson / Muir is not unique. Muir's Scottishness provides difference, but their similar readings of women's position and commitment from young womanhood (and earlier) to feminism, their University educations, their marriages, and their working lives of professional writing and broadcasting, bracket them both in a world aware of wide social changes and possibilities. In her preface to *The Cause*, Strachey wrote:

> [T]he true history of the Women's Movement is the whole history of the nineteenth century; nothing which occurred in those years could be irrelevant to the great social change which was going on, and nothing was without its share of influence upon it. I have not referred to such events as the Indian Mutiny, the Franco-Prussian War, the Home Rule Agitation, or the Parliament Act, and yet I know that these things undoubtedly had a bearing on the problem and did their part, along with the whole progress of the world, in shaping this special development. (Strachey, 1928 5)

Muir takes a similarly broad view to the development of women's position, but in her case, she adds in the unconscious, the world of dreams, Freud and psychoanalysis. Strachey was a novelist as well, but her view of the changing world is more that of a social historian, while Muir's is that of an instinctive feminist and a writer rooted in the intellectual currents of her education and young adulthood. This chapter discusses Muir's feminism and its interconnections in relation to two pieces of her inter-war work, written between 1924 and 1936, *Women: An Inquiry* and *Mrs Grundy in Scotland*.

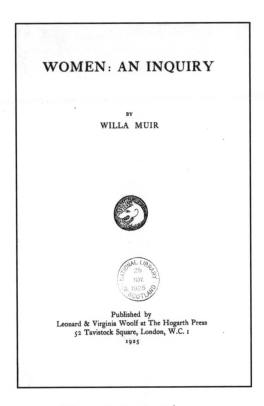

WOMEN: AN INQUIRY

BY

WILLA MUIR

Published by
Leonard & Virginia Woolf at The Hogarth Press
52 Tavistock Square, London, W.C. 1
1925

*Women: An Inquiry,* title page

## *Women: An Inquiry*

*Women: An Inquiry,* published in London in 1925 and in New York in 1926, is Muir's first published work. Muir apparently began serious work on it during August 1924, Edwin mentioning to Sydney Schiff that she 'will get on to her book' (18 Aug. 1924; Schiff papers; Butter, 1974 41). Schiff apparently suggested to Muir, before he had read it, that it should be a short book rather than a Hogarth essay. Muir, disconcerted by Schiff's request for a synoptic index to the book, replies with a combination of modesty and insecurity:

> I doubt if my essay can be resolved into such an index without making
> it sound pretentious, & a little absurd. For it is only an essay: I had not
> thought of it as a book, although Edwin says it would make quite a good
> small book . . . . I had thought of trying to place it as one of the Hogarth
> Essays, which, according to an advertisement, are not necessarily literary:
> but I don't want to take advantage of their kindness to Edwin . . . . I hope
> you like the essay. It is not good enough to make me feel confident: as a

matter of fact, I am a little twittery about it. If I had been a man I could have done it with less effort! (WM to S. Schiff, 25 Nov. 1924; Schiff papers; BL)

Muir's open acknowledgement of her lack of confidence, tellingly bracketed with the assumption that her gender makes it more difficult for her to feel confidence, is not just first-book nerves. It is true that the Schiffs were the first to read it apart from Edwin, and that they represent for Muir highly cultured and knowledgeable readers with access to the publishing and the literary world, while Muir at 34 is a writing and publishing novice. But Muir never loses her tendency to self-denigrate her work while writing, revising and after publication (in letters, journals or in *Belonging*), with an ultra-critical sense of her own capacities. This is part of her own innate sense of insecurity, of being an outsider, but is clearly also part of the problem of being a woman who, even when writing critically about gender relations, still grapples with her own lack of confident self-belief. But while her letter to Sydney Schiff contains her default position of an internalised lack of confidence (both gender imposed and specific to herself, if the two can be separated), it also contains a brisk defence against the idea of a synoptic index; the essay has already been condensed to about a third of its 'former size' and is 'closely packed'; 'some of the divisions' (it had ten sections) contain 'so much matter that it would be almost impossible to synopsize them briefly for an index. Also I doubt if any chapter could bear being read by itself: they all hang closely together — except perhaps VIII' (25 Nov. 1924; Schiff papers; BL). Violet Schiff sent her some suggestions after reading the essay and Muir wrote a characteristically cheerful and grateful letter back accepting some and resisting others. [1]

After an apparent failure by Sydney Schiff to interest either Constable or Chatto & Windus, it was finally sent to Leonard Woolf, January 1925 (14 Jan. 1925; Schiff papers; BL), and accepted by him in early March for publication by Hogarth Press; Muir tells the Schiffs that 'Woolf asks if I would shorten the essay somewhat: I shall find out what idea he has about the desirable size & see if I can do it or not' (4 March 1925; Schiff papers; BL). It becomes a thirty three page pamphlet in the first series of 'The Hogarth Essays' (number ten), just as Muir had originally envisaged it. The first pamphlet in the series, *Mr. Bennett and Mrs. Brown* (1924), is an early example of Virginia Woolf's interest in the difficulties of women in literature; it is also a discussion of the new writing and what was to be expected of it, the issue of 'character', and the evolving 'form of the novel, so clumsy, verbose, and undramatic, so rich, elastic, and alive' (Woolf, 1924 9-10). *Women: An Inquiry* is more of a generalised and philosophical exploration of differences between men and women. It is described by Sue Innes as 'an attempt to develop feminist theory, particularly ideas of gender difference in relation to psychoanalytic thinking' (Innes 114). It sets itself the task of searching out the 'essential difference' between women and men, rather than the analysis of socially proscribed differences which seems to underwrite much of Willa Muir's later writing. Despite including in the first paragraph the caution 'if it is an essential difference', the pamphlet is mainly rooted in an essentialist view of women, that is, the belief that gender differences and attributes are inherent, and, therefore, inevitable: 'One might reasonably expect the difference between them, if it is an essential difference, to be now capable of formulation. An essential difference would be a difference distinctively human, that is, spiritual as well as physical, and at the same time distinctively sexual' (1; all page references are to the Canongate edition). It is 'capable of formulation', clearly, because they have arrived at this point in the developing rights and changing positions for women. Muir concludes in the final paragraph that the 'present inquiry pretends to be nothing more than a stimulus to the further investigation of essential differences between men and women' (30).

Muir has been criticised by late twentieth and twenty first century critics for the apparent essentialism of her views, essentialism being assumed to be a trap for women, a means of containing them within what, in fact, are socially con-structed (and constricting) rather than 'natural' roles. Margaret Elphinstone sees it as 'an uncomfortable text', and finds it 'strangely conservative and "masculine"' (Elphinstone 405). Margery McCulloch views it as 'puzzling' (McCulloch 2007 91; see also McCulloch, 2004 384). Alison Smith, still critical but in a more positive way, describes it as containing 'the romantic hope . . . for the achievement of an ideal state between the genders, a harmonious balancing between men and women of what she sees as their essential attributes and differences'; she still finds it an essay 'paradoxical in its very analytical voice', with the analytical Muir deciding 'that women are essentially not analytical', but are stronger in the 'unconscious life' (A. Smith 43). Muir's work, non-fiction as well as fiction, is mostly considered by these critics in a literary context with some nods towards intellectual and gender history, with *Women: An Inquiry* mainly considered in the context of discussion of her novels and / or *Belonging*.  But Sue Innes has an extended discussion of Muir's *Women: An Inquiry* in the context of a social science exploration of feminist groups of the early twentieth century in *Love and Work: Feminism, Family and Ideas of Equality and Citizenship, Britain 1900-1939*. She considers it in the context of other contemporary feminists who were more obviously politically commit-ted than Muir (for example, Strachey, see above, and Holtby, see below). On the whole, even though she describes it as 'a problematic text' (Innes 114), she views *Women: An Inquiry* more positively than the literary critics. Innes believes that Muir's exploration of '[s]exual difference particularly in modes of thinking / per-ceiving' is 'acknowledged without entailing female inferiority' (Innes 114). She also sees the pamphlet as containing an 'inchoate radicalism', and interesting 'in its use of psychoanalytic ideas; and its attempt to develop a theory of complementarity applicable to all of life through an examination of gender differences in creativity and cognition' (Innes 116).[2]

The pamphlet clearly does have a tendency to explore a 'different but equal' position, but it is also concerned with resistance to essentialism and oppositions between essentialist views and socially constructed views of gender difference. Muir consistently uses caveats such as 'if', 'yet', 'rightly or wrongly' (1, 5) to limit her exploration in 'this artificially narrowed field of activity' of the 'essential nature of women' (5); she is concerned with equalising man's and woman's apparently differing roles: 'If man's energy is diverted more into conscious life, woman's energy is diverted more into unconscious life, and one is not more important than the other. It is a relative, not an absolute difference; both men and women are human beings, and all that concerns human beings is their joint affair' (7). This is not to say that some of Muir's oppositions do not seem straightforwardly and irritatingly essentialist:

> Unconscious life creates, for example, human beings: conscious life creates, for example, philosophy. If men are stronger in conscious life, and women in unconscious life, their creative powers must express their strength. Men should excel in translating life into conscious forms, women in fostering the growth of life itself. Men will create systems of philosophy or government, while women are creating individual human beings. (8)

While we might now reject Muir's oppositional position, the passage illuminates her view of the parallel yet interlocking processes of the conscious and unconscious. If we separate it for the moment from its female / male connection, we can usefully extrapolate from it onto her technique of inner and outer narratives in *Imagined Corners* in particular. The rational, sociological and anthropological approach belongs with that novel's narrator's analyses of the social structures and interactions of the society while the dreams, the hypnogogic states, belong with the unconscious and provide the interior of the novel and of the characters. After all, this is the Muir who writes to Gunn that 'the dreams I give my characters are meant to be at least as important as their waking actions' (Pick, introduction, *Imagined Corners* ix).

*Women: An Inquiry* begins with views of women in primitive societies and the present, fatherhood (and the difficulty of proving it) and motherhood (easily established), the unconscious, the state and the 'good woman' (not a term of praise in Muir's writing), men and their tendency to patterns and systems, public life for women (and its disadvantages), creativity and art, and the possibilities for women.

Looking at some of it in more detail, it is clear that preoccupations which occur in her later work are already present. Awareness of Freud's ideas and Frazer's anthropological work into primitive societies underwrite the first section: 'In men's societies of a primitive and arrested type where the etiquette of conduct betrays its origin, one can see clearly man's fear of woman. Woman possesses some mysterious power which must be averted by elaborate taboos' (3). She then considers menstruation and childbirth, and the way women are seen as dangerous 'even to-day' (4). The conclusion she draws from this is that 'men's fear of women proves only that women are not naturally inferior and subordinate. It does not prove that they are different from men' (4). She thus clearly lays down the position that women are neither 'naturally inferior' nor 'subordinate', while continuing her pursuit of her investigation into whether women and men are 'different'.

Discussing the way women had been 'regarded as mere receptacles, passive receptive bodies which created nothing', Muir suggests that 'motherhood was allowed by popular opinion to be a creative function, but of a purely physical nature . . . further defined as the sole justifiable function of women'. She moves from this to the point that in 'Oriental countries the still more logical conclusion is drawn that women justify their existence only by producing men-children. In a society committed to this point of view childless women are failures in life, and the unmarried woman is a ridiculous nuisance' (5). Writing as she was in the aftermath of world war one, where the position of the superfluity of unmarried women of child bearing age was much discussed, she adds in a brief Swiftian conclusion: 'If social remedies such as polygamy, suttee, infanticide, or euthanasia are not put into practice, the phrase "superfluous women" comes into existence, and the State is shaken by the problem of what to do with its superfluous women' (5). In *Imagined Corners* she expands on this, exploring the constricted role of the spinster in pre-world war one society, indicating an awareness (only hinted at here) that the problem of 'superfluous women' and attitudes to them is not something caused by the death of all their potential partners in the trenches. These attitudes pre-date the war and are part of the problem of women's unequal position in society. Muir is not alone in her views. In 1921 the *New Statesman*, writing critically of the attitudes implicit in the term, thought it 'absurd on the part of the Press to talk so much of the two thousand [sic, i.e. 2,000,000] "superfluous women", or "thwarted women", as though "superfluous", "thwarted", and "unmarried" were convertible terms' ('Woman', *New Statesman*, 24 Sept. 1921 669; cited Joannou, 1995 79).

The discussion of motherhood is a part of Muir's overall attempt to pin down the possibly essential differences of men and women; it is described at the start of section II as an 'artificially narrowed field of activity', although Muir still intends to look at it for clues as to woman's 'essential nature': 'Yet if motherhood can be defined, rightly or wrongly, as the sole function of women, it must be a function which in some degree expresses the quality of womanhood as distinct from manhood' (5). She then turns to the problematic issue of fatherhood, seeing it at the root of much of what she interprets as the differences between women and men, legally as well as 'essentially', since fatherhood, 'the more casual relationship of the two', could not 'be proved with the same certainty as motherhood':

> In a masculine State, where the father is the only legal parent, the institution of marriage is necessary to prevent fathers from successfully disclaiming their children. Maternity is not so easily denied, and in a feminine State it could be proved without the aid of a marriage contract . . . . As far as the race is concerned, all women are potential mothers, and must have the necessary reserve of energy for this function whether they intend to become mothers or not . . . . Thus men have more energy to waste on their own individual purposes than women. (6)

Marianne Dekoven, discussing Luce Irigaray's work on Freud, summarises woman's position: 'Her terrible power to engender life is repressed and reassigned to the man, who then appropriates all ownership of reproduction and powers of naming, and, therefore, of representation, under what Lacan calls the Name-of-the-Father' (Dekoven 179). Muir's approach is simpler, but similar enough to indicate that the problematics of dealing with the patriarchy, its assumptions, and the overarching power of Freud as intellectual father are as apparent to feminists in the first half of the twentieth century as they are to French feminist theorists in the second half. Muir places woman as being in touch with the unconscious, and man as more part of conscious life; she seems genuinely to see this as a characteristic division which gives power to the woman rather than condemning her to the 'instinctive', the 'intuitive', in a society which she shows as prioritising the 'rational' and the male:

> The unconscious is concerned with growth rather than with form; it is essentially emotional, spontaneous, and irrational. As far as we know, it is concrete in its thinking and not abstract; it creates living agents and not systems of thought. Thus, while conscious processes supply form and permanence in our world, unconscious processes supply growing vitality and change. The creations of unconscious life are wrought in mortal substances, those of conscious life in enduring patterns which are one step removed from life. Unconscious life creates, for example, human beings: conscious life creates, for example, philosophy. If men are stronger in conscious life, and women in unconscious life, their creative powers must express their strength. Men should excel in translating life into its conscious forms, women in fostering the growth of life itself. Men will create

systems of philosophy or government, while women are creating individual human beings. (8)

This is one of the lines of thought difficult for later twentieth century critics to swallow; for example, Kirsty Allen wrote in 1996 that the pamphlet as a whole is 'as entertaining as it is intellectually unconvincing' but 'it seems sadly dated and misguided' (Allen, 1996 vi). For Muir, the 'essential difference between men and women' makes 'them complementary to each other' (7). She continues with a straightforward expression of the equality of this difference:

> There can be no question of absolute domination of one sex by the other when the strength of each lies in a different direction. If man's energy is diverted more into conscious life, woman's energy is diverted more into unconscious life, and one is not more important than the other. It is a relative, not an absolute difference; both men and women are human beings, and all that concerns human beings is their joint affair. (7)

Her belief is in the importance of that 'joint affair', but her division between men creating 'systems of philosophy or government' while 'women create individual human beings' (8) remains troublingly (as opposed to descriptively) essentialist because it seems to undermine women as being fully part of intellectual or political society.

As befits a post-Victorian, post-Edwardian feminist, Muir analyses the complicity of the 'conventionally good woman', acquiescing 'in repression and punishment' in the male State while men praise her 'subserviency and unconsciously despise her'; Muir certainly sees herself as one of the 'fearless women' who do not thwart human life, who do not impose 'obscure dissastisfactions' on their men in private (11-12). Outcasts who have refused to conform to male systems of morality remain individuals to 'the women who love them' (21) and refuse to sacrifice them to 'a code' (23). As befits a modernist feminist, Muir sees 'any confusion produced by the action of women' as only adding to the 'rich confusion of life itself' (23). But Muir also posits an extremely narrow place for women in modern society. Because she defines the modern State as 'a highly organized system of government resting upon other systems, such as those of finance, law, and industry', ramifying 'downwards until they touch the lives of all the individuals who compose the nation' and her view of women's absolute commitment to the individual, this touching of the lives of individuals becomes the 'fitting point for the public activities of women' (25). But this is that very limited view of women's public role that helped contain twentieth century women in the 'caring' professions such as teaching and social work. Women who do take part in public life are then doubly handicapped by Muir's gendered oppositions:

A man can be formal and abstract without losing his human qualities or ceasing to be creative, since his energies are distributed in that way, but a woman cannot . . . . [B]ecause she has killed herself spiritually, a formal woman is twice as formal as a man, and her work is necessarily barren. Most women are instinctively aware of this danger and protect themselves from the hardening of traditional routine by simple indifference to their work and an escape into marriage as soon as possible. But this is merely an evasion of the problem which women must solve in the next generation or two, the problem of leavening the organized systems of society with human values so that mechanical routine is reduced to a minimum. (25-26)

This is a rigid division that condemns women who take part in the work structures of the mechanised world, while giving no indication that responsibility should also lie with men for changing an arid, damaging system. It also carries undercurrents of the barren woman being the unnatural woman, despite Muir's rejection of that idea earlier in the pamphlet. As Dorothy Porter McMillan writes, Muir 'works with some of the binary oppositions that we have come rather to distrust', although she also points out that Muir 'in no sense . . . countenance[s] the use of such distinctions to curtail women's potential' (McMillan 29).

The penultimate section of the essay also draws from standard assumptions that have curtailed women's perceived contributions to art, although it is here that Muir comes closest to Woolf's idea of an androgynous artist figure described in *A Room of One's Own* (1929) 156-57. Muir's artist, presumed to be male, must 'possess both masculine and feminine qualities; that is to say, he has immediate access to the intuitions of unconscious life, as a woman does, and he creates conscious form, as a man does' (27). But she then continues with an entirely gendered view of women's capacities in art: 'if women are handicapped in those arts, such as literature, painting, and the composition of music, where the finished product takes a permanent form detached from the human personality of the artist, they should have an advantage in arts like dancing, singing, and acting, where the actual personality is the medium of expression' (28). She exempts the novel from 'literature' on the equally prejudiced grounds that the 'more elastic the form, the more shapeless it is, the more women are able to use it for sustained work. In literature, at least, this seems to be true. The loose bulk of the novel makes it attractive to women as a medium of expression; and any long works of the first rank written by women are to be found in this form' (28). Muir's own later insecurities about her capacities as a novelist are all brought into play here. After she finishes *The Usurpers* and feels undermined by Edwin's lack of enthusiasm for reading it, she comments in her journal that 'in writing a book' she attends 'far more to the construction, the sequence of incidents, the feeling conveyed, than to the style, although I am not aware of neglecting the style' (14 April 1952; journal; Jan. 1951-Sept. 1953). We are told in the pamphlet that 'women are more likely to be influenced by its content than by its form' in their estimation of a work of art; Muir then 'hazard[s]' an entirely denigratory 'guess that in literature the vocabulary of women contains fewer unusual words than that of men. For the difference between spoken and written language is roughly analogous to the difference between women and men' (29). Muir's relationships to literature, the intellect, and gender relations remain complex and inconsistent all her life, and it is unfair to demand either consistency or a more 'positive' view of 'woman' from this pamphlet. As she writes in the short last section, the 'present enquiry pretends to be nothing more than a stimulus to the further investigation of essential differences between men and women' (30). Dekoven, again discussing Irigaray's work on Freud, writes that the 'vigilant repression and exclusion of the feminine "origin" of life results in the starkness of the familiar normative gendered self / other dualisms of Western culture: masculine / feminine, white / black, higher / lower, culture / nature are only the most rife with political implications of these pervasive dualisms' (Dekoven 179). Muir also deals with these 'pervasive dualisms', while trying hard not to hierarchise them so that the female appears lower than the male. That she should exhibit some tendencies towards inconsistency is unsurprising. Her attempt to place the female and male in equal but different positions is an impossible task, given the weight of patriarchal views, Freud's included, that woman is somehow the lower, the specific, to man's universal superior position.

The problem is not so much that *Women: An Inquiry* is essentialist, though it is, but that the binary oppositions set up by Muir are so rigidly conventional. Binary oppositions are troubling for feminist critics; Hélène Cixous' analysis in the nineteen seventies indicates why this should be so:

Thought has always worked by opposition,

    Speech / Writing

    High / Low

By dual, *hierarchized* oppositions . . . . Myths, legends, books. Philosophical systems . . . . And all the couples of oppositions are *couples* . . . . Is the fact that logocentrism subjects thought — all of the concepts, the codes, the values — to a two-term system, related to 'the' couple, man / woman? . . . The hierarchization subjects the entire conceptual organization to man. A male privilege, which can be seen in the opposition by which it sustains itself, between *activity* and *passivity*. (Cixous 90-91)

French feminists such as Cixous or Luce Irigaray provide later attempts to unravel the gendered oppositions of active / passive, male / female and the problematics of this for feminist analysis and thought. Muir's attempt comes in 1938 in 'Moving in Circles' when she discusses the opposition of 'straight-line' (male) and 'circular-minded' (female) thought systems:

> You will note that I am making my straight-liners masculine and my circular-minded people feminine. I do that partly because I am myself circular-minded and I tend to assume that it is a feminine attribute. Like all generalisations, it is perhaps inaccurate. Yet it is usually taken for granted in popular beliefs about men and women . . . . A woman is supposed not to be able . . . to go straight to the point . . . . I do not say that women cannot do these things; I only say that men naturally assume that a woman does not go straight. (*Listener* 603)

It remains troubling that Muir insists in *Women: An Inquiry* that women are innately more closely allied to the unconscious and assumes that women, not men, must be responsible for change in the future. Also Muir produces a pamphlet that, despite her vaunted display of logical formats and argumentative development, lacks logical development and 'retains an ambivalence about whether . . . [gender] differences are fixed and natural or a socially-constructed continuum' (Innes 147). In fact, as Dorothy Porter McMillan points out, '[l]ike many of her successors in this inquiry Willa Muir is better at defining the problems and asking the questions than she is at providing the answers, but as theoretical underpinning, her essay remains a significant landmark' (29). *Women: An Inquiry* is further evidence of the difficulty of disentangling gender characteristics that are constructed from those that might be innate.

Muir herself clearly saw the pamphlet as part of the argument for feminism and change in women's position and was very disappointed in January 1926 by the lack of response from her peers:

> My old essay has fallen very flat. I don't think people realise its implications — perhaps because of its purposely moderate & reasonable tone. *The Nation* said it was as unexciting as boiled rice. *Time & Tide* has not reviewed it at all! I thought women's societies and associations would have been interested. However — I shall launch bombs next time! (F. Marian McNeill; 26 Jan. 1926; NLS; McCulloch, 2004 201).

She perhaps did not know about the review 'The Future of Women' in the *Times Literary Supplement*; this admires the essay as 'significant because all her material, however familiar, is consistently and freshly seen' and thinks it is 'a substantial contribution' to the question of the 'true relations of men and women' (*TLS*,

26 Nov. 1925 790). Interest now in *Women: An Inquiry* lies partly in its being Muir's earliest work. But it also lies in it being part of that strand of modernism which writes polemically as well as imaginatively, and part of that general movement of work by feminists of the nineteen twenties and nineteen thirties whose childhoods (as Muir said later of herself) 'lay in the backwash of the nineteenth century' ('Moving in Circles' 603). In 1922 Cicely Hamilton is afraid that the backwash to feminism after the gaining of the vote would be problematic for women's advance (Hamilton 2:853). But this other backwash, 'of the nineteenth century', is an essential component of all the changing 'isms of the early twentieth century. *Time and Tide* itself, founded in 1920 as a feminist and left wing periodical (supported by Hamilton and Rebecca West among others), is part of this movement for change. Dekoven comments on the interconnection of Victorianism, modernism and feminism in terms closely related to Muir's themes in *Mrs Grundy in Scotland*: 'feminists were in fact just as committed to overthrowing the Victorian ideal of closeted, domesticated, desexualized, disenfranchised femininity as they were to overthrowing its attendant cultural ideal of high moral insipidity' (Dekoven 177). The women who write non-fiction feminist critiques of society (often from differing standpoints), incorporate into their work psychoanalytic, particularly Freudian, political and social discussions. *Women: An Inquiry* is part of this British cultural exploration of women's changing roles. The process / struggle of Muir's grappling with issues of essentialism, hierarchies, equalities, social constructions, consciousness and unconsciousness is itself the point, rather than whether she is right or wrong, with something heroic being shown in her effort.[3]

Another feminist grappling with the issues is Winifred Holtby in *Women and a Changing Civilisation*, published in 1934 as part of John Lane's 'The Twentieth Century Library'. (Naomi Mitchison's *The Home and a Changing Civilisation* (1934) is also part of this series.) Holtby's work is a more extended piece than either *Women: An Enquiry* or *Mrs Grundy in Scotland*, including two appendices, 'Some of the Laws passed in England since Women obtained Political Enfranchisement' and 'Women's Suffrage in the European Countries' (195-99) and a bibliography which includes Olive Schreiner's *Women and Labour* (1911), Ray Strachey's *The Cause* (1928) and Woolf's *A Room of One's Own* (1929) but not Muir's *Women: An Inquiry*. More discursive and wide-ranging though her book is, Holtby is still writing from similar contexts to Muir with similar attention to working out gender issues. The introduction is headed 'Is there a Woman Problem?', and the conclusion ends with 'The Conditions of Equality', while the title of section III, 'The Inconveniences of Transition' acknowledges both the complicated nature of women's changing roles and resistance to them; this section also shows the effects of psychoanalysis in its chapter headings, including 'The Inferiority Complex', 'The Chivalry Complex', 'The Slump Complex', 'The Modern Girl'. The debate about the superfluous woman (*Women: An Inquiry* 131) recurs in 'Are Spinsters Frustrated?' against which Holtby argues vigorously (Holtby 125-33). In her conclusion she problematises the whole question of female or male characteristics, adding in sexuality, something that Muir avoids discussing in her published non-fiction:

> I think that the real object behind our demand is not to reduce all men
> and women to the same dull pattern . . . . We do not know how much of
> what we usually describe as 'feminine characteristics' are really 'masculine',
> and how much 'masculinity' is common to both sexes . . . . We do not
> even know — though we theorise and penalise with ferocious confidence
> — whether the 'normal' sexual relationship is homo- or bi- or heterosexual.
> (Holtby 192)

But, as Innes indicates, Holtby also 'refers quite straightforwardly to women's "biological tendency to preserve rather than to destroy' (Holtby 50; cited Innes 130) adding weight to Innes's sensible point: 'Whether a view of essential gender differences is espoused or not, and however you explain it, in 1925 most women and men's life circumstances were different' (Innes 131). This view can be read as a mild rebuke to all of us who, as late twentieth and early twenty first century feminist critics, too easily dismiss Muir's views in *Women: An Inquiry* (and elsewhere) as essentialist and neglect the real intellectual courage Muir shows in her explorations.

*Mrs Grundy in Scotland* back dust cover.

## *Mrs Grundy in Scotland*

Although *Women: An Inquiry* was eventually published as part of the Hogarth Essays Series, as has been seen, it was not a commissioned piece. *Mrs Grundy in Scotland*, on the other hand, is part of a commissioned series. Lewis Grassic Gibbon had been invited by Routledge to edit the series 'Meanings in Scotland' (which became 'The Voice of Scotland'; for the front dust cover of *Mrs Grundy*, see 54). Gibbon was going to write on Burns, Compton Mackenzie on Catholicism and Scotland, A. S. Neill on education (for the full list of titles, printed on the back dust cover of *Mrs Grundy*, see above). According to MacDiarmid in January 1935, 'the final set of titles, authors to approach, etc. were the result of a pooling of our various suggestions — in particular, the Whisky one for Gunn, the Sex one for Willa Muir, and the Lenin one for myself were my own suggestion' (Bold, 1984 537). Perhaps listening to her hold forth in St Andrews on 'her favourite topic — phallic symbolism', however much he disliked it or her (see Bold, 1988 333), led to MacDiarmid's suggestion for 'the Sex one for Willa' (although Valda Grieve's anecdote (see 'Life and Context') is dated by Bold as relating to the period in which Muir was already writing the book). Muir was to dedicate *Mrs Grundy in Scotland* to Grassic Gibbon; 'planned for the delectation' it 'can only be dedicated instead, humbly and sorrowfully, to his memory' as he died suddenly in February 1935. Much later she writes of him: 'Unlike Christopher Grieve, he didn't just lift other people's work; he wasn't a master jackdaw of that kind; he had a fertile imagination. (He was a dear chap, and I liked him very much)' (WM to Tom Scott, 20 June 1966; NLS). MacDiarmid inherited Grassic Gibbon's advisory role to the series. Edwin Muir, by this time, was also working on *Scott and Scotland* (1936), his contribution to the series that proved the breaking point in his friendship with MacDiarmid, containing as it does views inimical to MacDiarmid's on Scottish literature and the viability of Scots as a language for intellectual thought.

Joy Hendry, in a brief consideration of Muir's work in 1987, describes *Mrs Grundy in Scotland* as 'an appeal for a reappraisal of women's roles, and of the relation of the individual to the environment' (Hendry 303). Although these can be found in the work, appropriately for the series the discussion in *Mrs Grundy in Scotland* centres more on the repressions and shortcomings of Scotland than on a re-examination of Muir's feminist analysis in a Scottish context. Awareness of the specific repressions of the patriarchy underpin the work and it deals explicitly with issues of gender and nation. There are also attacks on capitalism (as befits a work commissioned by the Marxist Grassic Gibbon), religion (particularly its Scots Presbyterian manifestation) and sustained attacks on the Victorian age, suitable for Muir's modernist post-Victorian position. It is more expansive than *Women: An Enquiry*, consisting of Muir's exploration of Mrs Grundy, the archetype of female sanctimony and social hypocrisy, and her interconnections in Scotland where, according to Muir, there already exists an earlier, powerful version in Mrs MacGrundy. Muir begins with the origin of Mrs Grundy in Thomas Morton's play, *Speed the Plough*, first performed in the Theatre Royal, Covent Garden, 1798. Chapter one, 'Dame Grundy', starts with her first 'appearance' which turns out not to be a literal appearance on stage, Thomas Morton's 'stroke of sheer genius' (1) being 'that the figure presented in the play was not the actual Dame Grundy selling her butter and hectoring her neighbours; it was something more formless, more pervading, more universal; it was the sinister image of Dame Grundy in the consciousness of her neighbour, Dame Ashfield, the bogey that haunted the less successful woman wherever she went' (2). Mrs Grundy moves from this first presence in absence to being a ghost haunting and permeating society; 'from being an imaginary menace in the mind of a farmer's wife, in the minds of a theatre audience' she becomes 'gradually . . . a convenient symbol to express the sum of social forces that surround and often threaten any individual in the world' (3). This idea of Mrs Grundy's figure as 'more formless, more pervading, more universal' (2) is powerfully threatening and Muir connects it with her historical examination of the patriarchy and the role of women in post-Reformation Scotland. Mrs Grundy was generally used as a kind of representation of Victorian hypocrisy and repression for women and Muir is not alone at this time in connecting Mrs Grundy with the position of women. Ray Strachey calls her final chapter of *The Cause* (1928) 'The Death of Mrs Grundy'; she gives no reference in the text of the chapter to the 'Mrs Grundy' concept, so confident is she of the name's resonances. Chapter one of Muir's *Mrs Grundy in Scotland*, exploring Dame Grundy's progress through the nineteenth century in England, concludes with her capacity to 'put a new face on things'; being ousted by 'the amoral power of money . . . from her strongholds in the social life of London', she retreats to the provinces from 'whence she sprang'. If threatened there, 'she can always find a home in Scotland' which she had begun visiting with Queen Victoria, finding 'a new lease of life' there (9).

'Mrs Grundy comes to Scotland', chapter two, was published in the January 1936 issue of *The Modern Scot* (4:289-96). Suitably for that radical journal, it contains attacks on the established church of Scotland, the bourgeois social hypocrisies upheld by that church's attitudes and the class divisions to be found in nineteenth century Scotland. Muir states that the individuality of the protestant tradition meant that 'Pride and poverty walked hand in hand' and that the lowland Scot, 'jealously vigilant over his individuality', would not have allowed a 'native Mrs Grundy — no Mrs MacGrundy' to emerge on the stage (11). But she then briskly gives Mrs MacGrundy a previous 'existence concealed behind the veil of that Bride of Christ, the Scottish Kirk': 'The Scottish Kirk might claim to speak with the tongues of men and of angels, but its voice became more and more unmistakably the voice of Mrs MacGrundy. Mrs Grundy from England had only to ally herself with the Kirk Sessions of Scotland' (12). Mrs Grundy and Mrs MacGrundy have an equal presence in the remainder of the book, sometimes sisters under the skin, sometimes rivals. Muir presents Mrs MacGrundy as 'a negative, thwarted perversion of what might have been or might yet become a genuine national consciousness' who, like Mrs Grundy, 'can create nothing new; she is merely obstructive and deforming, where she is not a passive reflection of the *status quo*' (31).

By setting up Mrs MacGrundy as separate from (rather than a Scottish manifestation of) Mrs Grundy, and also as representing a characteristic that predates Mrs Grundy's manifestation in England in the late eighteenth century, Muir undoubtedly contributes to some inchoateness at the heart of her argument. Her chronology of Mrs MacGrundy and Grundy is sometimes confusing and her 'Church history', according to Catherine Carswell's review, is 'here and there . . . a trifle rough and more than a trifle partial' (*Spectator*, 22 May 1936 946). It is certainly the case that Muir's hostility to Presbyterianism and Calvinism is apparent in *Mrs Grundy in Scotland*. But although her main hostility is towards the Presbyterian church (whether Free or Auld Kirk), she is somewhat even-handed in *Mrs Grundy* as she also attacks the establishment of whichever Kirk was in power, pointing out that when the Episcopalians were in power they were as violently intolerant as the Presbyterians:

> It is the congregations I propose to look at rather than the clergy who min-istered to them, for these ministers were the victims as well as the products of the Kirk. It is the emotional fervour of the congregations that is really important. And the first thing to note is that the congregations were as fanatically gloomy and violent under Episcopacy as under Presbyterianism . . . . In fact, a crowd yelling at the referee in a Glasgow football match to-day strongly resembles in temper the congregations of the various churches of Scotland at the end of the seventeenth century. If this violent feeling, which existed throughout Scotland independent of creed, was religious, it was religious in a very dark and primitive sense. (20)

Muir does not specify what it might be in Scotland that leads to 'dark and primi-tive' religious fervour. She grounds Mrs MacGrundy in chapter three (called simply 'Mrs MacGrundy') in seventeenth century religious controversies, and traces the congregations' demand for excitement in their religion, 'which in other countries has usually given birth to dramatic art': 'And the Scottish congregation got more thrills out of the performance than any audience in a commercial theatre: the spate of bad rhetoric was no mere rhetoric where every member of the congregation was personally involved in the drama of Heaven and Hell. Theirs was a fearful exhilara-tion' (22). This 'almost savage exhilaration' dwindles in the eighteenth century into 'Sabbath Observance' (24).

Alongside the attacks on religious hypocrisy, the book contains class-based political analyses. Discussing the enforcement of 'a monstrously inflated Sabbatarianism' (16) by the Free Kirk in 1866 on a compositor excommunicated because he set up the *Glasgow Herald* on a Sunday evening, she argues that this rigidly sanctimonious approach led directly to the setting up of the Socialist movement in reaction:

> And, indeed, the wage slaves who had jobs to lose soon ceased to trouble the church. They were well crushed beneath the wheels of advancing capi-talism and they retaliated by forming Radical associations. The old fervour which had originally made the Scottish Kirk a genuine, though peculiar,

expression of Lowland Scottish initiative now passed into the Scottish Socialist movement. (17-18)

The separation of the troublesome working classes into the new religion of Socialism meant that the new middle classes were free 'to assimilate themselves more and more to the respectable bourgeoisie of England' (18). Thus Muir presents Grundy and MacGrundy as separately sourced but irredeemably linked by the developing cross-border class structures of the Victorian age. In 'A Spot of Detective Work', Muir refers in passing to an idea akin to Gregory Smith's 'Caledonian antisyszygy', discussed in *Scottish Literature* (G. Smith, 1919 4) and developed by MacDiarmid in the nineteen twenties, that there is a particular split in Scottish sensibility. Later in *Living with Ballads*, Muir expresses the idea of a dualism in Scottish culture as negative:

> As long-lasting have been the more subtle effects of the split in the Scottish personality between open profession and furtive indulgence. A self-conscious split of this kind falsifies, by putting on the defensive, what lies on both sides of it: the open profession can become sanctimonious, the furtive indulgence can grow coarse with bravado. The resulting dualism in Scottish culture has been noted by many critics. (*Living with Ballads* 195)

But in *Mrs Grundy* she explores its origins more, interpreting it as coming from the repressions of Mrs MacGrundy, who bricked 'over the ancient fervour' with 'censoriousness and self-distrust' (33). Muir continues:

> Of course there is a split in the Scottish consciousness; Mrs MacGrundy officially took over the control of Scottish passion, throwing Scottish intelligence behind her, but the split cannot extend to infinity. As a matter of fact, Scottish intelligence has here and there drawn out the ancient fervour, despite Mrs MacGrundy, so there must be an underground communication between the two. For a while the Radical movement in Scotland, developing into Socialism, tapped the ancient reservoir of passion, and individual Scots, escaping from Scotland, have shown both passion and intelligence and thus achieved distinction in a world where a combination of these two is becoming more unusual. (34)

It is only through flight that those individual Scots can find themselves, a solution that both Muirs took, and also given by Willa Muir to the non-conformist characters in *Imagined Corners* and *Mrs Ritchie*. Escape or die seems to be the solution for Muir in her fiction, such was the strength of her rejection of the stifling bourgeois respectability of small town Scotland. She posits only one possibility for those individuals who remain in Scotland:

[I]f you do manage to grow up among the middle classes of Scotland without striking solemn or facetious attitudes . . . you must suppress your intelligence to keep from hurting their feelings; if you set honesty above kindliness you rouse ill-will and suspicion so easily that social intercourse becomes contentious . . . . Too often the middle-class Scot who is both intelligent and kindly escapes from the dilemma by retiring within himself or within the shelter of a small group of like-minded people, and so ceases to be an effective element in public life. (35-36)

The Muirs had been part of one such group in Montrose in 1924 and were now part of another in 1935, the radical, nationalist group centred round James Whyte's periodical *The Modern Scot* in St Andrews. But their reactions against Scottish society always carried them away again, from the 'retiring' Scot, living as best as they could in Scotland, into the expatriate Scot.

Much of *Mrs Grundy in Scotland* is clearly part of the modernist impulse to reject Victorianism; this is most explicit in 'The Victorian Age'. Muir's definition of 'the Victorian problem' (42) seems to be England waking up 'to find itself largely industrialized, in the grip of colossal forces which dwarfed mere humanity' (38). She presents the advance of Mrs Grundy in Victorian England as part of that protectiveness of the home which was the corollary of the advancing empire of capitalism and industrialism. Mrs Grundy 'reassured herself about God by dabbing little bits of Christianity over herself as ornaments, excrescences of a muddled mind very like the ornaments she dabbed on her furniture or on her houses or her clothing . . . . She padded and draped the stark facts around her; she put twiddly bits all over the functional structures of capitalism and then folded her hands complacently' (38). This metaphor of the 'twiddly bits' is part of the standard misconception that the Victorians chose to disguise piano legs as part of a repression of sexuality. Later in *Mrs Grundy*, Muir apparently moves from metaphor to straightforward assertion:

The generous baroque curves of the legs of the Victorian grand piano suggested unspeakable seductions, and Mrs Grundy veiled these legs in discreet skirts. Sexual licence peeped at her from behind everything . . . . The word 'freedom' suggested to Mrs Grundy only the idea of sexual freedom; she tabooed, therefore, freedom of thought or observation or expression, even freedom of movement. (48)

Matthew Sweet, in *Inventing the Victorians*, explores the extent to which this post-Victorian 'orthodox view' about the covering of curves, although 'cited with impressive regularity in both popular and scholarly writings', is based on a misunderstanding (Sweet xii). He argues that not only is there 'no evidence that the custom was ever practiced in the period, except as a means of protecting valued furniture from damage', but also that 'this little paradigm of prudishness existed for the Victorians much as it exists for us — only they told it as a joke against the perceived refinement of middle-class Americans' (Sweet xiii): 'the synecdochic relationship that now [2001] exists between Victorian sensibilities and the clothed piano leg is wholly fraudulent. It persists, however, because the story is useful as a way of dismissing the Victorians' experience as less honest, less sophisticated, less self-cognisant than our own' (Sweet xv). As Sweet points out, Lytton Strachey's *Eminent Victorians* (1918) contains one of the earlier attacks in the modernists' rejection of the preceding age, part of 'Bloomsbury's poison-pen letter to the past' (Sweet xvi). Muir is also participating in this movement against the Victorians. But Muir's attack quoted above is a symbolic rather than an actual assumption that all curves must be covered. It enables Muir to continue with a satiric response to a late Victorian representative of womanly virtues and her supposed fear of the new in women's attitudes:

> She had learned to tolerate railway lines, which ran, after all, on rigidly straight lines although they were not obviously bridled like horses, yet the freedom of bicycles on the roads shocked her, and the more dangerous freedom of the New Motor-carriage, which made a first tentative appearance a little later, at about the same time as the New Woman, startled her profoundly. I have no doubt that Mrs Grundy would have prescribed, if it had been in her power, a red flag to be carried in front of the New Woman. (48)

The railway age had contributed to the development of the modern age, its timetables dependent on the new regulated time of the Greenwich Mean which permitted the increasing capacity of the world to define what was happening exactly when. As Galison notes in *Einstein's Clocks, Poincaré's Maps*, '[l]inked clocks of the late nineteenth century covered the world. Circles of such wide-spanning technologies pulled each other along. Trains dragged telegraph lines, telegraphs made maps, maps guided rail-laying. All three (trains, telegraphs, maps) contributed to a growing sense that long-distance simultaneity made the question, What time is it now somewhere else? at once practical and evocative' (Galison 313). Muir had first developed the image of railway lines as representing security for Annie Rattray, who saw them as 'promised lines of certainty cutting through the bewilderments of life' (*Mrs Ritchie* 41). But here, the image links Mrs Grundy's fear of the new back to the early nineteenth century when men walked in front of the new railways with red flags, warning of the new and dangerous, reminding us of the circular and continuous nature of both history and fear of the modern.

Muir is able to position herself with the superior modern in attitudes to gender in 'Scotswomen'. Discussing 'the fears of the Victorian age' (45), she explores its attitudes to women in the family, the separation between inside and outside the family, the oppositions between business and home, man and woman:

> The men were very busy and important on the scaffolding of new constructions, but their souls were shivering. From the chill abstraction of possibly agnostic thought and certainly amoral science, from the cold logic of finance, they returned to their homes in need of warm slippers, large comforting meals at large and permanent-looking family tables, the general assurance of solid domesticity . . . . The more ambiguous business morality became, the more anxiously they looked for a stage setting of inflexible virtue at home. (45)

She moves into a criticism of the idea of women as 'environments for their families' (44), the women enveloping their men, so that the men failed to understand 'that women too might be individuals with a turn for adventurous enterprise' (46), concluding in a superior way: 'We have an unfair advantage in considering this mid-Victorian scene; we look back on it along perspectives which make its complacency faintly ridiculous; but we cannot blame the average man of that time for not realizing that his attitude to women was a little fatuous' (46). She then makes another division between England and Scotland when she claims that this idea of 'women-as-environment', in opposition to 'women-as-individual' (47), could not work in the same way in Scotland:

> The austere Lowland Scottish tradition, which for each individual drew a straight line from earth to heaven terminating in the Day of Judgment, had deeply affected the status of women . . . . The father-image of mankind sanctioned by the Kirk was as absolute and solitary as its presumable prototype in heaven. None of your environmental nonsense in Scotland. Ilka herring had to hang by its ain tail. Man was an individual reaching to the skies: woman, being more akin to the earth, a lesser individual stopping short of the skies and therefore not to be trusted, even with her own children, unless she obeyed the precepts of the Kirk. (49)

'*Grundy* versus *MacGrundy*' gives an analysis of the introduction of visible class signifiers that led to distinctions that were previously unrecognised (or unknown). Again Muir posits an opposition between the middle class and bourgeois respectability of Mrs Grundy and the older sexual wars of Mrs MacGrundy: 'The Kirk, then, and Mrs MacGrundy had already established a code of sexual propriety more severe and denunciatory than Mrs Grundy's' (54). But Mrs Grundy taught the middle-class Scotswomen 'a lesson in class-consciousness. She taught them how to differentiate themselves in externals from their poorer sisters. Mrs MacGrundy of hallowed tradition served as a guarantee of general moral respectability, but even the very poor or the very ignorant could keep the Sabbath devoutly; to mark the difference between class and class Mrs Grundy was needed. It was her task to comb the tangled individual threads of Scottish society into smoothly classified strata' (56). Muir devotes 'MacGrundy in the Highlands' to an attack on the Clearances, basing it on her notes from Alexander Mackenzie's *The History of the Highland Clearances* (1883).[4] This was the section that Catherine Carswell most admired: 'that part of Mrs. Muir's book . . . in which we read of the eloquent Highland silence that followed in Mrs. MacGrundy's wake, contains the saddest, if also some of the finest, passages between its covers' (Carswell, 1936 946).

'Interlude on Strychnine' moves to the heart of Muir's angry rejection of Mrs MacGrundyisms:

> We can now see Mrs MacGrundy in her true perspective. She represented
> the rigid hardening of a violent revulsion from earlier cultural values . . . .
> Mrs MacGrundy, in a sense, was born out of the Reformation; in a sense
> she was carrying out an historical process . . . . The Reformation was a
> kind of spiritual strychnine of which Scotland took an overdose. Instead of
> acting as a tonic on the individual Scot, it cramped him in a tetanic rigour.
> And that cramped stiffness was perpetuated in the tradition which I have
> called Mrs MacGrundy. (74, 75-76)

This is where she most clearly places the ills of Scotland at the door of the Reformation. It is the same view of post-Reformation Scotland as essentially sterile that leads to Edwin Muir's poetic rage against the architects of the Reformation in 'Scotland 1941':

> But Knox and Melville clapped their preaching palms
> And bundled all the harvesters away,
> Hoodicrow Peden in the blighted corn
> Hacked with his beak the starving haulms.
> Out of that desolation we were born. (Edwin Muir, 1965 34)

Edwin had already written in similar terms in *John Knox: Portrait of a Calvinist* (1929) (dedicated to 'Hugh M'Diarmid'). His appendix on the relation of Knox to Scotland contains only a grudging recognition of any positive effects the Reformation might have had: 'As for the more general effects of Calvinism in Scotland, who can compute them? Knox's religion, it is probable, stiffened the independent political spirit of the people'. Otherwise, he sees it as imposing 'a spiritual and moral tyranny' (E. Muir, 1929 307) and as being a 'narrowly specialized kind of religion'. His conclusion is that it was:

> [A] peculiar religion — a religion which outraged the imagination, and
> no doubt helped, therefore, to produce that captivity of the imagination

in Scotland which was only broken in the eighteenth century . . . . What Knox really did was to rob Scotland of all the benefits of the Renaissance. Scotland never enjoyed these as England did, and no doubt the lack of that immense advantage has had a permanent effect. It can be felt, I imagine, even at the present day. (E. Muir, 1929 308-9)

Edwin Muir writes in his *Autobiography* that his book 'was not a good one . . . too full of dislike for Knox and certain things in Scottish life' (E. Muir, [1954] 1993 226).

In *Living with Ballads*, Willa Muir refers briefly to interconnections between Calvinism and the older Scottish communities and is almost positive about them:

> The Calvinist creed . . . chimed in with some of the deeper resonances in the imagination of Ballad audiences. The preachers, moreover, proclaimed the doctrine dramatically, staging performances in the pulpit which excited the congregations and reminded them that they were participants in a cosmic drama. (*Living* 191)

But Edwin's anti-Reformationism is entirely shared by Willa Muir; at times in *Mrs Grundy in Scotland* it almost over-rides her concern with the position of women in Scotland. Reviewing *Mrs Grundy in Scotland* (along with Mackenzie's *Catholicism and Scotland*) under the title 'Counterblasts to Knox', George Scott Moncrieff recognises this emphasis on Presbyterianism and enjoys Muir's presentation of Mrs MacGrundy as a personification of 'a medley of unpleasant social phenomena': 'Mrs. Muir's bogus biography is a delightful piece of work. It is a squib, sparkling and well-aimed. It is no easy feat to maintain a note of ironic humour throughout the development of a complex theme, or to personify a medley of unpleasant social phenomena' (*New Statesman*, 27 June 1936 1040). Following Muir's eight pages of notes from Mackenzie's *History of the Highland Clearances* in her notebook, she jots a plan for *Mrs Grundy*:

> Mac / Grundy / Sanctimonious Observance-Attitudes / Censorious / Timid / *Women* — have to supply lacking social community sense in Scotland / private — each a mother to her husband / *Money position* of women / girls & men take each other as they find them — no / girls must be 'adapting' themselves to men's desires / where community valued / women valued' (Notebook; St Andrews).

This plan signals that her exploration will interconnect religion, social morality, women and Scotland. The book, of course, is not about 'Sex' (in MacDiarmid's term) and Scotland, but gender and Scotland. As befits a book on the hypocrisies of both Mrs Grundy and Mrs MacGrundy, any direct reference to sexuality is repressed, and references to sex are in the context of social and religious repression.

Many of the strands of *Mrs Grundy in Scotland*, particularly those on religion and Presbyterianism, are taken up and developed further in *Living with Ballads*, Muir's penultimate prose book.

Elphinstone's view is that *Mrs Grundy in Scotland* is 'perhaps Muir's most overtly radical work, insofar as she tackles the combined issue of gender and nationality for the first time (I think) in the history of Scottish critical or political theory' (Elphinstone, 1997 413). As a judgment this disguises problems that occur in the book where the development of the argument can seem repetitive and sometimes unclear. Innes thinks that in *Women: An Inquiry* Muir 'often has three or four arguments running at once and rarely pauses to disentangle them' (Innes 119). Possibly the same problem is part of *Mrs Grundy* with Muir being too entrenched in her material. In this later book, she circles and returns to various parts of her argument, contributing to the feeling that it lacks a completely logical development, although her argument for circularity in 'Moving in Circles' might be her own defence against this charge. The different but linked symbolic natures of Mrs Grundy and MacGrundy provide the convenient peg for Muir to hang her attack on the Victorian age, bourgeois respectability, the Kirk, gender assumptions and its accompanying restrictions of possibilities for girls. For Muir, 'the history of Mrs Grundy in Scotland is only made interesting by her ceaseless struggle with Mrs MacGrundy. I have said that the two figures coalesced, but the partnership was an uneasy one' (61). The somewhat forced exploration of their respective histories allows her to re-explore some of the ideas that had already appeared metaphorically in her two novels, the railway line from earth to heaven of *Mrs Ritchie* (cf. *Mrs Grundy* 48) and the idea of the symbolism of the house:

A house must always stand as a concrete symbol of the woman-as-environment, and although these Scotswomen persisted in thinking of themselves as individuals, Mrs Grundy had hopes of recalling them to a more feminine frame of mind by playing on the symbolism of the house' (58-59).

The use Muir makes of these symbols in her novels is explored in the individual chapters on *Imagined Corners* and *Mrs Ritchie*.

Chronologically written before and after Muir's two novels, this discussion of Muir's two polemical essays has considered them at length because of their intrinsic interest. But it also lays the groundwork for further exploration of Muir's interlocking preoccupations. As will be seen, concerns shown in these works are present everywhere in her writing productions, fiction and non-fiction. There might be complaints about essentialism in *Women: An Inquiry* or about illogicality or historical inaccuracy in *Mrs Grundy in Scotland*, but both essays provide important and interesting explorations of Muir's preoccupations with gender and society. The earlier *Women: An Inquiry* is also of interest because of its difficult ambivalences about women and the unconscious and men and the conscious. The greater length of *Mrs Grundy in Scotland* allows space for an interestingly complicated and interwoven consideration of Scotland and England, of religion and Scottish society. Susan Manning rightly sees Muir as 'an important figure of Modernism'; Manning's judgment is that Muir's 'radical essays, though to an ear attuned to more recent formulations of the "woman question" . . . [they] may seem deeply confusing in their analysis, remain significant documents of early feminism' (Manning 6). By placing *Women: An Inquiry* and *Mrs Grundy in Scotland* within their contexts of inter-war Scotland and of British feminism, their significance is confirmed.

## Notes

1. Muir's reply to Violet Schiff about *Women: An Inquiry*, 28 November 1924, is an entirely typical example of Muir's direct and warmly engaged style in her letter-writing; I give most of it here as an example of that style, but also to illustrate Muir's processes in relation to the essay and her willingness to change but also to defend: 'I cannot thank you enough for your heartening letters. I have been walking on air! Your suggestions are all just: and I shall act on them — with this reservation that in calling housewifery *relatively* unimportant I did not question its importance, but considered it less important than an independence of moral values. I see what you mean by the jibing note: I believe one or two things of that kind crept in because I feared the essay might be dull without a sauce piquante. But since you find it the reverse of dull, I shall remove these unnecessary frills! I entirely agree with you: if the work alone makes its effect, they are superfluous & disharmonious. Also I shall do marginal headings — quite a different task from the synoptic gospel or index. (*I* don't know if it's synoptic or synoptical!) // I should never have written it if it had not been for meeting you (besides condensing the old essay I re-wrote it entirely) and I think I would not have been so encouraged to do so if I had not met in the flesh a woman with a genius for womanhood — I mean you, madam . . . . I don't say that it is entirely a study of Mrs Schiff, but she enters into it largely! I would very much like to dedicate it to V. S . . . . Of course I should be transported with joy to make some money: and if it could be published in America too I might: but if I get £250 out of it altogether that will exceed my expectations . . . . I agree that the Hogarth Essays are not so good a medium as book publication: only I did not

believe that it would be accepted as a book. That's all . . . . ' (Schiff papers; BL). *Women: An Inquiry* is dedicated to Violet Schiff.

2. Sue Innes and I had many enjoyable discussions about Muir and biographies of other Scottish women as she worked on *The Biographical Dictionary of Scottish Women* (Edinburgh: Edinburgh University Press, 2006). A long time feminist writer and journalist, Sue Innes died on 24 February 2005.

3. This sentence is based on points made by Kathy Chamberlain in an email discussion (18 Oct. 2006).

4. There is also a second edition of Mackenzie's *The History of the Highland Clearances*, altered and revised by Ian MacPherson, 1914. Muir's notes do not indicate which edition she used.

BEJANT GROUP, SESSION 1907-1908.

T. RODGER, St. Andrews, Fife, N.B.

Professor Scott Lang. Principal Sir James Donaldson. Professor Burnet.
W. L. Stuart. Colin Hill. H. D. C. Craig. W. Stewart.
W. Paton. A. S. Lowson. J. L. Smith. E. Davidson. W. J. Macdonald. A. J. L. Wallace. W. L. C. Duff. W. L. Anderson. R. T. Wishart.
D. C. Duncan. M. S. Henry. H. R. Irvine. R. M. Stobo. M. Anderson. E. A. Hood. M. B. Barkley. M. L. Wynd. M. W. Henderson. A. Craighead.
W. A. G. Stevenson. L. A. Beveridge. J. A. Thomson. E. W. Hampton. J. Mann. M. H. Smith. M. C. Hay. M. G. Nicoll. A. Cuthbert.
E. J. Herbage. D. K. Brown.
T. P. Buist. P. D. M'Laren. M. A. Robertson. F. B. Harris. J. L. Maclean. M. J. H. Ferguson. G. E. Buist. R. G. Herd. M. A. C. Bell. D. C. Barron. W. G. E. Findlay.
J. B. P. Ferguson. J. B. Scrimgeour. M. M. K. Goldie. K. M. Stuart. E. Coward. E. L. Lowrie. T. P. Hogg. J. Marshall.
A. Cumming. F. W. Millar. W. Sanderson. J. Cape. C. H. Brown. W. T. Buchan. D. A. Duncan.
C. W. Soutar. W. Suddler. A. R. Hamilton. D. H. Auchterlonie. K. M'Lay.
Professor Purdie. H. Rode. A. Burt. J. C. Kydd. A. D. Butchart. L. A. Sutherland. Professor Lindsay.

Bejant group, St Andrews, 1907-8.

# *Imagined Corners*[1]

*Imagined Corners*, Muir's first novel, had a long gestation. She begins serious work on it when the Muirs are living in the South of France, first in St Tropez and then in Menton. Edwin Muir writes to Sydney Schiff in May 1926 that once they have finished their work on the 'prodigies' of translating Lion Feuchtwanger's *Jew Süss*, they are going to take a week's holiday, 'before we sit down to our novels' (11 May 1926; Schiff papers; Butter, 1974 56). By 21 November 1926, Edwin is reporting to his sister and brother-in-law, Elizabeth and George Thorburn, that 'after a summer of very hard work . . . Minnie' has written 'about half of [the novel] she is still writing' (Butter, 1974 58). But Muir is soon pregnant with Gavin who is born October 1927. The following years are taken up with moving back to Britain and more translating. Muir writes to Marion Lochhead in 1933 with some notes for an article that Lochhead proposed for her series 'Scottish Women Writers of To-day' in the *Bulletin and Scots Pictorial*: 'How do we live? Translating from the German, reading German books for publishers, doing anything that turns up. // How do we want to live? On the proceeds of our own creative work. Apparently quite impossible' (3 March 1933; see Appendix I). On 8 July 1929, Edwin writes to Schiff that an advance from Heinemann for his novel, *The Three Brothers* (1931), will allow them both 'fairly complete leisure for 4 or 5 months; and Willa is going to take advantage of it, too, to finish her novel, long since begun, and well under way. I am greatly struck with what she has written of it, and by the whole scheme' (Schiff papers; Butter, 1974 67). *Imagined Corners* is finally completed and published by Martin Secker in June 1931 (with a second printing, August 1931); the *Glasgow Herald* and the *TLS* both review it, 2 July 1931. Care of Gavin (as well as the demands of earning money through translating) may have prevented her completing *Imagined Corners* sooner, but, after reference to her two published books and to *Mrs Ritchie* that would be 'much better than my first novel', Muir gives Lochhead what is probably the most positive description of her son Gavin that appears in her letters or journals: 'I think my best piece of work is Gavin — a large, well-made, healthy clever boy!' (3 March 1933; see Appendix I).

The title, *Imagined Corners*, the only one of Muir's titles that is metaphorical, has hints of both containment and the infinite reach of the imagination. The other titles, *Women: An Inquiry*, *Mrs Grundy in Scotland*, *Mrs Ritchie*, *Mrs Muttoe and the Top Storey*, *The Usurpers*, *Living with Ballads*, are all literalist in their descriptive content. Only the last prose work *Belonging* seems as suggestive and redolent with possibilities; but that has *A Memoir* as part of the title to identify its category. The phrase *Imagined Corners* is from John Donne's 'Holy Sonnet' 7:

At the round earth's imagined corners, blow
Your trumpets, angels; and arise, arise
From death, you numberless infinities
Of souls, and to your scattered bodies go.

Donne's 'round earth's imagined corners' in turn refers to 'Revelation' in the *Bible*, 'I saw four angels standing on the four corners of the earth' (Rev. 7.1) and to judgement day, when Donne's 'numberless infinities of souls' and 'scattered bodies' will be brought together. Donne's poem provides the metaphoric framework for the novel, allowing Muir's title to suggest ways in which her fictional world, bounded by real and imaginary corners, also contains the infinity of the imagination and the unconscious. The novel itself combines in its narrative pattern the worlds of the unconscious and dreams with the social constructions and ideological framework of Calderwick, the community in which it is set. To encompass all of this, Muir adopts a fluid and multi-voiced narrative style. This style is part of what Elphinstone believes is a more consistent radicalism in Muir's novels than in *Women: An Inquiry* or *Mrs Grundy in Scotland*: 'after all, when Muir set out to write fiction, she was able to employ the literary construction of the inner self that Modernism offered her, and the psychoanalytical model of identity that her academic training had given her, in order to bring the plural, fragmented and radically subversive subject into the written text' (Elphinstone 406). Muir is one of those modernist writers who may appear to write in a more traditional style than Virginia Woolf or James Joyce, those representatives of Joseph Allen Boone's 'high modernist bravado' (Boone 5). Yet in *Imagined Corners* in particular, Muir produces a text that is 'infused with the rhythms and reverberations that evoke the power of libidinal activity and unconscious desire to shape not only human subjectivity but external "reality"' (Boone 5). The novel is both a contribution to this modernist strand, exploring the unconscious, dreams and sexuality and, in the more conventional part of the narrative, to the specifically Scottish anti-Kailyard tradition. Lochhead comments in her 1933 article on its anti-Kailyard connections, praising it for being 'neither steeped in the sentimentality of the Kailyard, nor . . . a protest in the manner of "The House with the Green Shutters"' with 'alive and credible' characters' (see Appendix I).

Muir later criticises *Imagined Corners* as having 'enough material in it for two novels, which I was too amateurish to realize at the time' (*Belonging* 163).[2] While allowing for Muir's over-developed tendency to defensive self-criticism, she is probably partly referring to its concentration on the interlocking stories of two clearly differentiated family groups, the Shand family: John and Mabel, Elise (Lizzie in her youth), Hector and Elizabeth, and Aunt Janet, and the Murray family: William, the United Free Church minister, Sarah, the unmarried, housekeeping sister, and their brother Ned, paranoid and unsettling, the failed University student. The 'plot lines' relating to the two families 'are thematically linked to create the dynamic tension that informs the novel' (Elphinstone 406) with the Murray family, firmly within the post-Kailyard tradition, leaning towards tragedy with no solutions other than death, madness or dependence on charity. The Shands on the other hand provide for possibilities of growth and change as well as an exploration of sexuality through Hector, Elizabeth and Elise, and of the socially constructed roles of women and men. A novel concentrating solely on the Murrays would have referred back to the harsh anti-Kailyard world of George Douglas Brown's *The House with Green Shutters*. One dealing only with the more expansive Shand family would have allowed a modern exploration of gender and sexuality; linked with Catherine Carswell's *Open the Door!* (1920) and D.H. Lawrence's novels, it might have become one of those novels too influenced by what Drew punningly criticises as 'this new delirium dreamens' (Drew 60). But by intertwining the two different kinds of novel through its narrative patterns and process of doubling and pairing characters (Elizabeth with William, Sarah with John, Ned with Elizabeth and Hector, Hector with Elise, Elizabeth with Elise), Muir ensures that the Murrays' lives provide a dark undertow to the Shands'. The narrative of growth and change accompanies the narrative of unfulfilled lives, madness and death, the novel's scope widening beyond the parameters of either tradition. Elphinstone sees Muir's technique as a use of psychologist's training:

> [S]he very deliberately brings psychological paradigms to her construction of fictional characters. She uses tensions between the conscious and the unconscious in fiction, by aligning them with tensions between the actual and the imaginary. One might say that she integrates Freudian psychoanalysis with one of the traditional tenets of Scottish literature: the polarity of the ordinary and the marvellous, the inner world inhabited

by ghosts and dreams, and the outer world of appearances which seem to be real. Hence Muir's insistence on the importance of dreams in her fiction. (Elphinstone 404)

This reading is another articulation of the intertwined strands of *Imagined Corners*. Like my reading, it gives a much more positive interpretation of Muir's complex novel than it is ever credited with by Muir herself.

As if to counteract the imaginative mystery of the title of the novel, book one of *Imagined Corners* is called 'Calderwick, 1912'. From the perspective of the novel's publication date, 1931, this dating carries the inevitable reminder that an apparently static world was shortly to be changed unimaginably by world war one. The opening paragraphs of the first book provide a satirical description of the 'burgh of Calderwick'. But the opening lines of the novel, '[t]hat obliquity of the earth with reference to the sun', and the 'arguable uncertainty of the sun's gradual approach and withdrawal in these regions' (1), ensure that the burgh, Scotland, and the novel are all included within a universe where the sun has an uncertain relation to the earth, the solidity of the town is contrasted with a flow and lack of boundaries in nature with the larks, crows and gulls not even knowing they are 'domiciled in Scotland'(2). By naming book one 'Calderwick, 1912', Muir separates it from books two and three, 'The Glass is Shaken' and 'Precipitation', grounding it in the pre-war town of Calderwick on the north east coast of Scotland. But she connects the three by introducing on the second page the metaphors of a glass being shaken (water contained) and of precipitation (water natural and uncontrolled):

> Human life is so intricate in its relationships that newcomers, whether native or not, cannot be dropped into a town like glass balls into plain water; there are too many elements already suspended in the liquid, and newcomers are at least partly soluble. What they may precipitate remains to be seen. (2)

The life of the town is contained like a scientific experiment within a beaker, the rational detached tones of the narrator introducing the metaphor of change, observable but unpredictable. This metaphor of scientific observation is anticipated in Drew's 1926 study of *The Modern Novel*, where she describes the reader's role: 'the gospel of disenchantment in sketches from life where existence becomes like a drop of water seen under a microscope, a substance teeming with unsuspected activity, where the reader lives in a tensity of feeling, a keenness of perception and a pitch of sensitiveness — a complete heightened reality' (Drew 248). But Muir gives it a wider context, *Imagined Corners* becoming an exploration of Drew's 'unsuspected activity' in the unconscious as well as the conscious world. The narrative format of *Imagined Corners* allows for the intersection of both the inner and outer life of the society of Calderwick. The outer is examined through the exposure of the social forms of the town and an exploration of gender roles and their implicit oppressions imposed on the characters by the society of the time. The inner life is exemplified in the way the narrative point of view throughout the novel moves through the various characters' thoughts, the reader being drawn into an awareness of each character's thought process in turn. Over-identification with any one character is prevented. The inner life is also represented in the ongoing internal analyses by Elizabeth and Elise of their respective psychologies, and in the attention Muir gives to the dreams of her characters. For Muir, dreams represent a reality as strong as any in the conscious world, and she explores this in the novel through the dreams of her characters. She writes to Neil Gunn soon after the novel's publication: 'nobody . . . has seen that the dreams I give my characters are meant to be at least as important as their waking actions: that William Murray is another version of Elizabeth in different circumstances' (Pick, introduction, *Imagined Corners* viii-ix). She is intent on probing the psychological depths of the individual, exploring the manner in which all individuals are not 'individual' but products of the ideology of their time and of their particular society. These individuals are the 'countless disconnected existences, bound to their environment'(148) that Elise imagines on her train journey through France from her position of 'peculiar, almost a god-like, detachment from the lives through which she flashes' (148). Muir may create a structure with 'enough material in it for two novels' (*Belonging* 163) but this is essential to allow its complicated dual process of inner and outer life to be shown. This ensures there is no one consistently central focus for our attention, and that interpretation and response must shift and move along with the narrative.

The use of these methods of narration allows a combination of the 'realist' traditions of the nineteenth and early twentieth century novelists with the newer internalised writing of modernism, the looking within that Woolf had advocated in 'Modern Fiction' (Woolf, 1925 196; 1966 2:106). Muir chooses an observant narrator with characteristics shared by the psychoanalyst, the anthropologist, and the scientist: a standing back to assess the culture and the characters, the dissecting, examining and enlarging as through a microscope, the analysis of unexpected conjunctions. Muir was in St Andrews when J. G. Frazer gave the Gifford Lectures there in 1911 and may well have attended them. His articles on 'Taboo' and 'Totemism' had appeared in the ninth edition of *Encyclopaedia Britannica* (1875-89) and his ground-breaking work, *The Golden Bough*, was published between 1890 and 1915; Freud drew on his ideas in *Totem and Taboo* (1912-13, trans. 1919), and T. S. Eliot, critic and poet central to modernism, acknowledges *The Golden Bough* in his notes to 'The Waste Land' as a 'work of anthropology . . . which has influenced our generation profoundly' (1922; 1969 76). Muir's armchair anthropologist in the novel is Karl, Elise's recently dead husband; he had 'looked at facts as if they were hieroglyphs', and had left behind him seven books, written 'in his study surrounded by mountains of reference-books, without once visiting the countries whose ciphers he unriddled . . . . Karl should have written a book about the primitive people of Scotland . . . . He would have inspected their mythology as if they were Tlinkit Indians. He would have explained their ideology to them. Ideology was a favourite word of his' (149-50). Instead it is his widow Elise who comes to examine her past and her town, to synthesise her earlier rebellious self with her later European self. But Muir's narrator can also be read as a social anthropologist like Karl, assessing the taboos and structures of Calderwick and its inhabitants, as Frazer had assessed and compared the magic and religious ritual of primitive societies in *The Golden Bough*. The narrator provides the cold eye of Frazer's 'dispassionate observer' (Frazer 56) and the voice that interprets and analyses throughout the novel. The approach to systems of beliefs, customs and narratives used by anthropologists provides Muir with the method for studying the conflicting narratives of the characters and the interwoven beliefs and customs that entrap them, the 'ideology' of the place. Alison Smith identifies one other objective voice with that of the narrator of *Imagined Corners*: 'Muir's book, in the very analytical tone of the narration (the narrator almost has the voice of a patient lawyer for the defence, explaining and arguing for her characters at every turn), is a book about the analysis of emotion' (A. Smith 40). While I agree with Smith's view of the novel as an 'analysis of emotion', Muir's narrator, organising the reader's response by her observations, seems more akin to Frazer's 'dispassionate observer', the social anthropologist, than to a psychologist observing patients or Smith's 'patient lawyer for the defence'.

The wide-ranging, cross-disciplinary intellectual curiosity of Willa Muir and her contemporaries in the early twentieth century is illustrated by Edwin Muir with his description of early discussions with friends in Glasgow (before meeting Willa in 1918), and of his interest in Freud and Jung:

> We . . . discussed everything under the sun: biology, anthropology, history, sex, comparative religion, even theology . . . . We followed the literary and intellectual development of the time, discovering such writers as Bergson, Sorel, Havelock Ellis, Galsworthy, Conrad, E. M. Forster, Joyce, and Lawrence, the last two being contributed by me, for I had seen them mentioned in *The New Age* by Ezra Pound . . . . For some years *The New Age* had been publishing articles on psychoanalysis, in which Freud's and

Jung's theories were discussed from every angle, philosophical, religious, and literary, as well as scientific. The conception of the unconscious seemed to throw new light on every human problem and change its terms, and . . . I . . . snatched at it as the revelation which was to transform the whole world of perception. (Edwin Muir, *Autobiography* 115-16, 150)

Similar feelings about the unconscious are described in Willa Muir's account in *Belonging*; referring to 1933, they apply equally well to the Muirs' earlier years in London: 'our thoughts and feelings reached out into the cosmos and into the unconscious with a sense of natural freedom, and the whole world of books was ours' (1968 170). She explores this reaching out into the unconscious in her characters' dreams in *Imagined Corners*. Frazer had written that '[w]e seem to move on a thin crust which may at any moment be rent by the subterranean forces slumbering below', meaning the 'solid layer of savagery beneath the surface of society' (1922 56). Muir uses the same volcanic image to express Elizabeth's fragile control of thought over feeling: 'her thoughts congealed like a crust over her feelings . . . . In another moment her emotions would break their crust and come bubbling up' (114-15). This metaphor for the uncivilised and for emotion, each pressing uncontrollably on the thin crust of surface civilisation or social control, becomes in Freudian terms the unconscious and the subterranean feelings which surface in dreams. Freud and Frazer, both equally part of the intellectual currents of the nineteen twenties, are implicitly present in *Imagined Corners* when the narrator refers to Elizabeth's 'half-conscious taboos of her youth' (222) and when Elise wants to tell Elizabeth about 'the possible symbolic meaning' (246) of her maid Madeleine's fear of snakes, that she had earlier described to her brother and sister-in-law: 'She's full of queer superstitions about animals, almost all of them about the peculiar dangers women run. She thinks that men haven't nearly as much to fear. It must be a very old belief, as old as the affinity between Eve and the serpent; but it's not a belief in companionship; it's a sexual fear of some kind, perhaps' (159).

When John Shand writes to ask Elise / Lizzie to visit, not having communicated with her in twenty years, '[s]omething hidden very deep seemed to have come alive again' (37); his hidden feelings for the sister (rejected because she ran off with a married foreigner), suppressed for twenty years, are expressed in a dream as he drifts 'into sleep with the vague idea that he was stumbling through a dark forest of lofty trees, pursuing a brilliant butterfly that would dart off at a tangent and not keep to the path' (26). His 'dark forest of lofty trees' (26) is expressive of tangled sexuality and the uncatchable, unpredictable butterfly that is his sister. Though Muir does not explore explicitly any sexual feelings John may have had for Lizzie, it is made clear that she was and is the emotional centre of his life in a way that his wife Mabel, married to him for his social position, cannot be. Sarah, William Murray's oppressed and unhappy sister, has a dream equally emblematic of her psyche, at a time when she is exhausted by her brother Ned's madness. In an example of narrative analysis early in the novel, Sarah's and Mabel's opposite senses of themselves had been typified through the image of a web:

> Sarah, if she had pictured a web of the world, might have regarded herself as one of many flies caught in it by God, her sole consolation being the presence of the other flies and the impartial symmetry of the web, but Mabel lived at the heart of her own spider's web, and every thread from the outside world led directly to herself. (8-9)

But later, as Sarah approaches defeat with Ned, her unconscious rejects the comfort of an 'impartial symmetry of the web': 'Confused dreams ensnared her; the more she swept out corners the thicker she became entangled in cobwebs, and finally an enormous, hairy spider crawled over her shrinking body' (177). The impartial symmetry of God's purpose has been undermined, and exhaustion and despair entangle Sarah's unconscious in a threatening web. As well as exemplifying Sarah's supposed lack of access (as a spinster) to sexual feelings, the dream also presages her failure to save her brother Ned and the collapse of her whole system of being, her loss of her place in society. Ned himself is not represented through his dreams; his breakdown forces him to live his unconscious paranoia and madness, not dream it. He lives with his unconscious fears exposed, in a world off-centre to everyone else. We see Ned from the outside, through other people's reactions, his inner life invisible and apparently as mysterious and uncontrollable to himself as it is to his sister, even though it can have 'a glimmering of reasonableness in it' (29). To Elphinstone, his 'incarceration in the lunatic asylum is the epitome of all the spiritual imprisonments in the novel' and 'a *communal* rejection of the unruly unconscious' (Elphinstone 408). But his role is also to live out the collective fears of the other 'saner' members of his circle, providing unsettling evidence of the precariousness of the mind and the fragility of the human spirit.

Sarah Murray, the misunderstood, put-upon minister's sister, appears early in *Imagined Corners* and plays a central role in the anti-Kailyard strand of the novel. Muir uses her to explore the lack of options for older unmarried women, and the social negativity of their positions: 'If a celestial journalist, notebook in hand, had asked her what kind of a woman she was she would have replied, with some surprise, that she was a minister's sister' (2-3). This both represents Sarah's own attitude and the social reality of her position;

once her brother William has drowned, she has no right to a home in the manse and only a resented charitable action provides her with a place to live. But Muir also shows that Sarah and William Murray are both trapped in their time's gendered ideology. It does not occur to Sarah that, when the effort of lifting a tray was almost too much for her,

> William, being stronger and less tired, might carry the tray into the kitchen. Nor did it occur to William. He had not quite escaped the influence of his father, who had ruled his house, as he had ruled his school, on the assumption that the female sex was devised by God for the lower grades of work and knowledge, and that it was beneath the dignity of man to stoop to female tasks. But although this assumption lay at the back of William's mind it appeared so natural that he never recognised it; if Sarah had asked him to carry the tray he would have done so willingly; the assumption merely hindered him from thinking of such an action. (16)

This assumption of male superiority, 'devised by God', so internalised that it appears natural, is unrecognised by William or Sarah. Two other women who, like the Murrays, belong in the novel's anti-Kailyard strand are Mary and Ann Watson. They are sisters locked together in hatred and dependency, in a sibling relationship that mimics marriage in their differentiated roles of breadwinner and housekeeper. Their father having left the house to Ann and the shop to Mary, Ann locks Mary out of their shared house. Their minister, William Murray, attempting to persuade 'one bitter old woman to give shelter to another', reacts to the threatening appearance of the house; the kitchen window seemed to him 'a dim and evil eye; the cottage was, like himself, a body full of darkness' (101). To William the house appears as a symbol for his own spiritual struggle with the concept of evil; but it is also shown as the embodiment of the two sisters' imprisonment. The cottage's 'body full of darkness' can be read as emblematic of those 'dark places of psychology' that Woolf saw as the concern of modern novelists (Woolf, 1925 193; 1966 2:108); but it represents evil to William as well as the Watsons' stultifying relationship. Mary Watson inherited the draper's shop from her father but not his eldership of St. James's United Free Church: 'which was perhaps the reason why her moral vigilance, unremitting in general, was especially relentless towards the minister and elders of that church' (11).

Muir makes it clear that these women who think all control must come through their 'moral vigilance' are both suffering from and trapped by their gendered assumptions that men, however useless, had the automatic right to positions of power, and that women had access only to the manipulation of men, rather than their own public right to action. Sarah defines this resentfully after Ned's final breakdown: 'If it wasn't for the women the world would be in a gey queer state. And the women got little credit for it' (202); these women are passive victims caught in the web of society. Muir theorises this directly in *Belonging*:

> Male dominance had been my mother's creed and as a child I met it like a toad meeting the teeth of a harrow . . . . The patriarchal Law rated us as second-class citizens (we could not vote) and the patriarchal Church assumed that we were second-class souls (being suspect daughters of that Original Sinner, Eve, we had to cover our heads in church and could not hold ecclesiastical office). There was now no 'parity of esteem' as between male and female in patriarchal structures, whatever values they may have started with . . . . By the time I went to teach in England I was already alert to the comedy of my position as a woman in a patriarchally-minded country. (*Belonging* 140-41)

But in *Imagined Corners* the 'comedy' of women's position is expressed as a tragedy for women like Sarah Murray, the Watsons and Aunt Janet of the Shand family, with whom an ungrateful Sarah ends up living. They are narrow, limited, and without futures, condemned to insecure and socially rigid lives, unable to imagine escape or enact social change through their own actions, journeying 'from one infinity to another in such a narrow cage' (20), as William thinks of Ann. It is one of the reasons that Elise cannot stay in Calderwick. In a refraction of Muir's views, Elise tells John about the contrast between the 'thinking boy' and the 'thinking girl': 'Tradition supports his dignity and undermines hers. I can remember how insulted I was when I was told that woman was made from a rib of man, and that Eve was the first sinner, and that the pains of childhood are a punishment to women . . . . But I did suffer, all because of superstitions that are long out-of-date and still perpetuated' (216-17). Elise escapes a second time from Calderwick; but Muir allows no escape for the women who are spinsters, remnants of the kailyard, assumed by Muir to be asexual beings, tragically unaware of their repressed position in Calderwick and Scottish society.

Elizabeth, the young, newly married wife of Hector, is partly Muir's exploration of what might have happened if the young Willa Anderson had married her 'Rugby champion and gone to live' in Montrose (*Belonging* 125). Elizabeth carries an emotional force; she is a modernist heroine believing 'in something that flows through the universe . . . . It's not outside, it's inside oneself. And yet it comes suddenly, as if from outside' (72-73). She is shown working through the conflicts for an educated and intelligent young woman of that time, changing name, status and place by the act of marrying, who then sees the possibility of reclaiming her own identity only outwith Scotland: 'I could take my own name and leave Scotland' (124). Waking one morning beside Hector, she 'was lost and no longer knew who she was'; she moves into a hypnogogic state where the world stretched 'into dark impersonal nothingness and she herself was a terrifying anonymity' (64). The 'disordered puzzle of her identity' (64) is that she is both Elizabeth Ramsay and Elizabeth Shand; she fears becoming more and more 'inalterably' Elizabeth Shand, with the years of the future assuming the 'perspective of fields, each one separated by a fence from its neighbour . . . . But this was no longer time or space, it was eternity . . . perhaps a higher fence marked the boundary between life and death, but in the fields beyond it she was still Elizabeth Shand . . . . It was appalling' (64-65). Elizabeth's waking dream of this interminable succession of fences and fields shows the landscapes of her married future, stretching ahead of her, contained and restricted. But she also knows that, like Hector, 'in the ultimate resort she too was simply herself' (65). Muir shows Elizabeth's feelings for Hector fluctuating wildly, making clear the strength of their sexual attraction and their lack of intellectual connection. It is Hector's presence that confuses Elizabeth's clarity; in his absence 'her painful agitation subsided with incredible quickness' (115) and she can sit down to read a book by the French philosopher, Henri Bergson. Elizabeth Drew asserts in 1926 that she knows 'no single woman in fiction who can stand as an example of one who finds a life based on ideas or an intense creative energy an essential factor in her happiness' (Drew 112). Muir's connection of Elizabeth to Bergson and the comfort of intellectual excitement provides a partial riposte to Drew. Elizabeth's intellectual pursuit of Bergson is calming for her and acts as a reminder of her intelligence and connectedness to the intellectual currents of her time. But Muir also uses Bergson's ideas of motion and continuous change in the passage of time and the flux of consciousness, developed by Bergson in works such as *Time and Free Will* (1910), as an enabling image for Elizabeth's state of division: 'The whole of Elizabeth's world was in flux, although not exactly as Bergson had declared it to be, and instead of regarding the phenomenon with scientific interest she felt as if she were drowning in it' (115).

The Bergsonian idea of flux is opposed by the regulation of life by railway or school timetables, and of time itself by Greenwich Mean Time (introduced in 1884 in Britain). Sarah Murray's 'precisely regulated . . . scheme of life' (16) comes from her upbringing in her schoolteacher father's timetabled world. Sarah is disturbed if she cannot predict 'what was to be seen at any hour of the day' and she needs 'the orderly life of Calderwick' to keep pace 'with the ordered march of the sun'; it is Sarah who hears the 'prolonged whistle of the express from King's Cross . . . . punctual to the minute' (7). Of course, this is the train which drops the newly wed Hector and Elizabeth Shand into the mixture of Calderwick society, with all the attendant disturbances that they bring to the Murray family. Sarah's brother William has a more complicated relationship to time, as befits the character whom Muir describes as 'another version of Elizabeth in different circumstances' (Pick, introduction, *Imagined Corners* ix). The 'large white dial of a clock' (68) facing the pulpit in William's church is akin to Lawrence's 'great white clock-face . . . . the eternal, mechanical, monotonous clock-face of time' in *Women in Love* (1921; 1980 523). But William stares at the clock's 'expressionless white circle' as he preaches, not to regulate his time, but to lift himself 'through a kind of self-hypnosis . . . into a transcendental world favourable for sermons' (68). Towards the end of the novel, after his failure to help his brother Ned, and his own spiritual crisis, William dreams of navigating himself on a tea-tray down a yellow river that is both in China and 'the river of the will of God' (272), interpreting it as the necessity of resigning himself to God's will. As he later struggles through the storm to see a parishioner, he continues meditating on his dream as the 'stream of Time' and interprets his dream sea as '[t]he Pacific'. In his last moments, he is described as 'almost smiling in the darkness' as he imagines it as the 'sea of God's peace' (273). Muir thus shows William as reaching a kind of resolution of his religious doubts through the dream. But he is part of the anti-Kailyard tragedy of the novel, so the resolution is reached just before he falls into and drowns in the 'nasty, stagnant corner' (44) of the docks that Hector had earlier shuddered at: 'On a dark night . . . it would be easy to come down to Dock Street and walk right over the edge into that scum . . . . Better to drown in the open sea than in that stagnant muck' (44). Elise has a more positive relationship with the sea, as befits one of the characters shown as being aware of her identity, conscious and unconscious; she dreams of an open sea, the Atlantic, where 'an enormous, endless billow' was going to obliterate the children and herself on the shore (242). Her fear on wakening is then superseded by a strengthened sense of herself as 'an unassailable point within the compass of her body, the centre . . . of a dimly perceived circle . . . . The centre of one's being, apparently, was both tranquil and intrusive' (242). Throughout the novel, Muir uses water and the sea metaphorically to explore the unconscious and provide commentary on her characters' states of consciousness and identity of being.

Elise has a complicated function within the novel. She is the younger Lizzie who reacts to the unfairness of her gendered upbringing and who provides John

Shand's emotional life in childhood. She is also the sophisticated Europeanised Elise who, through her early study of Saint-Simonianism and Enfantin (256), her relationship with Karl, and her talk of teleology which 'led to queer conclusions' (231), represents questioning, radical, intellectual traditions, coming home to lay the ghost of her earlier self. She becomes a precipitating factor in the resolution of Hector and Elizabeth's relationship. Elizabeth, caught in a turmoil of feelings about being a married woman and about her essential identity, is 'looking for her other self' when she first meets Elise: 'since Elise was a woman Elizabeth did not know that she fell in love with her at first sight' (165). This is the Elizabeth who has an out of body experience as an expression of poetic and intellectual passion and who feels split in the space of 'thickened obscurity' (174) between body and mind; she thinks of the 'impersonal force' of Hector's sexual appeal, his 'grace and strength' expressed in the language of the 'Song of Solomon' (175; *Bible* 7.4). Her revelations come through the medium and language of sexual orgasm:

> Elizabeth went on stroking her body, almost mechanically . . . . [A]n image of herself grew before her . . . . It was an overlapping of vibrations rather than a solid form, and the vibrations extended beyond the farthest stars. One end of this shadowy projection had long, slow, full waves; that was the body and its desires. At the other end were short quick waves; these represented the mind. (174)

The frankness of Muir's approach to sexuality here prepares us for the possibility of Elizabeth and Elise's future relationship. It is through Elise's money that Hector is enabled to leave Scotland for Singapore, Elise acknowledging to herself that she may just be 'buying off' Hector (257) so that she can sweep Elizabeth off to Europe, as a 'brand-new daughter, or sister, or wife, or whatever it was, having carried her off like a second Lochinvar' (279). By invoking Scott's romantic hero ('So daring in love, and so dauntless in war', 'Lochinvar'), Muir ensures that we interpret the Elise / Elizabeth relationship widely. Alison Smith writes of Muir's 'analytical other Lochinvar' as 'highly ambiguous, in fact quite flirtatious. There is clearly a seduction of sorts happening here. It's the promise of other things; it's the romantic rescue of the self by the self from false role, from slow death by stereotype, the rescue of the emotional, naïve and passionate by the experienced, analytical and articulate' (A. Smith 44). Muir uses the imagery of pruning to bind Elise and Elizabeth together. Elise had meditated on the way that she had avoided commitment to Karl: 'fastidiously shaking herself free of entanglements, pruning her own emotions and ruthlessly lopping with the knife of reason every tendril that

> There are people like Elise who prefer to do their own pruning; there are many who submit to pruning by others; there are a few, like Elizabeth, who do not know that pruning is inevitable and do not foresee that their eager growth will be broken off by circumstance—pruned raggedly . . . instead of cleanly, by the apparent cruelty of chance instead of by design. (251)

As the train moves towards the south of France, Elizabeth sees vines for the first time ('those twisted little stumpy dwarf trees'): 'She had imagined something more lush . . . not this dry, bright landscape with those gnarled little trees, that looked as if they had been tortured . . . . Crippled, like herself' (Muir's ellipses; 281). Elphinstone, along with Elizabeth, interprets 'the very landscape' negatively as echoing 'the imprisonment of soul that has tormented Elizabeth in Calderwick' (Elphinstone 407). But the viewpoint is clearly Elizabeth's alone, Muir ensuring that Elise's own 'great content' at the sight of the vines, indicators of the Midi and the south, is present to balance Elizabeth's reaction. The imagery of the pruning that forms character that the narrator has already explored is extended at the conclusion of the novel by knowledge that only with pruning do winter vines produce summer abundance for harvesting and the very lushness that Elizabeth sought. Muir, having lived in the south of France as she was writing parts of *Imagined Corners*, leaves this to the reader's imagination.

The ending of the novel refuses closure, the sexual possibilities widening beyond heterosexuality even as Elise acknowledges that Elizabeth may later return to some man 'the exact antithesis of Hector' (281). The train, representative early in the novel of the timetabled world, controlled by the clock, is the medium that carries Elise first out of mainland Europe into her past through geography and dreams, and then back from that past into alternate, uncertain and ambiguous futures which may carry new imprisonment. The novel ends with Muir's own ellipses: 'Madame Mütze felt Calderwick receding farther and farther, for Ilya's conversation travelled even faster than the train . . . .' (281). This ending is a movement into disconnection. Like the larks that had not even known it was Scotland at the beginning of the novel (2), Elise and Elizabeth fly off at the end into the world of not-Scotland. Freedom for them is flight from the constrictions of the known society into the privileged and detached life of incomers in southern France. But it is a flight to a continent about to be submerged in war and Muir uses knowledge of the outbreak of war to ensure uncertainty beyond the end of the novel. She defends this ending vigorously to F. Marian McNeill:

> [Y]ou object to my letting Elise leave Scotland. Well, my dear, it was supposed to be 1913, when there was little Nationalism: also, I was thinking more of Elise, when I followed her, than of national sentiment: and Elise would not have stayed in Calderwick, however it might have benefited from her presence—which I don't deny. I was not describing what ought to be in Scotland, but what actually would have happened there in 1913 to the characters in my book: and I think I am right in conceiving that Elise & Hector were bound to leave it. Elizabeth was almost equally bound to come back: but all that I left to the imagination of the reader, being more concerned to present an illumination of life in Scotland than a reformation of it'. (21 July 1931; NLS; McCulloch 208-9)

Her letter to Gunn (cited above, probably written at about the same time as the letter to McNeill) also addresses the Scottish issue ('I was trying to illumine life, not to reform it; to follow my own light, not deliberately to explore blind-alleys in Scotland') but to Gunn she concedes that 'being Scottish, my approach to any universal problem is bound to be by way of Scottish characters' (Pick ix). The review of *Imagined Corners* in *The Modern Scot* in October 1931 agreed; it found the characters 'indubitably Scottish, in fact indubitably Angus. Where [Muir] scores over so many Scottish writers is that she uses such characters for the major tasks of literature' (*Modern Scot* 2:3 171-72). But clearly McNeill had complained about the novel not being committed enough to the idea of Scotland for Muir to defend herself in this way. Both letters provide evidence (if such is needed) that Muir is aware of the relationship of her first novel both to the historical period in which it is set and also to its inextricable connection to her own Scottishness.

The review in the *Times Literary Supplement*, while thinking the novel 'starts very promisingly' and that some of it is 'excellent' is ultimately critical of its development and of the Elise / Elizabeth characters: 'Instead of Calderwick, or a comedy, we get a chronicle of Elizabeth's woes and her reaction to them . . . . Mrs. Muir seems to involve herself far too closely with these two Elizabeth Shands' (TLS, 2 July 1931 526). The review in *The Modern Scot*, overwhelmingly positive as it is, also has some criticism of the Elise / Elizabeth relationship and of the structure of the novel:

> In concentrating the interest on these two characters in the concluding chapters, something is lost and the balance of the novel is to some extent upset, since some of the preceding events described at length

scarcely impinge on these two women's lives; but the psychology of the two women is so convincingly described that what is lost on the swings, so to speak, is made up on the roundabouts. (*Modern Scot* 2:3 172-73)

Janet Caird, in one of the first critical discussions of Muir's fiction in the nineteen nineties, using the reductive title of 'Cakes Not Turned', is less convinced of the novel's success; she finds it 'a teasing, irritating book, because one is aware of possibilities in it not realised' with a minimal plot 'a mere framework for the interplay of character' (Caird 12). Yet for Alan Freeman, Muir explores 'the paradox of endorsing a notion of community while rejecting social circumscription of its members' and, in *Imagined Corners*, her 'narrative and her attitude to women and society reach a new level of innovation' (Freeman 165). For some readers, *Imagined Corners* is flawed by the intrusive narrator. Following Muir's own sense that it contains enough 'material for two novels' (*Belonging* 163) that would have been improved by 'cutting and trimming' (Muir; Robb 150), the criticism is that Muir fails to join into an effective whole the movements of her narrative, the external and internal, the sociological and the psychological. But I find this all much too reductive of the novel's strengths. I hold the much more positive view that Muir takes the disparate strands of her narrative and interweaves them so that the novel becomes the proper sum of its parts; the stresses and disjunctions between the outer and inner explorations are symptomatic of the same stresses in society between the demands and repressions of the social structure and the inner worlds of the individual psyche. The main characters of the novel are shown as being fragmented sites of conflict between competing selves, constructed in contradictory ways by the demands of societal expectations, their unconscious worlds clashing in dreams with their conscious realities. There is movement and fluidity, echoing Bergson's continuous change and flux, in the characters' understanding of their selves, a grasping after unity or sense while they fail to attain any stable understanding of their selves. The novel succeeds as a sophisticated enactment of the conflicts between societal repressions and individual yearning for escape, allowing Muir scope to explore the links between conscious and unconscious worlds, illuminating the dreaming of realities in *Imagined Corners*. Its breadth and ambition are positive and exuberant. With her next novel, *Mrs Ritchie*, she narrows her focus into a rigorously powerful examination of the negative effects of gender and class inequalities and a repressive religion on one woman.

Notes.

1. This chapter is an extended version of 'Dreaming Realities: *Imagined Corners*' in Carol Anderson and Aileen Christianson (eds.), *Scottish Women's Fiction, 1920s to 1960s: Journeys into Being* (East Linton, East Lothian: Tuckwell, 2000) 85-96.

2. David Robb notes that Muir had written on the Dundee University Library copy of *Imagined Corners*, October 1937: 'A long time since I wrote this; it seems to me now it would be all the better of "cutting and trimming"' (Robb 150).

## THOMAS JUSTICE & SONS, LTD.
### DUNDEE
Makers of good, useful, and comfortable Furniture since
the year 1872

## THOMAS JUSTICE & SONS, LTD.
### DUNDEE
Makers of good, useful, and comfortable Furniture since
the year 1872

Furniture advertisments, *The Modern Scot*, 1931.

# Mrs Ritchie

Willa Muir's second novel, *Mrs Ritchie*, was published in July 1933.[1] She writes later of the press of work in the Muirs' Hampstead house and the 'many hours of hard work' on translations 'needed to earn a sizeable sum' (*Belonging* 162). It is in this context that she works on *Mrs Ritchie* in her study on the ground floor, subject to intrusions from all sides:

> Yet there was always a press of work, and so I reverted to a student habit of mine, working at furious speed late at night into the small hours, after the vibrations of the day had died down. During the summer I sat up all night once in a while, hearing the birds sing at dawn and tumbling into bed for a few hours' sleep after breakfast, but I did this only when a translation had to be finished in a hurry or proofs corrected against a deadline. (*Belonging* 163)

This habit of Muir's, fitting work into the quiet of night, represents the resourcefulness of the female determined to complete work against the demands of running a household, without the privilege of the solitary male study at the top of the house. It provides a counterpoint to the feminist analysis of Woolf's *A Room of One's Own* which rests more on the needs of the woman writer without children. Muir's articulation here is an assertion of her importance and centrality in the Muir household, rather than a straightforward expression of a male / female binary where the male writer is privileged over the female. It has been read as the latter by David Robb in 1990. Although he thinks that 'there are signs that Willa Muir, the wife of the poet Edwin Muir, is coming out from under the shadow of her famous husband', he also feels that her 'own creative output' was hampered both by her need to earn money with translations and by being the 'home-maker' of the household (Robb 149). It is against the domestic background of their life in Hampstead that Muir continues: 'I cannot now tell how I managed to finish a second novel, but it does not surprise me that I lost control of it in the second half, although the first half is quite good' (*Belonging* 163). As she was writing the novel, she had been more optimistic: 'I am finishing *Mrs Ritchie* of which I have some hopes. It is — or will be — much better than my first novel' (Marion Lochhead, 3 March 1933; see Appendix I). Her later denigration of *Mrs Ritchie*, rather than being a useful comment on the novel, confirms again Muir's own insecurity about her work. The paragraph in *Belonging* continues with a reference to her also having been 'too amateurish to realize at the time' that *Imagined Corners* contains too much material (163). The previous chapter shows that Muir's assessment of her first novel is much too negative, and this chapter will make clear my view that Muir's assessment of her second novel is also misleading.

The many strands of *Imagined Corners* include a study of repression and its effects. The novel's focus moves from telescopic to panoramic, from the unconscious to conscious, from one character to another. In *Mrs Ritchie*, a bitter antidote to *Imagined Corners*, Muir chooses microcosm over macrocosm, putting under the microscope the damage done by repression to the human spirit, as well as the damage done by repressed anger to those surrounding the repressed. *Imagined Corners* offers more possibilities, more optimism, for all its critique of small town Scottish society. But in *Mrs Ritchie*, set in the same small town of Calderwick, the concentration is first on Annie Rattray and her apparently inevitable trajectory towards becoming Mrs Ritchie, and then on the narrow intensity of Mrs Ritchie's focused rage and the effect of her rage on her family. The novel is ultimately unrelieved by any real hope or possibility of release. Sarah Annie's flight from her mother at the end of the novel is one of desperation, carrying far less of the promise of life (however uncertain) that exists at the conclusion to *Imagined Corners*. The Murray family strand of *Imagined Corners* can be read as part of an anti-Kailyard tradition established by George Douglas Brown's *The House with the Green Shutters* (1901) while the Shand family sections provide a more diverse and, at least partly, positive interpretation of early twentieth century Scotland. But *Mrs Ritchie*, from its first publication, has been seen as entirely belonging to the anti-Kailyard school of literary tradition. The negative review in the *Times Literary Supplement* places it within a tradition that was now 'a little worn', the path too 'well-trodden':

> The unpleasantness of people who are at pains to be virtuous is in fact a theme that grows a little worn; and Mrs. Muir's rehandling of it here has hardly, perhaps, sufficient freshness of treatment to vitalize its solemn inveteracy. Mrs. Ritchie (Secker, 7s. 6d. net) is the portrait, set in a Scots town of before the War, and framed for the reader in a pair of green shutters, of the typical self-righteous domestic despot of literary tradition, who drives her family to desperation in an atmosphere of hatred and high tea. (*TLS* 13 July 1933)

The reference to Brown's novel could hardly be clearer and the reviewer is keen to present this kind of work as passé and tired. But a more positive review in *The*

*Listener* finds it 'Greek drama in a kail-yard' although it thought 'the psychology and the psychological symbolism of the story as a whole are too complete and perfect' (*Listener* 16 Aug. 1933). Later critical opinion, while still seeing the novel in relation to the anti-Kailyard movement, has also been much more positive than the *TLS* review. *Mrs Ritchie* remained out of print after 1933 until its republication by Canongate in 1996 as part of *Imagined Selves*. Aware of its existence, with access confined to copies of the original two printings in 1933, criticism of the nineteen eighties to early nineteen nineties recognised its power and importance. Isobel Murray concludes her essay on 'Novelists of the Renaissance' with a claim for Muir's importance:

> If MacColla has received cursory attention, the novels of Willa Muir have received virtually none at all. Willa Muir is known to posterity as wife of the more famous poet, of course, and co-translator of Kafka and the rest . . . . But she wrote two novels of considerable interest and sophistication which have been unjustly neglected. Edwin Muir's novels are interesting to any student of his poetry or his work generally, but tend to be somewhat flat and lifeless: Willa's novels are full of energy. (Murray 115)

Ironically, it is now Edwin who is less studied in Scottish literature courses than Willa Muir because of the popularity of women's writing and the availability (since 1996) of her first two novels. Murray's essay (published in 1987 but written before *Imagined Corners*' reissue by Canongate, also published in 1987) appeared just before the time when both women's writing and Scottish writing were being republished and studied in literature courses in Scotland.

Murray contextualises *Mrs Ritchie* 'as a descendant of *The House with Green Shutters*, [John MacDougall Hay's] *Gillespie*, and [A. J. Cronin's] *Hatter's Castle*, a tale with all the bleakness of the anti-Kailyard' (Murray 115). With this bleakness now seen as powerful, rather than in the negative light of the 1933 *TLS* review, Murray points out the novel's central difference to its predecessors in anti-Kailyard:

> Here is another oppressive family unit where children are terrified of parents, and fears, of God, church and public disgrace, are the dominant weapons against rebellious, even in the last resort murderous, youth. The fascinating difference is that this time it is the woman who is the central monster, with a 'terrifying intensity of self-assertion' which is unrelentingly destructive of her family. (Murray 115)

David Robb (1990) (before *Mrs Ritchie* was republished) and Beth Dickson (2000) have both connected the novel in detail with Brown's novel and but also with the earlier Scottish tradition of the monster that is traceable in Walter

Scott's *Redgauntlet* (1824), James Hogg's *Confessions of a Justified Sinner* (1824), or in R. L. Stevenson's works, *The Master of Ballantrae* (1889), *Dr Jekyll and Mr Hyde* (1886), or *The Weir of Hermiston* (1896). Robb refers to the 'hard, pure sense of tragic inevitability' of 'this characteristically Scottish *genre*' (Robb 160). But as they are aware, it is the presence of gender as a central concern of *Mrs Ritchie* that separates it from its male predecessors. Margaret Elphinstone comments in the conclusion to her analysis of *Mrs Ritchie*: 'This kind of devil has appeared many times in Scottish literature. The innovation . . . is that for the first time the devil is a woman' (Elphinstone, 1996 410). Robb suggests that in 'a literature renowned for its oppressive patriarchs, the figure of the terrible matriarch' has its antecedent only in Scott's Lady Ashton in *The Bride of Lammermoor* (1819) and in George MacDonald's work, particularly in *Lilith* (1895), which 'most fully utilised the archetype before Willa Muir' (Robb 160). But the ongoing preoccupation of Muir with the injustices endemic in a patriarchal world structured against girls and women means that *Mrs Ritchie* cannot just be concerned with an exploration of the small town monster that (departing from the more usual tradition) happens to be female. The explanation of Mrs Ritchie's achievement of monstrosity does not lie with the inevitability of the male protagonist's tragic fall from grace that Brown suggests for John Gourlay in *The House with the Green Shutters* (and that is hinted at in all the male examples cited above). Mrs Ritchie's achievement of monstrosity is shown as stemming from her girlhood as Annie Rattray, carefully positioned, as she is, within the narrow world of Calderwick and shown as angrily but futilely rejecting her place in its class and gender structures. But where the novel does intersect with its predecessors is in the tragic inevitability of her horrific effect on the lives around her. The male anti-heroes of her predecessors die (except in *Gillespie* (1914), which contains perhaps the closest parallel to Muir's protagonist), while Mrs Ritchie survives (even triumphs by her own reckoning) in a state of deluded madness, her men folk dead and her daughter fleeing for her life.

*Mrs Ritchie* spans the period from 1886, when Annie Rattray is 'only eleven and three-quarters' (5), to post-world war one when her son, John Samuel, has returned from the front. It is structured in four books, 'The Child', 'The Girl', and two titled 'The Woman'. The first two, dealing with Annie Rattray's schooldays and her time as a housemaid in a bourgeois household of three spinster sisters, make up less than half the book. They provide a detailed grounding for the family, class, and gender positioning of the adult Mrs Ritchie. All of Mrs Ritchie's male predecessors are to some extent placed within their family and social or political / historical background, providing some apparent explanation of their monstrosity. But the psychological and sociological detail of Annie Rattray's positioning by Muir makes *Mrs Ritchie* entirely a novel of the modernist period, however much it can be linked to its predecessors. Alison Smith typifies it as 'a novel where the Victorian closed, sure mind meets the modernist shell-shocked mind' (A. Smith 45). Muir the psychologist ensures that we see the insecurity and fear behind that 'closed, sure mind', tracing the freezing of possibility in the bright young Annie Rattray by virtue of her gender and class disadvantages, while also making clear that there was something inevitable about her struggle for power and dominance over all around her. The last two books trace in detail the married life of Annie Ritchie and her destructive effect on her husband and two children. The narrator as sociologist is also present. Chapter 28 begins with a long and detailed pæan of praise to Scottish baked goods, specifically to draw comparison with what is not available in the Ritchie household (179). The description itself is one of the most obvious examples in this novel of Muir's habit of incorporating sociological observations into her work, even more prevalent in her next work, *Mrs Grundy in Scotland* (begun in 1935 and published in 1936).

Muir the feminist later writes in *Belonging* about her awareness of the gendered expectations of the patriarchy:

> As a schoolgirl I shrugged my shoulders at the gap between the self I knew and the female stereotyping expected of me, but when I moved to the university I began to find the discrepancy comic. There was no lack of discrepancies affecting all the women students, not merely myself; the arbitrary conventions made eccentrics of us all. The patriarchal Law rated us as second-class citizens (we could not vote) and the patriarchal Church assumed that we were second-class souls (being suspect daughters of that Original Sinner, Eve, we had to cover our heads in church and could not hold ecclesiastical office). There was now no 'parity of esteem' as between male and female in patriarchal structures, whatever values they may have started with. (*Belonging* 140-41)

She has already positioned Eve in *Women: An Inquiry* as a threat to 'organized theology': 'So it happened that Eve, a creative woman vindicating the importance of individual moral values and of an individual conscience that should make each man the equal of God, was necessarily abhorrent to an organized theology' (*Women* 21). Muir writes later of 'the comedy of my position as a woman in a patriarchally-minded country' (*Belonging* 141). But her fictional exploration in *Mrs Ritchie* of a woman who follows 'systematic morality' (*Women* 21) too rigidly is entirely serious. Annie's route to the Calvinism that Muir believes kills the spirit is initially through her rejection of a more secular patriarchal law. Mr Boyd (the head-master who offers Annie the chance of a bursary) is shown as an example of this law:

> How could he assume — as he did — that the four-square structure of law and order, which he believed to be the very masonry of the universe, rested solely on the pillar of his will, and that if he failed to uphold his will even against one puny scholar the whole fabric would collapse? (29)

Once Annie has seen that the headmaster is 'but a mortal man', far from 'sup-porting the weight of the universe', then the 'temple of law and order' becomes 'an insubstantial fantasy' (29). Her challenge and rejection of his 'whole weight of authority' when he takes the tawse to her, symbolically returns her to the body of the class in a way she had never previously achieved (30). The scene is set for Annie's ultimately fruitless attempts at control of her environment, satisfying her urge for furious control of all around her. Her rejection of one kind of patriarchal law fails to protect her against the patriarchy of God in Scotland. Patriarchy's imposition of the 'pervasive dualisms' (Dekoven 179) of mind and body, heaven and hell, and attendant suspicions of female sexuality, feed into the example of the pathology of the repressed and the religious (the two shown as almost syn-onymous) that Mrs Ritchie becomes.

The title page of each book includes epigrammatic lines of dialogue:

### Book I: The Child

*The Child*: God of my Fathers, an abyss has opened
between me and myself.
*The Answer*: I clove that abyss.
*The Child*: How shall I bridge it?
*The Answer*: Throw a tight-rope across it. If you fall,
you fall.

### Book II: The Girl

*The Girl*: A hand has been stretched out to me.
*The Answer*: Take it.
*The Girl*: But if I lose my balance?
*The Answer*: Shake yourself free.

### Book III: The Woman

*The Woman*: I must be the best tight-rope walker
in the world. Look, I am more than half-way across,
although the rope shakes.

*The Answer*: I am shaking the rope. If you fall, you fall.
*The Woman*: It is my Enemy who shakes the rope.

**Book IV: The Woman**
*The Woman*: I have reached the other side. God of my
Fathers, where are You?
*The Answer*: Thou fool; I am in the abyss.
*The Woman*: I heard no answer. There is no one here
but Myself.[2]

These lines underpin the start of each book, suggesting both inevitability and insecurity. When read together, they make up a harsh poem to fear and the impossibility of belief in the existence of any God. Alan Freeman suggests that the 'book's division into four sections mimics the catechism with its questions and answers preceding each one' in an 'ordered, closed, arbitrary' way (Freeman 173). Taken together, they also remind us that the struggle in Annie Rattray and Mrs Ritchie, child to woman, is one familiar to Robert Wringhim in Hogg's *Confessions of a Justified Sinner*, that is, the struggle to find 'God' who then turns out to be the very devil that has been being resisted so strenuously. It is the world of the self elected to a delusory grace. The split self of the child, 'an abyss has opened between me and myself', is the precursor of the God in the abyss, and the 'enemy who shakes the rope', the devil who proves there is no God when the woman reaches the other side: 'There is no one here but Myself'. We are in a world where faith is impossible, and Mrs Ritchie's frantic pursuit of justification and election means that, like Robert Wringhim, she is condemned to fail in her extirpation of the devil, wreaking havoc on herself as well as on those surrounding her.

Muir's tight pattern of development of Annie's life underpins the 'concentrated linearity' that Robb sees in the narrative (Robb 151). This linearity is built on a complicated and dense exploration of the detail of Annie's history. The novel is also bound by its imagery: of slave narratives, of railway lines, of God's gaze, of house as body, with Annie Rattray / Ritchie tightly coiled at its centre. The novel starts with Annie's father, one of the town drunks, waiting outside the school, lost in a happy primitive world, broken by the confused roar of a school letting out; something 'black and bulky' (3) stirred in his midriff. When Mary, her older sister, takes him up the road, Annie is consumed with rage at her father and sister 'shaming' her. Despite her physical difference from them, Annie's 'black and bulky rage within her' (4) subliminally links her with the father she rejects with such disdain. The school she attends, with its new kerbstone 'fitted in exact squares' (4), is a regulated and desired world, opposing her father's world which belongs with the 'broken cobbles in the mud' (4) where the Rattrays live. The chapter ends with Annie in the chaos of her home on an ironing day with the washing that Mrs Rattray took in spread all around. But on her way home Annie sustains herself with an internalised rant, then with a fantasy against her family and her schoolmates. Her sister 'was just a black', and, lest we mistake this for some specifically Scottish denigratory use of 'black' ('In Calderwick at that time any detrimental was referred to as a black'), Annie thinks: 'A fine family to be born into. Worse than the blacks of Africa or America' (5). This small, ferocious girl (who from the outside seems 'just an ordinary little girl' (6)), eases her 'feeling of suffocation' by imagining her father and sister cowering in the 'ice-bound wastes' of the 'pitiless cold' of Tierra del Fuego; she 'changed the snow into sleet and then into hail: her rage drove the hail until it was lashing her father and sister on their naked, shivering bodies'; while she 'exulted in the sting' of the hail, 'the others were beaten to the ground' (5). She then transmogrifies herself into a 'queen of that far-off savage land . . . . more devastating than any hail. They crawled before her — father, mother, sister and schoolmates — while she sat on a throne with a whip in her hand and her feet on the naked back of a brown slave' (6). Brought out of her fantasy by Miss Julia Carnegie, her Sunday-school teacher, the 'dream folded its shining wings and plunged into some hidden abyss, taking with it the flicker of anger roused by the interruption' (6). Miss Julia is someone Annie admires, and partly responsible for Annie's imperial fantasies with her tales of missions in Africa, so the dream and anger is put away for a time. But it is the first mention in the text of the abyss of the novel's epigrams and it is into an abyss, in the end, that the adult Annie Ritchie will be lost.

Muir makes clear early in the novel that one of the reasons for the adult Annie's repressed self is the thoughtless, gendered nature of the limitation of possibilities for Annie as a girl. Her mother rejects out of hand the head teacher's suggestion that Annie was bright enough to go on to the Academy with a bursary: 'The bursary wadna pay me for your keep . . . It's no' even as if you were a laddie. Na, na, my leddy, the minute you're fourteen you gang to a job' (23). At this response, Annie's passionate rage, 'so bulky, so oppressive', becomes a volcanic flood that 'obliterated the neat scheme of rational activities' which she had been set to follow 'under Mr Boyd's guidance' (23). It leaves Annie 'withdrawn into a darkness where the sole reality was the assertion of a primal self . . . a self that acknowledged nothing but its own will to be' (24). Annie resurfaces from her 'bottomless pit of darkness' (24), and, in a 'cold fury' decides that 'she was going to assert herself as never before, not in the trivial world of school, but at the very centre of the world' (25). The dissonance between Annie's megalomaniac expression of her will and her actual life after school, a housemaid and then a wife and mother, is not emphasised by the narrator. Annie's cold fantasy of ice resurfaces in her dreams that night: 'she dreamed . . . that she was walking on thick clear ice, beneath which the faces of her mother, her father and Mary looked up at her. She stamped on them' (25). The novel's introduction to Annie, with the extended and concentrated imagery of exaggerated punishment, is emblematic of the extremity of her response to the world around her.

The first two books mainly take place from Annie's point of view, though intermittently, as on the first page with Jim Rattray, we are given the thoughts or feelings of other characters. The other main player is the narrator, present to ensure that we understand what we are reading (as often with Muir). After Annie's withdrawal into 'a primal self' (24), discussed above, the narrator as psychoanalyst comments that the 'more complex the personality the less easy it is to withdraw into that primal self' (24). The narrator also functions as sociologist. Annie, we are told, was 'a closed, secretive creature, cherishing a private dream of supremacy' (9). At the start of chapter two, we see both the reality of Annie's powerless position ('she discovered that to be Annie Rattray was to be of no account whatsoever') and her individual consciousness of intense individuality ('she was inwardly aware of nothing else') (9). The narrator then discusses the sociology of play in the primary schoolyard (something Muir later expands on at the start of *Living with Ballads*):

> [T]hey were drawn together as if for security . . . now spinning tops, now bouncing balls, now playing hopscotch; for although they seemed to be engrossed in a common occupation, each of them was isolated in a separate dream, a dream, perhaps, of achieving equilibrium in an unstable and incomprehensible world. (10)

In a rhetorical flourish, the narrator concludes that for children, unlike the 'incomprehensible, arbitrary, and possibly malicious' motives of 'the larger humans':

> [T]he unstable top is less elusive, for its spinning can be controlled to a dreamlike equilibrium; the rolling ball is less elusive, for it can be bounced in a chosen spot; the game of hopscotch is less elusive, for its scheme is clearly outlined in chalk on the concrete and all one needs is a firm balance on one leg. (10)

But Annie plays among, rather than with, the other little girls, and her 'dream of simple and savage supremacy' over her world leads to greater feelings of isolation; she looks at her classmates at play 'as a stranded mariner on an island peak might watch the gyrations of savages in the sea around him' (11). Only the 'ordered life of the class-room' (13) provides security, because 'the world of knowledge was impersonal, enduring, raised above the transiency of daily life into precision, into dogmatic certainty' (12). Annie's determination to protect herself with excellence within the classroom leads to her winning a prize for general proficiency. This prize allows the narrator to reflect on a possible 'moment of compunction' by the teacher, selecting a cookery book 'as he thought how ignorant she was of her destiny as a woman' (14). Annie's ambition, fed by the prize, 'flared up in an ephemeral, fierce blaze that, like the Jubilee bonfire, made more palpable the darkness preceding and following it' (14). Annie's ambition (thwarted both by her gender and class) is connected by this simile to the late, fierce fires of the 1887 jubilee celebrations of Victoria, empress of that empire which was moving inexorably through exploitation of its far flung lands towards failure. No hint is allowed that Annie, as fierce as the Jubilee blaze, might escape the inevitability of her own fall into palpable darkness.

Muir gives a rare description of the natural world when she describes the 'crystalline, transparent veil of light over the bare and reticent contours of the duneland around Calderwick, and a whispering wind from the sea ruffled the sharp bent-grass and the fragile harebells that rose from among dwarf thyme and eyebright' (15). But its purpose is to emphasise that Annie is *incapable* of noting these things, cut off as much from the natural world surrounding her as she is from her contemporaries. During the summer holidays her only consolation is to hear the Sunday-school tales of Miss Julia:

> Annie liked to hear about the black slave-gangs, and the floggings, and the lions that sprang out of the tall jungle. She was particularly struck with the story of an escaping slave-mother who was carrying her baby on her back and met a lion face to face; the woman raged and scolded and abused the lion with such vehemence that the creature retreated in bewilderment before her fury, step by step, while she shook her fist at it, until the jungle grass closed on it again and the slave-mother reached the mission station in safety. (16)

Beth Dickson points out that 'Empire forms a constant, if fitfully expressed, background to *Mrs Ritchie*' and sees Muir as repudiating, along with most modernist writers, 'the values of Victorian and Edwardian Britain' (Dickson, 2000 99-100). But neither Muir nor other modernist writers were free of ingrained prejudice about other than European races, however liberal they may have felt themselves to be. Muir is positing African complicity in slavery when she has Annie's queen place her foot on the 'naked back of a brown slave' (6) rather than presenting any absolute repudiation of empire. Her repudiation is of the idea of mission (that is, a religious mission) within the empire. This is consistent with Muir's own hatred of social hypocrisy and Calvinism. But, as Dickson points out, a clear connection is made between female sexuality and Africa. She notes that Muir 'may be following Freud's use of Africa in its Western appellation the "Dark Continent" as a metaphor for female sexuality in *The Question of Lay Analysis* (1925-1926)' (Dickson, 2000 100). Annie goes to work for Miss Julia (the middle class spinster living in bourgeois splendour with her two elder sisters), leaving school at fourteen just as her despised sister had before her. The confusing characteristics of late-nineteenth century Africa as presented to children in Sunday-school are developed further when Annie begins to help Miss Julia in her mission work for the Free Church of Scotland. When she sees the slave-mother who had faced down the lion on the cover of one of Miss Julia's books, she asks 'Please, Miss Julia, can I have Africa?' (71). Muir then moves into a passage explicitly foregrounding the connections of sexuality to Africa for the girl and the spinster:

> Africa was indeed a Dark Continent, and Miss Julia's voice took a deeper, a more solemn note as she expounded to Annie the degradation of the torrid zone. The map of Africa became a dark blot on the round belly of the earth, a devil's mark upon the belly of the earth. Annie and Miss Julia drew closer to each other over the polished table, and in their virgin minds hippopotami rolled their vast bulk, crocodiles heaved their obscene heads, insatiable lions sprang from cover, and cruelty, lewdness and murder roamed unchecked. It was a hot, savage night of lust that Miss Julia called up'. (71-72)

Dickson points out: 'Two narratives are being blocked here. What was the slave mother's story? And was the involvement of nineteenth century Scotswomen in missionary work merely a narrative of repression?' (Dickson, 2000 100). For Dickson it is 'entirely problematic' for us to interpret 'an African slave woman's short narrative as a metaphor for the rage and frustrated sexuality of free white women . . . showing the customary hierarchy of white over black' (Dickson, 2000 100). This is an entirely valid point, informed by Edward Said's analyses in *Orientalism* (1973) and *Culture and Imperialism* (1993). But Muir is writing not that long after the publication of Joseph Conrad's *Heart of Darkness* (1902) and in the Freudian climate of the early twentieth century. The complexities of sexuality, the empire, Africa and race written more eurocentrically than can be done more than a hundred years later, Muir's concern is to explore the awakening of sexuality in Annie via the route of Miss Julia's missionary obsessions. So, while Miss Julia thinks she is keeping Annie on 'the straight path of female propriety', she in fact leads Annie 'by a natural transition . . . from the sultry passions of heathendom to reflect upon her own sexual functions as a potential wife and mother' (73).

'Africa' is important in the pattern of imagery in *Mrs Ritchie*, closely interlinked as it is with sexuality. But linked with sexuality also are the Freudian connections of the novel's use of the unconscious. Muir hints at the 'subterranean forces slumbering below' (Frazer, 56) already used in *Imagined Corners* (see previous chapter). When still at school, Annie had wanted to surrender to the 'dark, irresponsible force' of the conscienceless world of the unconscious, discarding 'all the burdens of civilization', returning 'to a passion that is old and strong as the earth' through the 'thrilling game' of mesmerism (35). Annie is the best at descending into 'the dark cave' (36) among her schoolmates and gains a rare feeling of being part of the group. Her 'performance became more and more impressive . . . when she "woke up" . . . she never forgot to disclaim all knowledge of her actions during the frenzy' (37). This pre-figures her daughter's identification later of her mother's 'play-acting' (257). When Sarah Annie again identifies Mrs Ritchie's theatricality, the narrator specifically draws the reader's attention back to this childhood scene of Annie 'disclaiming responsibility for what she had done' (263). Annie takes it too far one day and, having been 'ower rough' (37), is cast out once more. Annie's precarious connection to her social world effectively ruptured, *Mrs Ritchie* moves into its other major thematic concern, the complex intertwining of God and the devil in any religious 'call'. Annie, resisting her impulse to jump from the railway bridge, 'gazed at the straight, inviolate track of the permanent way and . . . her spirit followed her eye along promised lines of certainty cutting through the bewilderments of life' (41). It is at this moment of interpretation of the rigid railway lines as a longed-for certainty, that Annie is 'called' to 'God':

> The red eye of the sun peered from a rift in the clouds, and as if a ray had penetrated her, Annie felt that God was looking at her, and almost in the same moment she knew that until this very evening she had been giving herself to the devil . . . . [i]t was a last temptation of the devil that had nearly drawn her to fall from the bridge. The solemnity of death and the solemnity of God — or were they one and the same? — filled the darkening world around her, and she was hushed in awe, uplifted in spirit as in body . . . . God was greater than any citizen of Calderwick . . . . And He had singled out Annie Rattray . . . . [T]he isolated dream that had cut her off from the others at home . . . now rose and joined her to the skies. God was her Father. In Mill Wynd she was a changeling. (41-42)

An essential component of Annie's religion is that if she is singled out for God's right hand, then the rest of her family will be 'cast into hell' (48). She will be selected as 'ane to heaven', like Burns's Holy Willie, while the others are going 'ten to h-ll' (Robert Burns, 'Holy Willie's Prayer', stanza one). Her 'isolated martyrdom' (51) within the family is for Annie a sign of her elevated status. Muir also roots Annie's pathology of godliness which requires 'unceasing vigilance and self-sacrifice' (50) in a rejection of dirt and chaos. 'Parsing and sums were like a barrier between herself and the devil; they belonged to the world of clean wake-fulness, not to darkness and dirt' (46); this order, previously sought in the world of school as a protection against the chaos of the outside world (whether of the playground or home), she now seeks in the narrow interpretation of religion that Muir presents as exemplified in the Free Church of Scotland. Once Annie Rattray casts herself loose from school and family and also, in time, from Miss Julia's household, rejected because its spinster state carried too low a status, Muir makes clear that Annie (now Mrs) Ritchie's adherence to pietistic Calvinism allows her to impose a terrible repression on those surrounding her, all in the interests of extirpating sin in the guise of normal bodily needs and functions.

Part of Mrs Ritchie's ceaseless battle against chaos is her attempted withdrawal within the safety of the house she attains by marrying the joiner, Johnny Ritchie. Annie's urge towards marriage is shown entirely as a product of her uneasiness at sitting in church in a pew with no man at the end of it and her interpretation of the two remaining sisters in the Carnegie household as 'useless . . . like a spot of decay that threatened to spread' (101). Her desire, as she sat awake at the top of the Carnegie household, 'like a wakeful eye above a sleeping body', was for an 'orderly subservience of her territory' but 'that territory, narrow as it was, could not be kept inviolate' (99). Her marriage is an attempt to gain that inviolacy. The house, in one of the most persistent images of the novel, is her body. But con-nected to the body is the problematic nature of sex and childbirth, redolent of the 'lower' world of her father and dirt. Marriage may provide the house but it also opens Annie to the puzzling world of sex and children. On their marriage night, Annie is mentally kept 'vigilant' against the 'devil . . . stirring in her bosom' (126) by the text 'Thou God Seest Me' placed above their marriage bed with its 'largely opened eye whose rays spread into the remotest corners' (123). As Annie is literally penetrated on her marriage bed, she is metaphorically penetrated by God's gaze, as she had felt at the moment of her religious epiphany (41). By linking this sexual imagery directly to Annie's religiosity, Muir intensifies the connections between sexuality, repression and religion in the pathology of Annie Rattray.

Johnny Ritchie has his own fear of sex from boyhood after hearing his mother's cries in a childbirth that brought 'a death of screaming agony' (111). He finds lit-tle comfort in Annie's arms, failing to find any 'warmth' or 'answering, absolving tenderness' in their sexual encounter. Annie's sexual being is 'locked up like the prim, clean house' whose key he cannot find, leaving him 'an intruder, a defiler, leaving unwanted filth behind him' (126). Despite the birth in due course of two children, John Samuel and Sarah Annie, Mrs Ritchie effectively freezes Johnny Ritchie out of his own home. John Samuel's request at sixteen for a latch key

Ritchie's attempt at control of her family. The negative *Times Literary Supplement* review clearly feels that this narrative control is problematic: '[d]islike, untouched by the humour that turns it to satire or by the humanity that gives the miscreant at least the semblance of a sporting chance, is a dangerous emotion for the artist'. Muir's apparent hostility towards her protagonist is 'not of the kind that vivifies creation', the novel's voice being like a lecturer's, 'precise and competent' but monotonous (*TLS*, 13 July 1933). While understanding this negativity, I take a much more positive position on *Mrs Ritchie*, Muir's narrative control giving the novel power and intensity rather than monotony.

F. Marian McNeill had complained about Elise's departure from Scotland at the end of *Imagined Corners*, presumably reading it as a criticism of the state of contemporary Scotland. After defending the departure, Muir adds 'I am proposing to write another novel about Calderwick, but you needn't look for Nationalism with a big N in it' (21 July 1931; NLS; MacCulloch, 2004 209). As Muir indicates here, any general application to 'Scotland' of *Mrs Ritchie*, centred as it is on the microcosm of the Ritchie household within Calderwick (Montrose), is even more oblique than in her first novel. Both novels are consistent with Muir's resistance to writing obviously 'Scottish' novels of nation. Her negative view of Scotland is strongly linked with her anti-Calvinism and her unhappiness with Scottish social constrictions' effect on the upbringing of girls and examination of these is important in *Mrs Ritchie*. Muir lacks interest in 'nation' as an abstract concept; her constant movement abroad into non-Scottish environments and her own resistance to the idea of a straightforward 'Scottishness' (possibly stemming from her sense of herself as an outsider to mainland Scotland, her parents' roots being in Shetland) mean that her writing takes no part in any overt debate about political power or nationalism in the Scotland of the time. The nearest that she comes to expressing nationalist feeling is when she and Edwin are the Scottish representatives at the 1932 PEN conference in Budapest (see 'Life and Context'). Helen Cruickshank, Muir's correspondent then, and F. Marian MacNeill are among women writers who lived and worked in Scotland, certainly feminist but perhaps prioritising things Scottish[3] whereas Muir's commitment is always to the importance of gender as a reality that underwrites everything. She resists the idea of talking, fighting and working politically for Scotland, 'being more concerned to present an illumination of life in Scotland than a reformation of it'. She continues to McNeill, 'it is indirect, not direct propaganda that literature provides' (21 July 1931; NLS; McCulloch, 2004 209). Despite this view, her quarrel with Calvinism and its followers in *Mrs Ritchie* and other works is so explicit that her attacks amount to 'direct propaganda'.

Muir would almost certainly have been in sympathy with the nineteen sixties and seventies' feminist slogan 'the personal is political', tending to exclude conventionally narrow political concerns from her areas of exploration. But despite her clear understanding of the sociology of gender and of ideas of environments that inevitably influence anyone growing up within them ('no individual grows independently of his environment' (Muir, 'Moving in Circles' 603)), despite her explorations in *Mrs Grundy in Scotland* and *Living with Ballads* of the all-pervading effect of the Reformation in Scottish life, her narrow assumption of what the political is means that she does not see religion itself as 'political' in any way. This leads to her underestimating the strength and directness of her assault on Scotland and the Calvinist strand in its religious life. Yet the powerfully negative analysis that *Mrs Ritchie* provides of the microcosm of Calderwick represents an attack on the social structures and institutions of Protestant Scotland that must have felt like the most direct and radical of commentaries on Scotland's state of being.

Notes

1. *Mrs Ritchie* (London: Martin Secker, 1933) had a second printing, August 1933. Muir gave a copy of the second printing to the Grieves, inscribing it 'To Valda and Christopher from Willa'. The copy (Edinburgh University Library) has the book plate, 'Ex Libris Hugh MacDiarmid'.

2. These epigrams are reproduced from the first edition; quotations are otherwise from the *Imagined Selves* edition of *Mrs Ritchie* (1996).

3. Helen Burness Cruickshank (1886-1975), born in Angus; like Muir, she attended Montrose Academy but could not afford to go to University; poet and civil servant; working first in London, she took part in suffrage activities there; returning to Edinburgh, 1912, she was a founder member of Scottish PEN (1927) and the Saltire Society (1936); friend of many Scottish renaissancists. Florence Marian McNeill (1885-1973), born in Orkney; writer and folklorist; educated Glasgow University, she taught in France and Germany; secretary of Scottish Federation of Women's Suffrage Societies, 1912-13; a founder member of Scottish PEN and a vice-president of the Scottish National Party in the 1930s; best known for *A Scots Kitchen* (1929), she had also worked as a researcher on the *Scottish National Dictionary* and published a novel, *The Road Home* (1932).

# THE WAR
## GOES ON

■ ■ ■ ■ ■ ■ ■ ■ ■ ■ ■ ■ ■

*By*

## SHOLEM ASCH

*Translated by*

WILLA *and* EDWIN MUIR

■ ■ ■ ■ ■ ■ ■ ■ ■ ■ ■ ■ ■

G·P·PUTNAM'S SONS
*New York*
1936

*The War Goes On* title page.

# Translating for a Living

Although Willa Muir only published two novels, she had an existence as a writer all her life. How this is dealt with can seem problematic when much of the evidence for this statement is unpublished and much of her translation work is confused by her joint by-line with Edwin Muir on the title pages. I have already considered separately her two novels and two polemics in the context of the nineteen twenties and thirties. Discussion of Muir's other works, published and unpublished, is less easily corralled into individual chapters. What approach can encompass her translation work (mainly done from the late nineteen twenties to the nineteen forties, with or without Edwin), her two unpublished novels, *Mrs Muttoe and the Top Storey* and *The Usurpers*, a few reviews and articles, all her letters (available mainly in collections in St Andrews University Library, the National Library of Scotland, and the British Library), her post-war journals (available in St Andrews University Library), and her poetry (scattered between manuscript sources and small privately printed limited editions)? I regard all of this work as a central part of Muir's writing life and am going to consider them in two chapters, beginning with the translations that constituted much of the Muirs' capacity to make a living for many years and on which so much of Muir's own public reputation was to lie before her novels were republished. The following chapter, 'Fragments of a Writing Life', will consider her unpublished novels, her journals and letters and her poetry. Her two final published prose works, *Living with Ballads* (1965) and *Belonging* (1968), I shall consider in a separate, final chapter.

## Willa Muir's translating

The Muirs are an important part of a process of nineteen twenties and thirties cultural exchange. This exchange has a far greater breadth than is always remembered in a retrospective gaze through the prism of world war two and post-world war two interpretations of Germany and Eastern Europe. Muir's own difficulty with the idea of translating German in a post-Nazi world is testament to this. She writes of this in 1959: 'I ought to say that the last war prejudiced me, I think, against the German language. I find myself disliking the purposive control, the will power dominating the German sentence'. She concludes her meditation on the German sentence with a typically Willaesque psychoanalytic conclusion: 'One can tell that the Germans are very bowel-conscious, or as the psychoanalysts say, anal-erotic. So the right image for the German sentence, I suggest, is that of a great gut, a bowel, which deposits at the end of it a sediment of verb. Is not this like the Reich desired by Hitler, who planned to make mincemeat of Europe?' ('Translating from the German' 95, 96). But in the intellectually curious climate between the two world wars, there was an assumption on the part of publishers who commissioned most of the Muirs' translations (initially Ben Huebsch in New York and Martin Secker and Routledge in London) that translations of contemporary writing in German were commercially viable. Once world war two began, this commercial motive was undermined, presumably for the same reasons of hostility towards Nazism that Muir later felt. Commissions for the Muirs dried up: 'We discovered what we might have foreseen but did not: publishers no longer wanted translations from German' (*Belonging* 205). But between the wars, the traffic in translating was an essential component in sustaining the Muirs' roving, freelance lives as writers, underwriting their own explorations (in both writing and living) with payment for their translations of contemporary European writers. Sherry Simon acknowledges that while their 'translation work was clearly inspired in part by financial considerations' it 'was also closely tied to their commitment to "Europeanize" the British world of letters' (Simon 1996 77). There was a cross-border excitement at intellectual and cultural possibilities, whether living on mainland Europe or in London. Muir writes of this pan-European feeling when they were living in Hampstead, 1932-35:

> We belonged locally to Hampstead, but did not feel cut off from Europe,
> which had become part of our consciousness; the Channel was no longer
> a barrier. Not only were we translating European books and writing letters
> to European friends, we were in touch with Europeans in London itself.
> (*Belonging* 167)

It is in this period that Edwin Muir and Janko Lavrin edit *The European Quarterly: A Review of Modern Literature, Art and Life* (only one volume, in four numbers, was published between May 1934 and February 1935) which carried Muir's translation of Kafka's 'First Sorrow' and Edwin's 'Bolshevism and Calvinism' in the first issue and his essay, 'Hölderlin's *Patmos*', in the last issue (1:241-55).

The Muirs financed their first travels in Europe with Edwin Muir's reviews for the American journal, *The Freeman*. But its suspension in March 1924 meant 'no more dollars'; providentially they were asked to translate 'three of Gerhart Hauptmann's plays into English blank verse' at $100 a play (*Belonging* 101 106). This marks 'the beginning of a period when we turned ourselves into a sort of translation factory' (Edwin Muir, *Autobiography* 217). These translations then become an essential part of their ability to live their peripatetic writing lives, their capacity to work with intense commitment to fulfil their commissions giving them money to live on and time to write what they want. Of their time in Montrose in 1924, when she was thinking about what was to become *Women: An Inquiry*, Muir wrote later:

> I was revising the translation of a Hauptmann play, and later translating
> a fantastic novel of his: *The Island of the Great Mother*. From now on,
> it can be taken for granted that I was always translating something and
> any other work I did was sandwiched between translations. In the same
> way Edwin was always writing reviews: all his own work was sandwiched
> between reviews. If there were a troublesome dead-line for a transla-
> tion, and if he had time, he helped with it. This was the pattern of our
> working life until I had our baby [1927]. It was rather like subsistence
> farming, although we did earn ourselves intervals of freedom. (*Belonging*
> 114-15).

This passage both expresses the reality of their life in the unexpectedly rural image of 'subsistence farming' and introduces the problematic question of who did the translating. They are given joint credit on nearly all of the works but throughout *Belonging* Muir is far more ambiguous, moving between 'I' and 'we' in many of the passages dealing with translation. Translation is something Muir feels competent to do from 'many years' translating Greek and Latin into English: 'I was well trained in accuracy, at least, and that was all to the good, for Edwin's interpretation tended to be wild and gay. We hammered out our blank verse [for the Hauptmann plays] and it was rhythmical enough' (*Belonging* 106). Edwin Muir writes in 1924 of this same commission: 'Both my wife and I have been writing from morn till night this last week translating these Hauptmann plays, typing them and correcting, and it has completely tired us out' (Schiff papers; Butter, 1974 39). Butter dates this letter '[June 1924]'. But by later that summer, Edwin is writing to Schiff that Willa alone is now work-ing on the Hauptmann plays: 'Poor Willa has not yet got to her work on wom-en yet; she has been condemned to the revision and typing of Hauptman's play which she will not allow me to touch' (10 Aug. 1924; Schiff papers; BL). By 18 August 1924, he reports that she has finished the translation 'to the profound relief of us both' (Schiff papers; BL). For their first commission, then, it seems clear enough that they both initially worked on it fairly equally with Muir then taking over. In winter 1924-25, their translation of Gerhart Hauptmann's novel, *Island of the Great Mother*, was commissioned by Secker; of this Edwin reports they were to get $500 for it: 'Willa says she is going to do most of the work, and talks of finishing it off in 2 or 3 months' (11 Dec. 1924; Schiff papers; BL), indicating the extent that Edwin credits Muir with much of the work on these early translations in his letters to Sydney Schiff. Muir's later comments in *Belonging* continue the ambiguity. They recommended Feuchtwanger's *Jud Süss* for publication and were commissioned to do it, early 1926: 'While Edwin was finishing *Transition* [his collection of essays] I was getting on as fast as I could with this translation' (*Belonging* 122). But by 1928 Edwin writes to Schiff that '[o]ur year has been spent pretty much in keeping the pot boiling: that is, we have translated three plays by Feuchtwanger (he seems unending) and part of a new novel by him, which will continue engaging us for some time' (6 Oct. 1928; Schiff papers; BL); this confirms the way that their translating work was 'subsistence farming', pot boiling to finance their lives and own work, but also implies joint credit for the hard work. The Muirs went to live in St. Tropez with the intention of writing their novels, but 'if we were to get to our novels, we had to polish off *Jew Süss*. That seems an apt phrase, for I cannot say that we translated *Jew Süss*; what we produced was a polished rendering of it. In Montrose I had already begun to tailor the style to what I felt better suited an English public, and in St Tropez we went on doing that, cutting out adjectives and shortening sentences' (*Belonging* 125). This seems to imply that Muir produced the basic translation and then they polished it together. Edwin Muir's biographer, P. H. Butter, resists this idea as denigrating Muir's talents: 'it would be wrong to suggest that she brought only linguistic competence, and he added the grace of style. I think she did as much, perhaps more than, he to make the best of their translations works of art, conveying something of the originals and, especially in Broch's *Sleepwalkers*, the stylistic variations of the originals' (Butter, 1990 61). Muir refers directly in *Belonging* to this issue of credit, describing the way on their return to England in 1927 that 'Edwin was hailed everywhere as "the translator of *Jew Süss*", which amused me but irritated him' (*Belonging* 126). But Muir also straightforwardly uses 'we' in relation to Broch's *The Sleepwalkers*: '[w]e spent nearly a whole year of our lives translating this trilogy' (*Belonging* 152). Sherry Simon makes no comment on any division of labour other than that it is 'unfortunate that Willa Muir chooses not to describe this collaborative work with her husband, with whom she had a rigorously egalitarian relationship' (Simon 1996 77); this implies an acceptance by Simon that the work, when credited to both, was a joint production.[1]

The one work for which Muir famously describes their method is Kafka's *The Castle* (worked on in 1929):

> People have often asked me what was our technique in our joint Kafka translations? It was simple enough. We divided the book in two, Edwin translated one half and I the other, then we went over each other's translations as with a fine-tooth comb. By the time we had finished the going-over and put the two halves together the translation was like a seamless garment, for we both loved the sinuous flexibility of Kafka's style — very unlike classical German — and dealt with it in the self-same way. (*Belonging* 150)

This comment is placed chronologically in *Belonging* at the translating of their first Kafka novel, *The Castle*, though it implies other Kafka works as well. Catriona Soukup confirms that the method also applies to *The Trial* in her memoir 'Willa in Wartime'. Her conversations with Muir in Edinburgh took place because she, then a student and recently married to a Czech, Lumir Soukup, was interested in learning Czech in order to translate its literature. She asks Muir for 'tips' as their translations of Kafka 'read as novels in their own right' while Czech translations that she had read seemed 'stiff and unnatural'. Soukup then gives an extended description of the Muirs' general practice and their practice in relation to Kafka specifically:

> Willa read German quicker than Edwin did, so she read the book first. Then, after discussing it, they decided together whether they would translate it. When they decided to translate *The Castle* and *The Trial*, they tore the books in two (though she assured me they didn't normally do this to books). They then tossed a coin to see which half each of them would take. After translating their own part, they exchanged halves, and went through them carefully, correcting each other's mistakes. After the mistakes had been put right, the real work began. (C. Soukup 24)

Soukup reports that '[i]ncreasingly, as the years passed, it was Willa alone who did the translations, leaving Edwin free for his own writings' (ibid.). Clearly the source for both Soukup and *Belonging* is Muir so the one cannot be used as corroboration for the other. But nonetheless they do give a picture of some kind of joint process in the business of translating, however much both Muirs apparently acknowledge that the journey-woman work was primarily done by Muir while Edwin worked on his own writing, commissioned or otherwise. But Muir's earlier, less well known, description of this division of manuscripts to be translated seems to corroborate the extent that division of the work was the norm:

> [W]hen we translate a book, we divide it in two: after we have finished, Edwin goes over my half ruthlessly, and I go over his half ruthlessly, and the combined effort is put together. We have no hesitation in cutting each other's versions to pieces in the interests of the final product. (Lochhead; 3 March 1933; see Appendix I)

In *Mrs Muttoe and the Top Storey*, Muir's protagonists Alison and Dick are clearly based on Willa and Edwin and, while being cautious in using one of Muir's novels as evidence on this issue, it clearly illustrates some of Muir's own feelings in fictional form. In this unpublished novel there is a dialogue about the division of labour and the pressures of literary production for money:

> 'Can't you finish it by then? Shall I give you a hand?'
>
> 'Oh no, Dick, you've got to finish your own book. It's up to me. I took it on and I'll do it'. 'Don't go pottering around the house so much' . . . . Pottering, indeed. Pottering with Alice in the morning; pottering out of doors in the afternoons; pottering with translation in the evenings . . . . Damn money, said Mrs. Muttoe to herself, beginning to translate at high speed . . . . 'I'm translating it well; I'm putting a polish on it; but that only means putting a gloss on what is essentially cheap wood. It wouldn't be worth doing but for the money'. 'I know, darling. All the same, it will sell a good deal more than my book of essays', commented Dick Muttoe ruefully. That was the problem. The delicacy and clarity of Dick's literary gifts delighted only a small circle of appreciative readers. (*Mrs Muttoe* 132-33; St Andrews)

Muir here shows that the pressure of translation deadlines belongs to the female half of the partnership while the assumption of artistic worth lies with the male half; blame is not attributed; it is the fact of Alison and Dick's working life.

This issue of their division of labour would not be so compelling if Muir had not written in her 1953 journal about her resentment at the assumption that Edwin was the main translator, including her own feminist interpretation that she is a woman writer whose work has been subsumed into the male's area of credit. Her tone of hurt rage in her journal is far from the subsequent report in *Belonging* of her amused tolerance of the assumptions about which of them had translated *Jew Süss* (*Belonging* 126; see above); Edwin is central to blame in this passage:

And then I told him that even the translations I had done were no longer my own territory, for everyone assumes that Edwin did them. He is referred to as 'THE' translator. By this time he may even believe that he was. He has let my reputation sink, by default; so now I fear that if the Feuchtwanger publishers are told that I am prepared to do his beastly novel, they will refuse unless Edwin engages to do it, or to put his name to it. // And the fact remains; I am a better translator than he is. The whole current of patriarchal society is set against this fact, however, and sweeps it into oblivion, simply because I did not insist on shouting aloud: 'Most of this translation, especially Kafka, has been done by ME. Edwin only helped'. And every time Edwin was referred to as THE translator, I was too proud to say anything; and Edwin himself felt it would be undignified to speak up, I suppose. So that now, especially since my break-down in the middle of the war, I am left without a shred of literary reputation. And I am ashamed of the fact that I felt it as a grievance. It shouldn't bother me. Reputation is a passing value after all . . . . And yet, and yet, I want to be acknowledged.' ('*Why I am to be described as a mess*'; 20 Aug. 1953; journal; Jan. 1951-Sept. 1953)

The passage concludes a long section, provoked by Edwin's failure to read Muir's draft of *The Usurpers* (which she had completed in February 1952, and then revised). He was busy working on his autobiography and Willa accused him of intending to leave out the 'the Gerda episode' on Lake Garda ('Yes, indeed he would, he said'). The whole passage from the journal is available in Patricia Rowland Mudge's 'A Quorum of Willas' (Mudge 4-6), in the same issue of *Chapman* (1992-93) as Catriona and Lumir Soukup's reminiscences. It was Butter who first drew attention to the passage in his 1990 essay on Muir in the context of her feeling 'at times . . . that her own work was undervalued'; reading the journal passage as 'a characteristic mixture of assertiveness and modesty' (Butter, 1990 58), Butter leaves out Muir's reference to the 'whole current of patriarchal society' which is to omit Muir's grounding of her emotions in gender analysis. The emotional force of the passage is fuelled by her capacity to still 'call up vividly the emotions of that terrible time' on Lake Garda. But she is clear in the journal that it is also part her general lack of literary self-confidence. She writes about her earlier confidence in her translating abilities, 'so began doing it without arrière-pensée at Sonntagberg': 'But I had no general self-confidence, — in writing literature, at least, — and was easily cast down & shaken' (20 Aug. 1953; journal; Jan. 1951-Sept. 1953). Edwin's ignoring *The Usurpers* reminds her of his earlier failure to encourage her writing of a play in contemporary language on Noah's Ark when they were in Dresden. She self-analyses as she goes in the journal: 'And when Edwin ignored *The Usurpers* —— !! Then I unpacked all the unhappiness that had made my life bitter after finishing that novel. —— Then I perceived well enough that the earlier bitter feelings had been only an excuse for releasing the later. I really did let them all out' (20 Aug. 1953; journal; Jan. 1951-Sept. 1953). The passage is much more than 'wistfully regretful' (Allen, 1996 xii) and its power undoubtedly influenced Butter to concentrate in his essay on the importance of Muir's role in the translating. But its forceful description about the translation of Kafka in particular is contradicted by Muir's own words to Lochhead and to Catriona Soukup (see above) and in *Belonging* (150; see also above) where she talks three times about the physical division of the books for work on them. In the end the weight of the evidence seems to be that they did divide the translating although Muir may have done most of the preliminary work, particularly of the less inspiring translations, and that Edwin acknowledges this. Lumir Soukup told her that 'Edwin had told me many times, that she had "slaved" over translations of books she did not really like, in order to make it possible for him to devote his time to writing' (L. Soukup 33). In the period when their translations of Kafka were pre-eminent, Willa Muir had no real public existence other than as co-translator, her last novel having been published in 1933 and *Mrs Grundy in Scotland* in 1936. In post-world war two Britain and the United States, despite their equal credit on the translations' title pages, Edwin Muir's greater credit (in relation to Kafka in particular) probably comes from his writing of several short introductions to some of the Kafka translations, from his reputation as a literary critic and as a poet influenced by Kafka: 'He seems to have learnt how to transpose thought into image from Kafka' (Robertson, 1987 140; see also Robertson, 2000 109, 112).

Butter cites Muir's solo translations of Hans Carossa's four works between 1929 and 1933 as evidence for her specific skills as a translator: 'I find Carossa a writer of great beauty as translated by Willa Muir . . . . Her translations show more than linguistic skill. Penetration into the minds of these strange and difficult writers called for psychological insights and the persistence in her of that sensitive dreaming "me" beneath the exuberance' (Butter, 1990 63). Muir supposes that she is 'a "natural" for translation', since she 'never thought of theories when translating'. This is written in reaction to the seminar in Harvard on translation where she was 'bored by the abstract analytical quibbling. I would rather do translation for two hours, I felt, than attend for one hour to an intellectual dissection of its problems' (*Belonging* 300). But there is a curiously gendered feel about her claim that she did not intellectualise about the theory of translation because her skill was 'natural'. Her intensely personal reactions against German in a post-war world in her essay 'Translating from the German' are also like an expression of female 'natural' feelings, particularly coming, as they do, after Edwin's judicious poet's view of translating, with his section of their essay beginning 'Translation is obviously a difficult art: I use that word, for if translation is not an art it can hardly be called translation' (E. Muir, 'Translating from the German' 93). Their short commentaries, published as one essay under the title 'Translating from the German' (I, signed E. M., 93-94, and II, signed W. M., 94-96) were written for a book of essays *On Translation* after their attendance at the seminar on translation in Harvard described above. They are possibly based on interventions in the seminar itself. Indeed, Willa Muir's exaggerated anti-German language statements (see above) may have been in reaction to her boredom at the seminar, a kind of 'shocking the academic' auto-reaction. Butter is certainly correct when he foregrounds her claims to real admiration as a skilled translator. For all her insistence, Muir is aware of the theory as well as the practice and does at times analyse translating skills:

> Translating from a foreign language into one's mother tongue is as fatiguing as breaking stones, but there the resemblance ceases. One is not dealing with blocks of words that have to be trimmed into other shapes, one is struggling with something at once more recalcitrant and more fluid, the spirit of language, which makes thoughts flow into molds that are quite different from those of one's native speech. The very shape of thought has to be changed in translation, and that seems to me to be more difficult than rendering words and idioms into their equivalents. (Willa Muir, 'Translating from the German' 94)

She had written similarly in *Mrs Muttoe* of Alison's methods of translating, though here she characterises it as an art more connected to the unconscious:

> For about twenty minutes after that she worked steadily, writing in a child's jotter with a book propped open before her. Each foreign sentence on the printed page entered her mind, found a meaning there, flowed more or less sinuously into it and came out again, altered in shape, as an English sentence, a process which always seemed mysterious to Mrs. Muttoe, although sometimes she claimed it was as exhausting as stone-breaking. (*Mrs Muttoe* 19)

That these are a continuing part of Muir's ideas about translating is shown by Catriona Soukup description of Muir's advice (given to her in wartime Edinburgh) about the act of translating:

> One must never, Willa said, depart from the original, but at the same time, one should not stick to it slavishly. It is not so much translation — each language after all has its own syntax — as finding equivalents

and transposing them from one language to the other. Sentences must, if necessary, be abbreviated or lengthened, or turned around. Paragraphs and sentences have to 'go native' — there should be no trace of the original, foreign construction. A dictionary sometimes helps, but the inner ear must be the final judge which dictates the easy flow of the sentences and eliminates any jerkiness or awkwardness in the prose. (C. Soukup 24)

Walter Benjamin similarly asserts that '[a] literal rendering of the syntax completely demolishes the theory of reproduction of meaning and is a direct threat to comprehensibility' ('The Task of the Translator' 78). Taking Muir's three passages on technique together (one signed as her own direct views on translating, one fictional and one reported), they give some idea of both Muir's practice and theory of translating and indicate the strength of her grasp on what was, after all, the main part of her writing career for many years.

The bulk of their translation work was done for financial reasons and most of this work was felt to be hard labour; this is undisputed. I am not going to consider in much detail most of the works that they translated, preferring to concentrate rather on the act and purpose of translating as I have done above. As Edwin Muir wrote to Schiff about their first commission in 1924, 'I really think it has not been the labour which has exhausted us so much as the stupidity of the original. We did not choose Hauptmann for translating (we would never have thought of doing so); it was the publisher's suggestion' (Schiff papers; Butter, 1974 39). Then in 1928 he wrote, also to Sydney Schiff, that 'Willa and I have just finished translating three plays of Feuchtwanger, a rather painful and disagreeable task, for they are quite worthless' (26 April 1928; Schiff papers; BL). He presumably refers to Lion Feuchtwanger's *Two Anglo-Saxon Plays*, published in 1929, and *Success: Three Years in the Life of a Province* or *The Ugly Duchess*, both published in 1930. This translating that they did of Feuchtwanger was used 'to cover the expenses of moving and furnishing' and for Muir it represents a negative experience: 'When one is not interested, uplifted, exhilarated by the material one is translating, so that the unconscious delights in doing the work, the quick of oneself is responsive to the quick of the foreign writing, the labour of digesting sentences can become drearily depressing' (*Belonging* 149). Their work of translating Hermann Broch and Franz Kafka is in the different, positive category to the 'worse than breaking stones' or 'subsistence farming' kind of translating that Feuchtwanger represents to them (*Belonging* 149 115). Broch's and Kafka's works were those that fully engaged their intellect and enjoyment. Much of the Muirs' reputation as translators still rests on their being the first translators of Kafka into English and, with their work on the Austrian Broch and the German speaking Czech Kafka, a more 'responsive' note enters both Muirs' comments, Kafka because of their admiration for his work and Broch because of their friendship with him as well as their admiration of his work.

Hermann Broch was born in 1886 in Vienna; arrested in 1938 after the German annexation of Austria, he spent eighteen days in prison. He then emigrated first to the Muirs in St Andrews, August to September, then to the U.S., October 1938. He died in New Haven in 1951. The Muirs' translations of Broch's three volume novel *The Sleepwalkers* was published by Martin Secker in 1933 and of *The Unknown Quantity* by Collins in 1935.[2] It is clear that Broch influenced them both in their view of the developing political situation in mainland Europe, his pessimism eventually overriding any unfounded optimism they might have felt. Muir sees the 'real theme' of *The Sleepwalkers* as 'the inevitable break-up of civilization in contemporary Europe . . . . We spent nearly a whole year of our lives translating this trilogy, and so were bound to be influenced by its pessimism' (*Belonging* 152). Broch's style and its relationship to Joyce and Eliot are touched on by Muir in one of the few direct discussions of modern literature in *Belonging*:

> Broch, who admired Joyce's experiments with form and language (especial-
> ly *Finnegan's Wake*) had experimented with the form of his own narrative
> in the third novel, breaking it up into disconnected pieces, set down side
> by side, much as Eliot in his poetry had set side by side disparate aspects of
> experience; perhaps Eliot, too, had fragmented his observations as an im-
> age of disintegration . . . . [W]e did not agree that the unconscious should
> be despised as Broch despised 'the irrational', and the notion that it could
> and would overwhelm European civilization in a cataclysm like the break-
> up of an ice-floe gone rotten was entirely repugnant to us, even unthink-
> able'. (*Belonging* 152)

Edwin Muir gives his response to *The Sleepwalkers* in 1959:

> [T]he first book is written in one style, the second in another, and the
> third in a whole medley of styles, the object being to reproduce by these
> verbal fluctuations a sense of the disintegration of values in Germany in
> the years leading up to and following the first World War . . . . [D]ifficulty
> itself became an essential quality of his prose; his attempt to show the
> almost inexpressible. (Edwin Muir, 'Translating from the German' 94)

The differing styles of the books with their attempts to express fragmentation and disintegration, clearly made the task of translating Broch challenging, however much they appreciated his work and his friendship. George Steiner writes later that the Muirs 'excelled even their own standards' in *The Sleepwalkers*. He extends the Muirs' views of the complexities of Broch's novels, reading 'the sum of his fiction and philosophy as an extended metaphor of translation: between present tense and death, between classic values and modern chaos, between verbal expression on the one hand and music and mathematics on the other' (Steiner, 1975 319). As a consequence of the Muirs' friendship, Broch was to translate poems by T. S. Eliot, James Joyce and Stephen Spender, as well as by Edwin Muir (see Huberman, 1989 52). Elizabeth Huberman looks at the Muir / Broch relationship and methods in some detail in her two essays drawing on Broch's letters to the Muirs between 1931 and 1940 and the few surviving letters from them to Broch. She thinks that the correspondence gives some illumination to the question of the Muirs' translating techniques, at least in the case of their work on Broch. The bulk of the correspondence was with Willa Muir and Huberman suggests that she 'may well have also borne the greater burden of the translating' (Huberman, 1990 48). But Huberman also cites evidence for joint translating when she quotes Muir's letter to Broch, 7 July 1931: 'If we seem to have translated the books [*The Romantic* and *The Anarchist*, the first two volumes of *The Sleepwalkers*] at shameless speed, it is only because we are both doing it, and doing it with zeal' (Huberman, 2000 52). The problem for the Muirs in 1931 was that Broch was still writing the third volume, *The Realist*, which was sent to them in parts. Broch also extensively rewrote at proof stage which in turn involved them in retranslating (see Huberman, 2000 53-54). His judgement on their translation comes in 1932 when he writes that it is 'magnificent', and that he finds the volumes 'still more perfectly arrayed in their new dress than Kafka's *The Castle*' (Huberman, 2000 55).

Franz Kafka lived for much of his life in Prague; he was born in 1883, making him a contemporary of James Joyce (born 1882); he died in Kierling, lower Austria, 3 June 1924, and was buried in Prague. Muir notes that when they were first in Prague in 1921, their circles were entirely Czech and they 'never got even a hint that Kafka or his friends had ever existed in the city' (*Belonging* 62). Perhaps this is unsurprising given the difficult relationship between the German and Czech speaking parts of Czechoslovak society at the time. Kafka was also part of the Jewish community (which was mainly German speaking) in Prague. Kafka himself had made the choice to write in German though his spoken German was apparently recognisable as Prague inflected (N. Murray 54). Despite this, and his fluency in Czech, Nicholas Murray in his biography of Kafka comments that 'it is clear that Kafka, notwithstanding his respect for Czech language and culture, elected to see himself as a German writer and his models were the classical German writers such as Goethe' (N. Murray 55). In *Belonging* Muir writes that 'by good luck we now struck a book which we thought worth translating', Kafka's *The Castle* (149). They were living in Crowborough; Edwin, having just completed *John Knox*, persuaded Secker to publish *The Castle* and they began to translate their first Kafka work. Edwin had found Rilke's *Die Aufzeichnungen des Malte Laurids Brigge* at the same time as *Das Schloss* and writes about his reaction to Sydney Schiff; attracted by what Murray calls Kafka's 'imaginative, fabulating mode' (N. Murray 45), he sees Kafka's book as 'still more strange [than Rilke's] in its atmosphere: it is a purely metaphysical and mystical dramatic novel: the ordinary moral judgments do not come in at all; everything happens in a mysterious spiritual plane which was obviously the supreme reality to the author; and yet in a curious way everything is given solidly and concretely. The book was left unfinished when Kafka died a few years ago' (8 July 1929; Schiff papers; Butter, 1974 67). Both Muirs are excited by *The Castle* although there is a 'difference in emphasis' between their appreciations:

> Edwin was more excited by the 'whence' and I by the 'how'. That is to say, Edwin tried to divine and follow up the metaphysics of Kafka's vision of the universe, while I stayed lost in admiration of the sureness with which he embodied in concrete situations the emotional predicaments he wanted to convey, situations that seemed to me to come clean out of the unconscious, perhaps directly from actual dreams. (*Belonging* 150)

In other words, they each took from Kafka what chimed with their own pre-existing preoccupations. Walter Benjamin, reacting with dislike to Max Brod's 1937 biography of Kafka, also expresses the duality (and binary opposition) of mysticism and reality in Kafka that the Muirs experience between them: 'Kafka's work is an ellipse with foci that are far apart and are determined, on the one hand, by mystical experience (in particular, the experience of tradition) and, on the other, by the experience of the modern big-city dweller' (Benjamin, 'Max Brod's Book on Kafka' 139). But as has already been seen above, they both 'loved the sinuous flexibility of Kafka's style — very unlike classical German — and dealt with it in the self-same way' (*Belonging* 150), Edwin Muir writing that Kafka's 'style never strikes one as being acquired by study and practice, but simply to be there, like the intonation of a voice. So our main problem was to write an English prose as natural in the English way as his was in his own way' (Edwin Muir, 'Translating from the German' 93). What they seem to miss, or do not comment on, is Kafka's 'mordant strain of social satire' that George Steiner sees as present throughout his work but 'most notably' in *The Trial* and *The Castle* (Steiner, 1992 xi).

There were several more Kafka translations to come (see Willa Muir Bibliography). Edwin writes to Stephen Spender while working on *The Trial* in 1936 that 'I admire him more and more: his fascination is simply endless: and a feeling of greatness comes to me in every sentence' (Butter, 1974 93). George Steiner's view in 1992 is that this translation (published in 1937 by Gollancz) 'took on a classic aura' which he sees as 'regrettable' because of the novel's unfinished nature and the 'argument about the order of various chapters' (Steiner, 1992 ix). Max Brod, Kafka's literary executor, famously refused to follow Kafka's instructions to destroy his literary manuscripts; he put together versions of Kafka's works, notably of *The Trial*, which then formed the published texts. In an epilogue to *The Trial* he defends his actions, saying that Kafka is responsible for the chapter divisions and their headings, but that for their arrangement 'I have had to depend on my own judgement . . . supported by actual recollection' of Kafka reading him 'a great part of the manuscript' (Brod 255). The Muirs' relationship with Kafka's works is entirely based on Brod's versions of Kafka's posthumously published works; however much Steiner regrets this, he acknowledges that it is the 'Muir version, with its stylistic distinction and freshness of encounter, which, so far as the English-language world goes, remains canonic' (Steiner, 1992 ix). A more recent view is that of Karl Leydecker, in his entry on nineteenth and twentieth century German fiction in the magisterial *Oxford Guide to Literature in English Translation*; he concludes that the Muirs' Kafka translations, 'for all their brilliance and continuing popularity', have 'two drawbacks': inaccuracy and the fact that Brod's 'idiosyncratic original German editions . . . have since been superseded' (Leydecker 332). He also notes that Edwin Muir's introductions to the translations were 'highly influential' in spreading 'Brod's essentially religious and allegorical interpretation of Kafka's works in the English-speaking world' (Leydecker 332). Because of Brod's approach and their own allegorical and psychological tendencies in interpretation (Edwin Muir reading 'out of a kierkegaardian Calvinism'), Kafka as 'social satirist, a craftsman of the grotesque, a humourist with an eye to farce and slapstick' is omitted from the Muirs' picture (Steiner, 1992 x, xiii).

The Muirs' translations were essential in the introduction of Kafka to the anglophone world but perhaps the limitations (as defined by Steiner and Leydecker) are connected to the commercial nature of all their translating work. However much they appreciate Kafka as a fascinating European writer and enjoy the translating, their work on both Kafka and Broch is not part of their 'own creative work' (Lochhead; 3 March 1933; see Appendix I). It is part of the commercial enterprise (their 'literary living' (*Belonging* 305)) that allows the Muirs to finance their lives and their writing. Effort and commitment go into all her translating work, but the writing into which Muir pours her spirit, imagination and intelligence is her personal writing, the novels, poetry, journals and letters.

Notes

1. The position of their respective names on the title pages varies although by far the majority of the early editions list Willa Muir first; see the list of translations in Willa Muir bibliography.

2. Although *The Unknown Quantity* is credited to both on the title page, Sherry Simon identifies it as translated by Willa Muir alone, following Muir's 'I was finishing translating . . . "The Unknown Quantity"' (*Belonging* 197); she thinks this may be one of the examples of a translation done mainly by Muir with Edwin being given equal credit (Simon, 2000 29).

The City of the Future

A Prophetic Portrait, by Arnold Ronnebeck, Based on Modern Tendencies in Architecture

The City of the Future, *Vogue*, September 1925.

# Fragments of a writing life

Muir's letters, journals and *Belonging* attest to the extent that she and Edwin Muir were part of a peripatetic and self-aware cultural group with strong cross-border and cross-continental links. Her life-writing, published and unpublished, provides an understanding of these links and their lives; it can also be used to give an underpinning of explanation to her other works. In this chapter (as elsewhere in this study) I use the private and public forms of her life-writing both to expand and explain her writing and her attitudes. But her works can still seem to have a fragmentary nature when compared to the apparent consistencies of Edwin Muir's work as a poet, critic and novelist. The contrast can be interpreted in a conventionally gendered way, Muir as a woman writing and thinking in circles, explored in her own broadcast talk, 'Moving in Circles' (1938), while Edwin thought and wrote 'logically', detachedly, his work contributing to a visibly connected 'whole'. Muir herself seems to subscribe to this interpretation when she writes of their novel writing in St Tropez in 1926:

> [I]n a way we were both treating the same theme; that is to say, having found the right kind of love we were now both writing about the wrong kind; but Edwin's handling of it [for *The Marionette*] was more detached than mine, for he had transmuted it into symbols while I [for *Imagined Corners*] was relying on the empathy of personal feelings and memories. (*Belonging* 126)

It is, even now, easier to interpret Muir as the 'amateur' female writer and Edwin as the 'professional' male writer, with her professional existence a satellite to his. During her life this was certainly how she was seen, though some of her friends recognised it as problematic. A. S. Neill writes to her in 1964: 'How are ye? How are the book plans? Time you cease to be known as Edwin's Frau' (4 Sept. 1964; St Andrews). Taking her most disparate works, this chapter explores Muir's two unpublished novels, the essay 'This Lop-sided World', her letters and journals, and her poetry, as fragments of a writing life that illuminate and attest to Muir's individual and longstanding accomplishment as a writer. These all seem more fragmentary than the Muirs' translations as they are inaccessible to most readers, surviving in their limited editions (in the case of *Laconics Jingles & other Verses*), manuscript or typescript forms in various libraries' collections. But these 'hidden' works show the extent of Muir's commitment to a writing life, a commitment disguised by the apparently small number of works that she published between 1925 and 1969, the start and end of her publishing life.

This and the next section consider Muir's two unpublished novels in relation to preoccupations that she explores in her published work; it also considers the question of their success. The typescripts of Muir's two unpublished novels, *Mrs Muttoe and the Top Storey* and *The Usurpers*, are in St Andrews University Library. The novels are first mentioned in Butter's 1990 essay (Butter, 1990 68). Robb writes, also in 1990, that Muir 'wrote three further novels . . . . They are reputedly inferior to the two which attained print' (Robb 155) and Smith follows him with 'there are, incredibly, three unpublished novels' (A. Smith 45), neither having read the novels. Robb's assumption that there was a third novel is possibly based on the listing in the catalogue of Muir's notebooks and miscellaneous papers of two typescripts for 'This Lop-Sided World' (99 pages and 82 pages long), Muir's extended essay on gender and ageism. Kirsty Allen and Margaret Elphinstone provide the first commentaries based on a reading of the typescripts (Allen, 1997, and Elphinstone, 1997). Muir's two published novels had explored the world of Muir's childhood in Montrose and North East Scotland. But the two later unpublished novels, both written in Scotland are grounded in her adult life, both set in the worlds outwith Scotland of Hampstead and Czechoslovakia. As well as both having strongly autobiographical roots, the first, *Mrs Muttoe and the Top Storey*, grapples with ideas of an intellectual / emotional binary in a private family sphere, with some exploration of gender, while the second, *The Usurpers*, is preoccupied with the concept of the 'Organisation' (that is, bureaucracy) in the public East European sphere, more centred on a male viewpoint, and concerned with politics rather than gender. They both combine social comedy and satire with a strong undercurrent of nightmare, reminiscent of Fritz Lang's 'Metropolis' at the end of *Mrs Muttoe and the Top Storey* and of a Kafkaesque world of Czechoslovakian bureaucracy in *The Usurpers*.

## Mrs Muttoe and the Top Storey

Muir wrote *Mrs Muttoe and the Top Storey* while living in St Andrews; she probably took the name of her couple from Muttoes Lane which runs between

Market and North Streets, only a couple of blocks from Queens Gardens where the Muirs lived. She was not keeping a journal when she wrote *Mrs Muttoe* so there is very little background information about its writing. On 17 May 1938, Edwin notes that 'Willa is writing a novel' (Schiff papers; Butter, 1974 100). It was completed by May 1940 as Muir wrote that date on the typescript's title page. This title page shows a good deal of indecision on Muir's part. The title, 'Mrs. Muttoe and the Top Storey', has handwritten additions written around it, 'London is Looney-Bin / A Tale of the Thirties' with other titles, all crossed out: 'Top Storeys and Looney-Bins', 'A Tale of London Family Life in the Thirties' and '(Between the Wars) (Life in Hampstead in the Thirties)'. Despite their address, 20 Queens Gardens / St Andrews / Fife / Scotland, being written on the title page for return of the typescript, there is no evidence that Muir ever sent it to a publisher. P. H. Butter, Edwin Muir's biographer, thinks the novel 'in parts quite amusing' but 'a slight affair', and does not know 'if Willa even tried to get it published' (Butter, 1990 68). For Allen, it is a 'thinly disguised documentation of her three happy Hampstead years' and a 'flawed work of fiction' (Allen, 1997 314).

The typescript of the novel is 284 pages. Ostensibly it is the story of some months in the life of a writing couple who live in Hampstead, very closely based on Willa and Edwin Muir's own lives there. The novel begins: 'Mr. and Mrs Muttoe, who lived in Hampstead, had been twelve years married and thought themselves quite grown up'. The first chapter is from the narrative point of view of a con-woman come to interview for the job of housekeeper, allowing an outsider to give the first, apparently objective, description of the Muttoes and their house: 'A shabby, kindly house . . . . The Muttoes must be like twins, doing everything together' (3). Mrs Muttoe talks of her need for an 'independent woman' (8) to run the house for them while they were '"busy all day at literary work . . . . The house . . . is our office"' (7-8). But the woman disappears from the novel, getting three florins for her bus fare and the point of view of the rest of the novel becomes mainly that of the 'literary couple' that she has apostrophised as 'Middle-aged kids' (9). While the con-woman has no particular place in the structure of the novel other than her introductory view of the house, and might be seen as part of the relative failure of the novel to use successfully variant points of view (as both of Muir's published novels achieve), her brief presence contains some vivid moments: 'She enjoyed sitting taut and alert, perfectly balanced, ready to cut a caper in any direction' (4). Here Muir has created a small precursor to Muriel Spark's later devilish con-man, Dougal Douglas, who cut capers in every direction throughout *The Ballad of Peckham Rye* (1960). Muir has her applicant give the name of the last woman she had been interviewed by: 'It was not mere thrift that made the visitor so economical with pseudonyms; she would have thought it blasphemous to reject good names already provided by Fate' (2). Her economy again links forward to Dougal who, we are told at the conclusion of *The Ballad*, was a frugal man who re-used the elements of his life in his novels: 'for economy's sake, he gathers together the scrap ends of his profligate experience — for he was a frugal man at heart — and turned them into a lot of cockeyed books' (Spark, 1960 [1988] 142). This small pre-echo of one of Spark's most Scottish novels (despite its London setting) can carry no more weight than a suggestion of the common Scottish backgrounds of Muir (b. 1890) and Spark (b. 1918), both alert to the mischief of creation, disguise and cutting capers.[1]

Muttoes Lane, St Andrews.

The rest of the novel is primarily from the point of view of Alison Muttoe with occasional interjections of Dick Muttoe's thoughts or the maid Alice's (chapter nine is from the point of view of all three, for example). It concerns the life in Hampstead of the writing couple. Alison is at the centre of the household, in a study 'at once more accessible to intrusion and more crowded', frantically translating for money, with Dick in 'a bare room on the top floor, containing little save an electric heater and a view of the sky' (15). Muir's later, more detailed, description of their studies in *Belonging* (162-63) makes clear how straightforwardly autobiographical *Mrs Muttoe* is. Chapter 14 of *Belonging*, 'Hampstead', is like a summary of some of the main plots of *Mrs Muttoe* given in sixteen pages. In *Belonging*, Muir describes one of their Serbian friends, Dimitri Mitrinović, contributor (like Edwin) to the *New Age*, as a self-elected seer and 'an egregious nonsense-monger' who would cry 'London is Looney-bin, no?' (clearly the source of one of Muir's tentative titles for *Mrs Muttoe*) (*Belonging* 41). By the time of the Hampstead chapter in *Belonging*, Mitrinović is established 'as the centre of a cult' and when the Muirs called on 'The Master', they find his voice 'portentous with self-importance. We non-joined his bogus cult' (*Belonging* 168). In *Mrs Muttoe*, the Muttoes visit Stefan Popovitch who 'used to be a welcome visitor of ours, before we went wandering round Europe' (77) but has now become the 'Master', a 'generalised symbol' (84, 85). Alison Muttoe sees people's responses to Popovitch satirically: 'All these people's minds . . . run in circles round the central fact of Popovitch. He is the rabbit under the cosmic hat' (82). The fictional character and his transformation into the 'Master' are hardly changed from the original, with an identical dislike expressed of the sham cult.

Elphinstone is critical of the closeness of Muir's unpublished novels to her life: 'Sadly, for Muir the relationship between fiction and autobiography seems to become a negative one after 1933' (Elphinstone 410). It is true that *Belonging* has a discipline that *Mrs Muttoe* lacks (see next chapter for a discussion on *Belonging* in more detail). *Mrs Muttoe* may fail as a novel because its narrative line consists of the fairly uneventful life of Alison and Dick over a few months, interspersed with Alison's resentful ruminations on modernity, London, gender, 'meditating on the queerness of being a woman' (97). It contains repetitions of and expansions on some of Muir's previously effective metaphors, notably the function of the house (see the chapters on *Imagined Corners* and *Mrs Ritchie*, for Muir's extensive use of the house as metaphor). In *Mrs Muttoe*, the house becomes entangled with Alison's extended meditation on her idea of the top-storey autocrat (the life of the mind) and the Centre (the body) in the rest of the house:

> The house, sheltering its sleeping inhabitants like a many-chambered womb, was acting as her deputy; she was free of family responsibilities and isolated in a chilly bed, the vague circumference of her personality shrinking to a focussed point of waking life, somewhere behind her eyes. I'm my own top storey, said Alison to herself. (98)

At this same narrative point, Alison feels entangled by her responsibilities: 'she had a sense of being harrassed, as if a ball of wool which she usually held easily in one hand had suddenly unrolled itself and entangled her' (105). A few pages later it becomes untangled: 'One smooth, continuous movement encircling the house, creating order, sealing everything up in safety. One circular movement instead of a multiplicity of disconnected detail' (108). Muir presents Alison as responsible for organisation because of her own expectations, in the same way that Muir herself always assumes responsibility in the Muirs' lives. This is the Muir of whom Patricia Mudge wrote irritably:

> While she detested the male dominance she saw all around her, championing the feminist cause wasn't her primary concern. Even if it had been, Willa's opinions were too inconsistent to be taken seriously. In another unpublished work, *Mrs. Muttoe and the Top Storey*, the main protagonist is a translator of books whose work is equal to her husband's . . . yet after pages of didactics on the relationship between mind and feeling, 'the top storey' versus 'the centre', the manuscript ends with the not-so-strong female clasping her husband's hand for support. (Mudge 3)

Despite Mudge's view, Muir does have a consistency in her opinions in all her writing, hence the re-use of metaphors and ideas. The re-circling of her preoccupations, first expressed in the nineteen-twenties and thirties, continues in her unpublished works of the nineteen-forties and fifties into the late works published in the nineteen-sixties. After all, around the time Muir was probably writing *Mrs Muttoe*, she publishes her article 'Moving in Circles' in *The Listener*: '[I]t began to dawn on me that a circular habit of mind might be a strength rather than a weakness' (*The Listener*, 22 September 1938 602). That article ends with Muir's essentialist call: 'For my part, if any man tells me nowadays that I do not think straight, I say: "And why should I? It's my business to think in circles, the wider the better. I'm a woman"' (*The Listener* 603) while in *Mrs Muttoe*, Alison replies to Dick with 'mock dignity': 'I get to it . . . because my mind moves in circles and not in straight lines like yours' (228). It would be more unexpected if further explorations or referencing of Muir's concerns did not occur in *Mrs Muttoe*, even if the novel as a whole is perhaps too much of a regurgitation of pre-occupations, combined with a not-very-interesting story of a few months. Failing imaginatively and smoothly to combine them, Muir intersperses realistic description of *Mrs Muttoe*'s life and feelings with meditations on the Top-storey and the Centre (themselves somewhat inconsistently developed) alongside hints of Muir's various theories.

While I agree with views that see the novel's lack of coherent narrative development as less than satisfactory, there are aspects of it that show an interesting relationship to modernist preoccupations not so readily apparent in Muir's other works. Taking Alison Muttoe's negative phrase about her house, that 'multiplicity of disconnected detail' (108) that she found so entangling and oppressive, and reading it positively, an argument can be made that Muir was trying to introduce something new into her domestic narrative, replacing the intense social and psychological analyses of *Imagined Corners* and *Mrs Ritchie* with everyday realism interwoven with social satire and indications of nightmare worlds. The 'multiplicity of disconnected detail' gives a suitably discordant representation of modern life, noisy, dehumanised, and uncontrollable, a kind of world that Muir dislikes but represents as modern. The novel is mainly set in London. Even when it moves to the country we are given the perspective of Alice the townie maid who finds it threatening and strange: 'It was a world of stalks, stems, trunks, of pushing branches, coiling tendrils, lurking thorns; a world of secretly running sap; a sinister, frightening world' (119-20). But, for Alison Muttoe, it is the 'multifariousness' of London that induces in her 'a nightmare feeling of distraction' (231). We see her walking down the pavements:

> [B]efore her roared the traffic of the Power Age. Motor vehicles shuttled up and down the asphalt roadway like smoothing-irons . . . . [Y]et she felt that the Power Age interfered unreasonably with her freedom of action, especially when she had to skirt her way past two chromium-plated monsters which stood in the open window of a new motor showroom thrusting their insolent blank eyes almost on to the pavement'. (33-34)

This 'Power Age with its chromium-plate, its concrete, its multiple stores' (34), all symbols of modernity, is held at bay in Hampstead by the little shops and 'crooked old buildings of irregular size' (34), but it lurks throughout *Mrs Muttoe*. Alison's mood darkens as the novel draws to a conclusion. Chapter 18 begins briskly: 'In and around other parts of Europe, meanwhile, human life was being machine-gunned, bombed, shelled and torpedoed out of existence. The queerness of the world more than matched the queerness of Mrs. Muttoe's mood' (241). She meditates on the shape of London as an 'orderly spider's web', 'designed to facilitate the making of money' (245); she concludes that '[s]tudying the Money fabric has given me scunner at London' (251).

Ever caught in her own autobiographical line, what Muir does in order to link the modern, capitalist London of Alison's 'scunner' to the concluding nightmare of the novel is to have Alison relate her recent 'nightmarish' feelings about her work translating 'Garta' (clearly Kafka):

> It was true that Garta's work seemed to come straight out of the region which evoked dreams and nightmares. He showed an uncanny skill in describing the twists and turns of frustrated feelings; merely to read him was like having an anxiety dream by proxy. And every incident in his stories, almost every phrase, carried so many implications that the translation

had to be done slowly, with extreme care. Yes, Garta is making me fearful, decided Alison Muttoe, opening her jotter. (252-53)

This provides an interesting footnote to Muir's own feelings about working on Kafka whose *Great Wall of China* they were 'to get out' at this time (*Belonging* 162). The idea of Kafkaesque worlds (as well as Fritz Lang's world of *Metropolis*) can also underpin the concluding nightmare of the novel when Alison moves around a many-layered city world, looking in on a capitalist structure, industrialised and mechanised, and out at an unattainable rural paradise:

> The arena of this pit was covered with a mass of moving humans, divided into sections by straight lines radiating like spokes of a wheel from some far-off central point. The curved side of the pit rose smooth and glassy above the moving masses, unscalable except for extremely short ladders that hung down here and there. (268)

This carries echoes of Jeremy Bentham's panopticon, the prison design which Foucault took as central to the prison-like control mechanisms of capitalist society from which there is no escape. In Alison Muttoe's nightmare, the lifts shafts of this world were only for the goods, 'Goods ascending' and 'Profits descending' (269). She moves around this worker-beehive factory, 'the farther down she slid, the closer she would get to the source of supply' (273) until she found herself in

> [A] blank, dreary passage-way, running between two high, glassy walls . . . . It was . . . an apparently infinite extension of monotony. But, for compensation, the transparent walls enclosing it allowed one to watch scenes of the most varied interest; on one side lay the vast pit in the basement of the Money fabric, on the other side a perspective of fields and woods, with distant mountains visible on the horizon. (278)

This concluding nightmare of an enclosed capitalist world harks back to the Utopian cities of the early twentieth century art of which there are many examples, such as Antonio Sant' Elia's 1914 'New City Apartment Building' (Wilk 66) or 'New City Aeroplane and Railway Station' (Wilk frontispiece), Mies Van der Rohe's 1921 Skyscraper Project, Berlin (Wilk 22), or Arnold Ronnebeck's 'On the City of the Future: A Prophetic Portrait' (*Vogue* (late Sept. 1925) 55; see 138); these utopian representations became the nightmarish mechanised and mechanistic city of Fritz Lang's 1927 film *Metropolis*. Muir's description of the visible city as an ant heap with transparent but impassable walls to an inaccessible country interprets the modern as dystopian not utopian, the only way out to wake from the nightmare (for the full text, see Appendix III). It is from this nightmare that Alison awakes and clings to

Dick's hand, the ending that so annoys Patricia Mudge: 'the not-so-strong female clasping her husband's hand for support' (Mudge 3). Perhaps this is the ending of a novel lacking a strong narrative arc that the novelist does not otherwise know how to end. But it can be seen as showing a turning away of the protagonist / narrator from the modern world to the simpler, older world, represented by Dick who, like Edwin Muir, yearned for the Middle Ages when the medieval Church provided 'a common mode of thinking and feeling that held society together' (161). It can also be read as a critical rejection by Muir of the modernist world with all its 'multifariousness' (231) and 'multiplicity of disconnected detail' (108).

## The Usurpers

On 30 January 1951, Muir wrote in her journal that she has 'had an inert period, where writing is concerned. But I have begun my book again, wi' deeficulty. The frost, cold, bleak, unsympathetic, made this room so cold I could not use my hands' (journal; 1951-53). This book is *The Usurpers*. It is based closely on the Muirs' stay in Czechoslavakia, 1945 to early 1948, when Edwin was director of the British Council Institute in Prague. The difficulty she feels at restarting work on the novel in 1951 during 'cold, bleak, unsympathetic' weather seems symptomatic of Muir's difficulties with the novel. In one of the typescripts (presumably the first) in St Andrews University Library the main protagonists are called Jamesina and Martin Russell. In the second typescript, Muir has altered Jamesina to Georgina by hand; both names reach for the masculine, perhaps underlining some uneasiness in this character's position, given a secondary role with most of the narrative point of view centred on the husband Martin out in the public world. Both typescripts are 377 pages long. I am using the typescript with Muir's first choice of name, Jamesina, as my text.

*The Usurpers* takes place in the mainly public field of the expatriate community in Slavomania. As in all of her novels, the narrative point of view shifts. The first chapter is from the point of view of Alexander Bower, the 'Chief of the Utopian Cultural Mission to Slavomania, while Martin Russell was merely the head of a lecturing and teaching branch' (7). The college, headed by Martin Russell, 'had dissociated itself, probably in self-defence, from the Mission and had come to be regarded as a separate body' (28). But, in his own mind at least, Bower thinks, in another echo of Jeremy Bentham's panopticon, that he should be the central controlling power:

As he trotted along the path he saw in his mind a diagram of the new
Cultural Centre he wished to organize. It was an impeccably regular
diagram radiating from a single central point — the Head of the Mission
— , with an inner ring of specialist officers fanning out to a wider ring of
secretaries and typists. It seemed to him beautiful. It was simple, logical,
and, above all, economical. (28)

This is expressed succinctly in *Belonging* as the 'new scheme of Council activities
radiated, of course, from the Representative at the centre of it' (*Belonging* 229).
This 'Representative' of the British Council in Prague was Reginald A. Close about
whom Muir wrote a satirical poem beginning 'Unhappy Reg' on official memo
paper sometime in 1948, heading it 'Subject The MisRepresentative' (see Appendix
IV). The novel is partly an exposure of petty bureaucratic manoeuvring for power
within an organisation itself surrounded by political change over which it has no
control. Muir describes this in *Belonging*:

And at the same time as these internal tensions were making life uncomfortable in the Council, a pattern of increasing tensions was being repeated
outside, as political intrigue and counter-intrigue mounted in the country,
in Prague above all, on the approach of a General Election. (*Belonging* 231)

Elphinstone sees the 'office reflect[ing] Europe in microcosm, and its individuals embody[ing] the politics of power, the struggle between communism and
capitalism and the threat of both to individualism. The tone is pessimistic, the
vision one of social disintegration' (Elphinstone 412). *Mrs Muttoe* ends with the
nightmare dream of capitalist society centrally controlled and bereft of individuality, both Fritz Lang and Franz Kafka. But in post-war Prague, Kafka's home city,
Muir had been translating his *Metamorphosis* during the events leading up to the
communist putsch in Czechoslovakia and the putsch itself. It is the bureaucratic
and political nightmare with no logic or rationality that is shown in her contemporary journal, in *The Usurpers* (written in the early nineteen fifties) and in the
Prague chapter of *Belonging* (written in the mid-nineteen sixties). Muir was clear
about the connection between the first and last when she wrote: 'I have selected
these samples of behaviour from a diary I kept during and after the Putsch, the
only diary I have ever kept, and I hope I have conveyed the nature and intensity of
the strains and stresses to which we were subjected' (*Belonging* 239). In *Belonging*,
Muir also cites a playwright in their Writers' Circle (that met every week in their
flat) who points out:

[W]hat a vast, anonymous fog of fear is generated by modern city life,
among industrial workers, clerks and other small people. Their lives are
governed by faceless forces, great factories, blocks of tenements; somewhere

unknown to them sit unknown men causing unemployment or employ-
ment, wage cuts, rent increases, shortages, directing everyone's life, so that
they are filled with vague anxiety, an insecurity which drives them to join
for protection any visible body that looks like Power. (*Belonging* 232)

She writes this speech into *The Usurpers*, giving it to Havran, one of the Literary
Group: 'Think how much unconscious fear lurks in the average man, an industrial
worker, say, or a clerk, who feels that he is surrounded and governed by unknown
forces'. The passage continues in similar vein until it concludes: 'And the more
they are afraid, the bigger and more blatant is the party they join. Hitler or the
Communists, either will do' (129). Jamesina thinks in reaction: 'That is the real
Nightmare . . . the darkness inside oneself, the fear and the hatred' (129). It is as
though the nightmare is so all encompassing that Muir cannot make sense of the
condition of Czechoslovakia even in relation to the small and the personal; when
the Muirs returned to Britain, Edwin has a breakdown and Muir's back is disabled
by 'alleged arthritis' (*Belonging* 239), as though they were expressing mentally and
physically the repressions and loss they had left behind them. She writes later that
the 'unrest, the flurries from pessimism to optimism, which ravaged the country,
ravaged Edwin and me as well' (*Belonging* 234). The flurries and confusion that
surround the communist takeover, Jan Masaryk's death on 10 March 1948 (whether
suicide or murder),[2] and the escape of various friends to the West, are present in
all three written records of Muir's post-war stay in Czechoslovakia, and may in
turn contribute to her lack of narrative control or her failure fully to fictionalise
the material into a novel.

Narrative sympathy in *The Usurpers* is clearly with the Russells even when the
narrative gives Bower's and other points of view. Bower's belief in a logical and
economical circular structure with power centred firmly on the Head is inimical
to the Russells. Muir indicates from the start that the inherent authoritarianism of
Bower is to be disapproved of as she shows the triumph of a wider authoritarianism in the communist takeover in 'Slavomania'. Martin Russell, listening to Bower
talk at a staff conference, thinks that his face 'was a talking mask, that there was no
human being behind it' (42), further establishing Bower as somebody suspect. The
narrative is of a couple adjusting to life in post-war Slavomania where an unstable
regime is inexorably overtaken by the enforced stability of the new Communist
regime. They are doubly sidelined, as foreigners in the country observing the painful political changes, and outsiders within their expatriate world, Martin as head of
the College, semi-autonomous from the Utopian Cultural Mission to Slovomania,
and Jamesina as the wife of Martin, with no formal role: 'Like many Mission wives
she had no clear view of the Organisation behind the individual functionaries.
She saw it only refracted, as by a lens, through her husband's temperament' (121).

Jamesina is the least pro-active of Muir's female protagonists, shown as reacting emotionally, apparently an example of the uneasily essentialist woman described in *Women: An Inquiry*. Elphinstone is particularly critical of Jamesina's lack of success as an imagined character: 'the narrator seems to be too closely created in her image to be able to transcend the limitations of this construct, or to fully enter the public sphere, even in the disguise of a pseudonymous man' (Elphinstone 412). But Jamesina's lack of clarity is something that Muir acknowledges in the novel, even if it is based on her own feelings when she was the accompanying 'wife of' rather than a fully functioning individual in the British Council in postwar Czechoslovakia: 'When Jamesina Russell was on the defensive, her nebulous personality condensed and changed its shape, shrinking until it focussed upon the immediate situation. At these moments one felt the force and weight in her persuasions' (229). While this description ends with an apparently powerful Jamesina, it is the wavering nature of her 'nebulous personality', condensing, changing its shape and shrinking, that seems prevalent in the novel, wife as a backdrop and a support (even if at times resentful) to the main protagonist, Martin.

Willa and Edwin Muir and students, Prague, 15 May 1947.

The first part of Muir's chapter 'Prague' in *Belonging* gives the background to the Muirs' life there, 1945 to May 1947, when Edwin was awarded an honorary degree by the Charles University of Prague, 'the high-water mark of Edwin's influence in Prague. From that time his troubles and the political troubles of Czechoslovakia together gathered momentum and moved towards catastrophe' (*Belonging* 227). This conflation of Edwin's troubles with Czechoslovakia's perhaps shows one of the roots of the unsatisfactory nature of the fictionalising of their experiences into *The Usurpers*. The story of the latter essentially appears in section ii of 'Prague', headed 1947-48. A new 'Representative' has been sent out to be 'a new broom', 'a bureaucrat to the finger-tips' (*Belonging* 227). This person, named as Reg in the journal, becomes Bower, despised head of the Mission, in *The Usurpers*. Much of section ii is concerned with describing the head's reorganisation of the Council's structure as a way to curb Edwin's popularity as head of the Institute, including the 'Great Tea-Room Row' (*Belonging* 231) where the head tries to ban locally appointed staff from using the tea room. In *Belonging*, Muir shows the ensuing 'tea-room boycott' as coming 'as a kind of comic relief' (*Belonging* 231) while also being representative of 'the change in the atmosphere of the Council Palace' where they are 'now divided from each other by the gradings of protocol, and also from the Czechs' (*Belonging* 231). Her fictional use of this and other crises in *The Usurpers*, leads Elphinstone to accuse the novel of having 'a curious lack of focus on the political struggle, and the voice of the narrator seems more impassioned on the subject of discrimination over the office tearoom, and which of the British workers should have access to scarce family accommodation, than about arrests without trial, interrogation, or imprisonment under an increasingly totalitarian regime' (Elphinstone 412). Muir undoubtedly explores the interconnections between the Russells' / Muirs' mental and physical states and the deteriorating world of Slavomania / Czechoslovakia. But she is also trying to make sense of the nightmare descent into post-war Communist control, contrasting her views and feelings for Czechs and their country with her pre-war experiences there. Allen believes *The Usurpers* fails to 'reproduce the terror, the inexorable tension, and the genuinely expressive immediacy which the journals evoke' (Allen, 1997 457). I agree that the unfolding political drama of the journals has a tension and powerful immediacy that *The Usurpers* does not duplicate. Muir's difficulty in turning the emotionally powerful events described in her journal (which also records meetings with visiting British writers) and in *Belonging* into a fully realised novel may come from the lack of a strong narrative force in the novel. But it must also come from a lack of distance from the events that she witnessed. Muir writes in *Living with Ballads* (1965) (in relation to the childhood songs that she and her friends sang) about 'a mode of setting a distance between us and them, which seems to be a necessary process in the making of any work of art' (*Living with Ballads* 29). It is this lack of 'setting a distance' in *The Usurpers* that prevents it being made into a 'work of art' as a novel, Muir remaining upset and involved in remembered events when she begins writing the novel in Newbattle barely three years later. By the time she comes to write *Belonging* in the nineteen sixties, she has the distance of time as well as the discipline of writing the events for a chapter rather than a full length novel.

Muir worked on the novel exclusively for a year, noting the 'vast gap of more than a year' in writing in her journal because of this. When she returns to the journal it is to record an outburst of resentment and pain that Edwin has not bothered to read it, a precursor of her long '*Why I am to be described as a mess*' passage (20 Aug. 1953; journal; Jan. 1951-Sept. 1953; see 'Life and Context' and 'Translating for a Living'):

> It is finished, but not revised. (*The Usurpers*) // I think, whiles, it's very good; surprised that I could have thought it out at all; then, whiles, that it's disjointed, ill put together, lacking proportion and style. // I had a fit of black despair and resentment when I had finished it, just because Edwin left it for days before reading it. I know he was tired and busy, but I had wanted him to show enthusiasm & interest; he *never said a word about it*, not even regretting that he couldn't read it, because his eyes hurt, or he had other work, or what-not . . . . It was his apparent utter indifference that got me down; I could see how little value he attached to the *expectations* he felt it would have. Perhaps he is right, thought I; this book I have been dreaming myself into, with such enthusiasm and delight, is really a very second-rate production: it won't matter to anyone'. (22 Feb. 1952; journal; Jan. 1951-Sept. 1953)

This passage typically combines Muir's own mixed analysis of the novel's success and her furious emotional response to Edwin's indifference. A page following the title page of the typescript notes that 'This story is a pattern seen in a sea of probability', apparently acknowledging its autobiographical roots. Muir follows this with the more customary disclaimer: 'The characters, the action, the country in which the story is set, are all to be regarded as imaginary'. Her use of the qualification 'all to be regarded as' rather than 'imaginary' alone somewhat undermines the effectiveness of the disclaimer. Muir's pseudonym for the novel was to have been Alexander Croy, perhaps thought more appropriate given the centrality of the male protagonist Martin and the 'public and political rather than domestic and parochial' nature of the novel (Elphinstone 412). The completed novel was offered to several publishers, all of whom turned it down. Muir, saving herself from assuming it was rejected because of its failings with the comment 'perhaps afraid of libel', withdrew the manuscript when she was identified as the writer (14 Oct. 1952; journal; Jan. 1951-Sept. 1953).

Assessments made by those critics who have read either of the novel's typescripts tend to confirm Muir's fear that it was 'a very second-rate production' (22 Feb. 1952; journal; Jan. 1951-Sept. 1953). Allen also sees it as 'almost libellously factual' (Allen, 1996 xi) and 'stylistically laboured, heavily overwritten, and beset by basic literary naivetés and immaturities' (Allen, 1997 457). Critics also tend to dismiss *Mrs Muttoe* as equally 'second-rate'. As has been mentioned already, Elphinstone thinks the relationship for Muir between fiction and autobiography becomes 'negative after 1933'; but she thinks it 'simplistic and misleading' to define the two unpublished novels 'as either fictional or autobiographical on the basis of subject matter alone. The point is that as novels they lack subtlety in narrative point of view, resulting in an apparent lack of perspective in the world presented, in comparison with the two published works of fiction' (Elphinstone 410). Her complaint, that the two unpublished novels are equally unsuccessful in accomplishment, is valid enough. Butter thinks *The Usurpers* 'more substantial' than *Mrs Muttoe*, but also feels that both novels lack the 'intensity and objectivity attained' in the two novels that went 'back to her childhood' (Butter, 1990 68). But equating the two in this way as equally 'unsuccessful' (as tends to happen simply because they are Muir's two novels that remain unpublished), disguises their difference unhelpfully. They may both be closely based on Muir's life for their subject matter, but the two periods, pre-war Hampstead and post-war Czechoslovakia, are so different that the novels are more dissimilar in narrative concerns than *Imagined Corners* and *Mrs Ritchie*. *Mrs Muttoe* may deal with the personal world of a Hampstead marriage, closely based on the Muirs' life of that period and place, but it also ventures into a nightmare world of modern urban life and capitalism, linking it to Naomi Mitchison and Wyndham Lewis's collaborative modernist fantasy, *Beyond this Limit* (1935), as well as to Lang's *Metropolis*. It may suffer from some narrative inconsistencies and unevenness of tone, but it remains recognisably within the novel genre with narrative development and interest independent of the Muirs' Hampstead life and is the more successful of the two. *The Usurpers*, on the other hand, is so dependant on dialogue (and so close to Muir's contemporary journal reports of events in Prague) that its success as a novel is undermined. This pre-eminence of dialogue is marked enough that it is as though Muir is harking back to her much earlier intention to write drama without her realising that this is the genre to which *The Usurpers* could have belonged. It could profitably be used as the basis for a screenplay for a political film or television series about the warring cultural British community in the imploding post-war Czechoslovakia. With underlying narrative drawn from Muir's *Belonging* and the dialogue from *The Usurpers*, a powerful narrative could be made of the destructiveness of the effect of the divisions imposed on Eastern Europe in the early years of the Cold War. But both novels are worth examination because of the way that they intersect with Muir's life and life-writing and, despite the qualifications that can be made, they succeed in carrying interest and some success as fiction.

## 'This Lop-sided World'

The Muir who consistently noticed and wrote about gender relations matches her early theoretical *Women: An Inquiry* (1925) with a late unpublished work on ageism and gender, 'This Lop-sided World' (ca. 1960 / 1961). Its title page has *This Lop-sided World* by Anicula; Muir may have sent the second typescript of 82 pages (a neater typing of the 99 page typescript) to the literary agents David Higham Associates as the typescript is filed in one of their folders. Like the later feminists Germaine Greer who moved from *The Female Eunuch* (1970) to *The Change: Women, Ageing and the Menopause* (1991) and Naomi Wolf, from *The Beauty Myth* (1990) to *Misconceptions: truth, lies and the unexpected on the journey to motherhood* (2001), Muir's attitudes expand to include her latest personal experience.

She begins: 'I was born a she and have stayed one for seventy years, so that I am now an old woman. But "old woman", I find is in use as a term of contempt' ('Lop-sided World' 1). She proceeds to analyse the position of women from the point of view of 'the old patriarchal myth which regards man as the centre of creation and woman as a secondary adjunct, an after-thought, a kind of lean-to tacked on to the main edifice. You will say that it is as out-of-date as the similar myth that our planet, Earth, is the centre of the Universe' (4). She refers to the experiences of women such as Florence Nightingale and Sophia Jex-Blake in the nineteenth century (17 18). She is critical of Freud and Jung:

> [T]hey are themselves subject to patriarchal distortion and are governed by prejudices already in the air. Freud, for instance, put out an absurd theory that a woman has a natural sense of inferiority when she looks down at herself and sees that she lacks a male organ. He did not argue that a man similarly should feel inferior when he notices that he has no breasts to speak of. One should, therefore, keep a sceptical eye on psychologists'. (43-44)

She writes against the 'concept of the Terrible Mother' as bedevilling too many women (45); it is sadly ironic that William Knox has most recently cast her into this role in relation to her son Gavin, his problems, in Knox's view, partly caused by 'the way that Willa never favoured him over Edwin' (Knox 196). She concludes the essay with her wish for 'a harmonious partnership between men and women such as already exists sporadically, a general climate of opinion in which all notions of dominance by either sex have been eliminated' (82).

In a decade which saw the beginning of a new fight for women's equality, the work is not startlingly radical but it is an intelligent consideration of women's place in nineteenth and twentieth century society and the continuing need for change in gender relations. What is also impressive is that this is a woman of seventy writing a political pamphlet analysing the damaging imbalances that persisted. Muir's ideas on gender and society began when she was a child observing the treatment of girls and boys: 'Male dominance had been my mother's creed and as a child I met it like a toad meeting the teeth of a harrow' (*Belonging* 140); they continued through university and her membership of the Women's Suffrage Society. Presented in shorter form in her first published work *Women: An Inquiry*, her exploration continues in this late unpublished work. Like *Mrs Grundy in Scotland* before it, it is an extended consideration of gender relations in a patriarchal society, refracted through observations on ageism. What is new is Muir's analysis of the denigratory nature of society's approach to 'old women', coming from her personal observations as she increasingly lived with the difficulties of old age. The practice of old age with its indignities and its sadness comes ten years later in Muir's late letters to Kathleen Raine but the theorising of patriarchy's attitude to old women and her irritation with the resilience of that patriarchy is the concern of the forceful analysis of 'This Lop-sided World'.

## Muir's journals and letters

Life-writing is the term now generally used for personal writing in letters or journals by women such as Jane Welsh Carlyle who did not define themselves as 'writers', who were never published in their lifetime, but who nonetheless wrote constantly in letters, journals or other forms of personal records or correspondence. Willa Muir is clearly in a different category; she is a woman who worked as a writer intending publication for most of her life. She writes to Lochhead in 1933: 'How do we live? Translating from the German, reading German books for publishers, doing anything that turns up. How do we want to live? On the proceeds of our own creative work. Apparently quite impossible' (3 March 1933; see Appendix I). But, alongside the work she writes for publication, whether commissioned like the translations or creative like her novels, are her letters, journals and notebooks. There are few similarities between Willa Muir and Jane Welsh Carlyle, Muir's un-peripatetic nineteenth century Scottish predecessor who lived nearly all her married life in Chelsea with Thomas Carlyle, except perhaps that they have been in the past more noted for their marriages to Scottish writers than for their own literary productions. Both have received more attention as writers in recent years, mainly due to a reconstituting of the literary canon into a broader field. But a similarity is that their unpublished, personal writings have survived. The Carlyle archives, mostly in the National Library of Scotland, may have survived because of interest in Thomas Carlyle and his works, but Jane Welsh Carlyle's letters and papers were collected together by Thomas after her death because he saw them as a great commemoration of her worth (and his recognition of it). Willa Muir survived Edwin and her expression of her love for Edwin, inextricably connecting herself into his Story, was to be published in her poems and *Belonging*. Perhaps unusually in one so peripatetic, she clearly believed in keeping drafts of her works, typescripts, letters and manuscripts.[3]

Other people's archives contain her letters; for example, Ernest and Janette Marwick's in the Orkney Library, Marion Lochhead's and F. Marian McNeill's in the National Library of Scotland. Violet and Sydney Schiff's archive in the British Library contains the Muirs' letters to the Schiffs as well as carbons of many of both Schiffs' letters to the Muirs. The National Library of Scotland contains notes and drafts for *Living with Ballads*, drafts and a typescript of *Belonging*, along with many letters to Scottish friends and her later letters to Kathleen Raine. St Andrews University Library has possibly the largest archive of her works, typescripts of published and unpublished works, of radio talks, short stories, as well as notebooks containing her post-world war two journals, and many letters to her, presumably deposited there at the same time as her books when she found herself adrift in St Andrews in October 1969 (for details, see Willa Muir Bibliography). I have used these journals and letters throughout the chapters of this study of Muir's work as commentary and information on her life, work and attitudes. In this section of 'Fragments' I consider them not as a hidden constant behind her published works, but as life-writing showing style and thought that repays critical attention.

Muir's journals were all written in small notebooks, mostly around 20 by 16 centimetres in size. The earliest, the 'Marmaduke' journal, about the first six weeks of Gavin's development in 1927 (with a few later additions), is written mainly in pencil. (For discussions of this journal and later references to Gavin's difficulties in other journals, see 'Life and context'.) The later journals begin after world war two when the Muirs were in Prague, and continue intermittently until their stay in New England in 1955. They are written mainly in ink but with some pencil entries and a few later insertions and corrections in ink. Muir's writing, in journals, notebooks and letters, is bold and clear,[4] seeming to express a certainty and confidence that her words do not always bear out, the same dissonance, perhaps, that existed between Muir's outward presentation of confidence and her inner insecurities. They contain a listing of events in their lives but also discussions and opinions, interspersed with Muir's feelings. In 1947 she meditates directly on her appearance in an apparently objective manner:

[Q]ueer that it should be important to wash ones hair and powder face & dress neatly, that one's appearance should be a reality. For it is. If I neglect my appearance I look ugly, and Edwin sees that I am ugly, and insensibly is affected by the fact. Even queerer that, left to myself, I am ugly; queer because I don't *feel* ugly. I feel that I am an attractive interesting well meaning me, and so I don't feel ugly. Yet I look ugly without some care. I think probably I always did. (13 June 1947; journal; 1946-47)

Yet, even though the meditation is inextricably linked with feelings of insecurity about her connection to Edwin, it also contains hints of recognition that appearance is influenced by more than surface: 'I feel that I am an attractive interesting well meaning me'. In other passages, there is apparent spontaneity of expression, illustrating the changeability of her moods and her insecurity in her relation to Edwin:

[A]fter supper I took a shivering & trembling fit, & couldn't stop. Lay in bed, teeth chattering, & cried, & felt miserable. Edwin sat in drawing room & came in after ten to tell me wireless news; but long before that I had convinced myself that he wasn't really fond of me at all (leaving me as I wdn't leave a dog!) but only habituated to me . . . that his nervous tension was partly caused by his inability to love anyone but himself! So I had decided to treat him accordingly, on the assumption that I had spoiled him by giving him fondness & expecting too little in return. All this vanished, of course, as we both recovered a bit the next day. (30 April 1948; journal; Jan.–May 1948)

There is also a more critical take on Edwin, witness the two passages reacting to his failure to read *The Usurpers* (22 Feb. 1952 and 23 Aug. 1953; see above and 'Translating for a living'). Sometimes there is specific criticism, showing her capacity to turn a critical eye on Edwin as well as herself. Recording a politic reaction by Edwin, agreeing that a boycott by some British academics was a pity 'with a masterly mild regret on his face', Muir comments along with some characteristic self analysis: '(Edwin is really often a little bugger. I must not stifle too much my hunches of disagreement with him: which I am afraid I have done)' (16 April 1948; journal; Jan.-May 1948). In *Belonging* the event is narrated but criticism of Edwin omitted (*Belonging* 237). Passages with open criticism of Edwin do not appear in *Belonging* (nor in her letters) and this one in her journal is a precursor to her impassioned belief in Harvard that she had damaged herself by her earlier belief: 'I must kill my "vanity", my ambition to write. My intelligent Unconscious now told me that in killing, or trying to kill, my vanity I had nearly succeeded in killing myself . . . . I decided that the U. was quite right, and that I must let my "vanity" flourish. All the Willas, the passionate little girl, the ambitious & vital student, the positive, hopeful & happy new wife, came back together & fused, as it were, in this glow of possible achievement' (1 Oct. 1955; journal; Sept.-Nov. 1955; see also 'Life and context'). But she also records at the ends of this passage that 'I felt warm and gay inside . . . and I got up and delighted my dear Edwin with the news', indicating the extent that their emotional life continued to be closely and warmly entangled.

Her journals record Muir's dreams in some detail; the long passage '*Why I am to be described as a mess*' is preceded by a 'vivid dream' in which she 'crossed the half-derelict, ruined piece of ground that recurs in my dreams . . . . [I]t seems to be in England, not Scotland . . . I always cross it on my way to somewhere else'. When she describes her dreams, she nearly always records some analysis as well and here she asks: 'Does it represent the ruined piece of my life in Hampstead when Gavin was run over and his nervous system ruined?' (19 Aug. 1953; journal; 1951-53). She notes a discussion with Edwin on waking after another dream, '[w]hat on earth could make me dream such a dream' and then follows with thoughts about possible sources of her dream in recent events (21 Aug. 1953; journal; 1951-53). While her references to sexuality are mainly oblique or metaphoric in her novels, in her journals she is analytic. She records when she wakes up with an orgasm after a dream about a train to St Andrews coming 'right into the station' (14 Jan. 1947; journal; Nov. 1946-June 1947). In 1953, after having a dream when 'two children came rushing in & I *couldn't* get them to go out . . . . The tension was very great, and then I had an orgasm! and woke up', Muir analyses the function of these orgasms:

> I suppose one manufactures excuses for tension in a dream. Is the tension the cause of the discharge? or the need for the discharge the cause of growing tension? An orgasm is probably the easiest & most direct discharge of tension, preventing hysterical or other morbid results? (10 Aug. 1953; notebook; ca. 1953)

In a similar way she analyses the function of a good cry in a letter to Raine: 'It's a wonderful discharges of stresses, a Good Cry, as I know: but it has to be violent and uninhibited while it lasts — nothing lady-like abt. it. One needs to howl like a naughty child' (24 Sept. 1961; NLS). In her journals she records her opinion of André Gide ('[f]undamentally sterile, all this French analyses of his sensibilities') immediately after noting the arrival of her underwear from Binns (2 Feb. 1948) and comments that Elizabeth Bowen is 'disconcertingly fashionable looking, ostrich feather hat, necklace earrings, polished look' (7 Feb. 1948; journal; Jan.-May 1948). Later she notes that A. S. Neill on a visit to Newbattle (shortly after her outburst at Edwin in August 1953) is 'less prickly than usual, warm with feeling'. 'Inverted ambition is what eats at Neill, I fear!' and she concludes that he is 'still fascinated by Lesbians, masturbation, & sexual perversities, as he always was' (21 Aug. 1953; journal; 1951-53). She makes waspish statements about old friends, describing Helen Cruickshank and Marion Lochhead in 1953 as 'these dim, well-meaning, intense & serious women' (2 Sept. 1953; journal; 1951-53). So the journals go on, treating the outside and the inside of Willa Muir, a combination of psychological observation, commentary on people met and works read, as well as a dream, emotion and event record. It is the directness of the style that gives the journals their feeling of spontaneity and illusion of access to her life unmediated by self consciousness 'writerlyness'. The sequence of events, feelings and analyses are presented with refreshing openness, and the clarity of her style lends support to Muir's performance of her self in this most private of mediums.

Muir's letters, more publicly directed even though still in a private medium, show a similar directness in execution. For examples of her direct and warm style, see her reply to Violet Schiff about *Women: An Inquiry* (see 'Polemics', note 1) as well as the mini-life up to 1933 that she sent to Marion Lochhead (see Appendix I). They both contain similar expressions by Muir of her insecurity about herself along with expressions of feeling and belief. Her letter to Lochhead begins with an amused take on the idea of a self-chosen biography:

Every woman her own biographer — wouldn't that bring out some highly-coloured histories! You tempt me, you know, to give my imagination full rein, and to lead you to believe that never was there a woman so cultured, so clever, so handsome, so beloved as myself. Well, well! The facts are very sober, on the other hand, and almost incredibly heavy reading. (3 March 1933; NLS; see Appendix I)

Muir picks out the concept of a Muir 'so cultured, so clever, so handsome, so beloved' as fiction, opposed to the sober facts of her life, and yet in a sense (real rather than wishful) this is an entirely valid description of Muir; the sadness is that she apparently has no sustained belief in it herself. The main collection of letters that I have used in the rest of this study is Muir's great series of letters to Kathleen Raine, the poet; in their detail about her life and in their emotional force, they seem more like a journal. Two of her last letters are printed in Appendix I and provide examples of her dramatic presentation of herself, dealing as they do with her intention to move to St Andrews ('I am now hurling a hand grenade at you'; 27 June 1969; NLS; see Appendix I) and then her cri-de-coeur about her cat Popsy when she thought Raine wanted Muir to take her back: 'I hope this letter is coherent, for I am not very!' (2 July 1969; NLS; see Appendix I). It is clear that Muir's expression of what she felt could be overdramatic. Raine makes a direct comment on this tendency on a note card she adds after the second letter:

> Willa misunderstood a letter of mine offering to return Popsy to her, as she had written me that 'Lovey' Scott had told her she could have a cat. I had neither the wish nor the intention to be 'rid' of Popsy. This emotional reaction was typical of Willa. The next letter dispelled the misunderstanding. KR. (MS: NLS 19703.211)

One of the reasons that Muir's letters and journals are so readable, so compelling as evidence of a female life as well as her specific life, is that they are such a successful 'never-finishing performance of the female self' (Vanacker 198), allowing us to witness a presentation of the life of the twentieth century feminist Scot that is Willa Muir.

I am perhaps less inclined to take Muir's letters and journals as literary artefacts than I have done in my approach to Jane Welsh Carlyle's writings.[5] This is probably because Muir left final drafts of works intended for publication in typescript and wrote all her personal letters and journals by hand, making a clear demarcation between the two kinds of writing, public and personal. But her life-writing in journals and letters is clearly part of her creative output. Even when Muir is questioning herself, commenting that when writing her books she attends 'far more to the construction, the sequence of incidents, the feeling conveyed, than to the style, although I am not aware of neglecting the style' (14 April 1952; journal; 1951-53) or lamenting, 'But I had no general self-confidence, — in writing literature, at least, — and was easily cast down & shaken' (20 Aug. 1953; journal; 1951-53), her directness and clarity constitute a style choice. Her observations and commentaries, exploring and articulating possibilities, whether of her dreams, Gavin, herself, show an elegant clarity. Her letters are dramatic and developed to be such. This is why so much of her personal writing can be used in commentary, why its presentation of self and ideas is so convincing. Her letters can engage in defence of her work, show attitudes to Scotland in passing, be a commentary on her current life, and include further developments of her ideas on gender. Her journals give information about her life, analyse her dreams, comment on people more dramatically and waspishly than in *Belonging*, all the while showing her emotional state in all its turbulence. The Minnie who cast her engagement ring into the sea in St Andrews when a student is essentially the same as the Willa who casts her lot in impulsively with Lilias Scott to escape the constriction of living in a nursing home (see 'Life and context' and Appendix I). What Muir provides in her letters and journals is an intelligent and honest account of her life as she lived it, performing it for herself and for the recipients of her letters, acting, re-acting and over-reacting throughout her life.

## Muir's poetry

Although Marion Lochhead had headed her article about Muir in 1933 with 'Translator, Novelist and Poet', Muir had not defined herself as a poet in her letter to Lochhead (see Appendix I). Up until 1969 her main poetic accomplishment in print had been her translation into Scots of *5 Songs from the Auvergnat* (1931). Lochhead prints 'The Wee Man' (Lou Pitchiout Omé) from this collection and Francis George Scott sets it to music.[6] Butter concludes his 1990 essay, 'Willa Muir: Writer', with two of Muir's poems, 'Coasting down the steep of your forehead' (drafted, 5 Feb. 1947; journal; 1946-47), and 'Illusion' from *Laconics*, one of her poems written after Edwin's death. He also prints a selection from her poetry with a short introductory note in 1993. Muir had written to Butter about her *Laconics Jingles & other Verses* (1969): 'I hope these trifles may interest and amuse you' (Butter, 1993 93) and included a characteristic down-playing of them in her letter: 'They were written before Christmas and meant to be a kind of farewell to my friends, since I thought a nice little funeral was on the way for me. Well, here I am alive, and will have to stand the consequences of printing these verses. Some are good, most of them are so-so' (Butter, 1990 71). Pick dismisses *Laconincs* as 'a slim book of genuinely amateurish poems' (Pick, introduction xi) while Butter in both his articles makes no particular claims for Muir as a poet although he does conclude that 'her best serious poems are nearly all to or about Edwin' (Butter, 1990 71). He also quotes Robert Lowell's letter to Muir: 'I am writing now because of your *Bottghe* [sic] poems, very masterful and firm and touching. I like particularly "Solitaire" and "Requiem". They are all true and right for you and what I might have expected from your conversation—only I didn't know what to expect' (11 Jan. 1960; St Andrews; Butter, 1993 93). (For 'Requiem', see Appendix IV; *Bottehge Oscure* also printed two other poems, 'Wartime, Old Style (An Old Wives Tale)' and 'Fuss at a Railway Station'). Lowell's point that Muir's poems are closely linked to her personality and character seems entirely the case. I consider her poetry as part of her literary production, illuminating her feelings and providing more performances of her self.

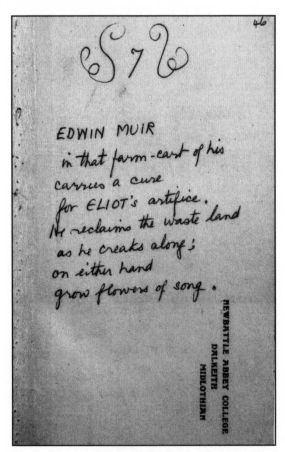

Poem to Edwin, Ephemeridae.

Muir wrote short poems into her journals and notebooks as well as two handmade little books of poems ('Ephimeridae') on Scottish and other writers for Edwin in the early nineteen fifties. Most of the latter poems are amusing doggerels, short squibs on the Muirs' fellow writers, satirical in intent, always sharp and sometimes unpleasant in tone, little effervescent jeux d'esprit to amuse Edwin with at least some of them extemporised in social gatherings. George Scott's description of her in St Andrews before the second world war describes how spontaneous the invention could be:

> Perhaps she would have fastened on a new word usage . . . . a classical tag,
> or a humorous verse invented calypso style for the occasion . . . . She used
> words as the currency of civilised intercourse and spent them lavishly but
> wisely, so that word play was never more serious yet entertaining. (Scott 38)

Scott cites some of her Ephemeridae as illustration (for further examples, see Ephemeridae, Appendix IV). The poems that she writes in her journals are more varied, playing with words; for example, the untitled poem that she writes on the inside cover of one of her journals where she lists the writers she does not read if she is depressed, concluding that she 'might give a boost / to Marcel Proust, / or start a-tippling / at Kipling' or her spoof poem on the British Council in the style of Gertrude Stein, 'What is the matter, baby mine?' (journal; 1947-Janurary 1948; see Appendix IV). But she also writes poems connected to Edwin in her journals. She writes 'To Edwin, absent' about her inability to feel at home without Edwin present, ending the poem with 'and yet I fit no pattern, left alone; / my home is in your bosom, only there'. 'Address to Edwin' is a poetic meditation on ageing, much more personal than her prose polemic, 'This Lop-sided World' (for both poems, see Appendix IV). But it also verges on the grotesque in its portrayal of how she sees herself becoming in the future, more aged than she is at 57:

> I hope that old age makes me merely comic,
> a funny, fat old woman with false teeth,
> that click or treacherously clack together,
> and bosom bursting from a straining sheath,
> vast hips and creaking knees and hobbling feet
> enveloped in a merciful skirt and cloak,
> a shameless old grey head, and mounted on it
> some foolish trifle of a hat or bonnet
> or even — God be good to us — a toque![7]

The second stanza, more serious, ends 'I hope you will forget the accidentals / remembering rather what I meant to be', leading Patricia Mudge to comment that if 'Willa . . . . [had] wanted to hide her insecurities, she failed' (Mudge 2). But Muir is laying claim to the reality of her life, ageing, depressed at times in the difficult situation in Prague, and dressing it up with humour to both amuse Edwin and remind him of their relationship.

One of her poems, 'In the Modern World', written after Edwin's death and published in *Laconics Jingles & other Verses* (1969) begins

My true Love lies alone,
a has-been,
picked clean
bone by bone. ('Laconics'; see Appendix IV)

The short poem is both a lament and a declaration that she is 'glad my true Love lies dead' because the world is so 'murderous' and confounding. 'My true Love' is a standard ballad phrase, but the poem's 'picked clean / bone by bone' echoes the macabre Scots ballad 'The Twa Corbies' with its concluding lines:

Ye'll sit on his white hause-bane,
And I'll pike oot his bonny blue e'en . . .

O'er his banes when they are bare
The wind sall blaw for evermair,
The wind sall blaw for evermair.

Muir shows here that the ballads are inscribed in her poetic memory. Some of the other poems in *Laconics* carry tones of anti-intellectualism:

so our intellectuals
all wear spectacles.

The question is; does what they see
make any sense to you and me? ('Jingles'; see Appendix IV)

Muir as usual defines herself in opposition to the intellectual. Given her connections with European intellectual life and her own intelligence and education, it always seems reductive that she should take such a conventional and pejorative attitude to intellectualism. But it is probably as much part of her gendered insecurity as of the attitudes of post second world war Britain where 'intellectual' is seen as an insult.[8] 'Not for Me' also includes a critique of modernism with its supposed angularity of architecture and ideas, before concluding with her preference for the curves of nature:

Not the urban towers
categorical with their ruthless right-angles,
cutting the living air into sections of nothing,
channelling its flow into false certainties.

Not the intellectual-isms,
categorical, sundering,

splitting personalities,
splitting hairs.

For me the curves of an embracing arm,
or the flowing contours of moving animals
the joyous freakish shapes of moths and flowers
on this well-rounded planet. ('Verses'; see Appendix IV)

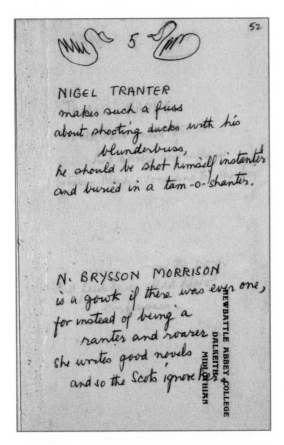

NIGEL TRANTER
makes such a fuss
about shooting ducks with his
blunderbuss,
he should be shot himself instanter
and buried in a tam-o-'shanter.

N. BRYSSON MORRISON
is a gowk if there was ever one,
for instead of being a
ranter and roarer
she writes good novels
and so the Scots ignore her.

Poems to Nigel Tranter and Nancy Brysson Morrison, *Ephemeridae* (2)

Her poems, particularly the satirical squibs, seem often to embody that very 'look at me' tone that clearly amused Edwin but so irritated some. But there is also a strength and vitality in the writing, along with a breadth of literary reference. *Laconics* includes some lyric poems, mainly connected to her grief at the loss of Edwin, but one untitled poem, perhaps harking back to that lost child of her miscarriage in December 1925, is also linked to loss and regret:

Where have you come from, shred of a daughter,
daughter I longed for and never bore?
Here you are in my dream
blown by what wind?

a shred, a wraith that cries in a piping voice:
'Don't leave me behind!' (see Appendix IV)

It is a poem effective in its perfect slightness, the ghost child incorporated into a dream. Certainly she uses her late poetry, just as she uses her letters, to express her great grief after Edwin's death in 1959. But all her poetry seems like a stream of consciousness expressing whatever she felt or was amused by at the time while each poem has the succinct and specific intensity of a poetic miniature. For me, her poetry is intentionally fragmentary, as linked to her preoccupations as any other of her writings, but giving a sense of her humour and wit not always apparent in her prose works.

Notes

1. For further considerations of Spark in Scottish contexts, see my 'Certainty and Unease in Muriel Spark's *The Ballad of Peckham Rye*' in C. Anderson and A. Christianson (eds.), *Scottish Women's Fiction, 1920s to 1960s: Journeys into Being* (East Linton: Tuckwell Press, 2000) 85-96, and 'Muriel Spark and Candia McWilliam: Continuities' in A. Christianson and A. Lumsden (eds.), *Contemporary Scottish Women Writers* (Edinburgh: Edinburgh University Press, 2000) 94-110.

2. Although a view persists that Jan Masaryk was killed by unknown communists, Muir insists in her journal and *Belonging* that he killed himself: 'there is no doubt that it was suicide; he told Lumir Soukup that he was going to do it. On this same afternoon there was the first meeting of the Parliament under the new Government, and he had been programmed to make a speech in the evening in the biggest hall of Prague, the Lucerna. He threw himself from a window of the Czernin Palace, and the whole country was convulsed with grief, a deep, human grief that came up against the impersonal, cold, synthetic system of Communist doctrine but could not overcome it' (*Belonging* 235). At the time she noted: 'To us it seems he must have done it as a grand gesture . . . . I think it will seem like the end of an era to the Czech people . . . . [A]n integral human act, M's suicide, versus synthetic power complex of C. P.' (10 March 1948; journal; Jan.-May 1948).

3. Before Muir moved to London, a list of the Muirs' books was made in the Cambridgeshire cottage, Aug. 1963, with a careful note of which were to be kept and which were to be passed to two women's colleges in Cambridge, New Hall (founded 1954) and Hughes Hall (1885-1973, after which date men were admitted) (WM-Raine, 8 Aug. 1963; NLS). The list survives in her archives in St Andrews allowing us to see what books she wanted to keep: all of Edwin's and her own and a wide variety of other works, including Elizabeth Drew's *Jane Welsh and Jane Carlyle*, detective stories by Ngaio Marsh, Dorothy Sayers and Margery Allingham, and many other works (including some by Kipling), mainly but not only literary (St Andrews; MS: 38466/6/17).

4. For examples of her writing, see Muir's verses on Edwin Muir (162), Nigel Tranter and Nancy Brysson Morrison (165).

5. See my approach in 'Jane Welsh Carlyle's Private Writing Career' in Douglas Gifford and Dorothy McMillan (eds.), *A History of Scottish Women's Writing* (Edinburgh: Edinburgh University Press, 1997) 232-45.

6. Francis George Scott, 'The Wee Man' (1931), *Songs: Thirty-Five Scottish Lyrics and other Poems* (Glasgow: Bayley and Ferguson for The Saltire Society, 1949) 11-13.

7. For Muir's hat (not a close-fitting toque) on the occasion of the award of Edwin's PHD at the University of Prague, see 150.

8. For more on twentieth century British attitudes to intellectuals, see Stefan Collini, *Absent Minds: Intellectuals in Britain* (Oxford: Oxford University Press, 2006).

Willa Muir's identity card photograph, Prague, 1945.

# Living with Ballads and Belonging

*Living with Ballads* (1965) and *Belonging* (1968), both published by Hogarth Press, were Muir's last prose works. They have a solidity and completeness attained by neither her unpublished novels nor her translation work; the connection to Muir of the latter is complicated by the question of who between the Muirs translated what, as well as by the ambiguous position translators hold in the field of creativity. Although her translation work was an ever present working reality for Muir in the nineteen thirties and nineteen forties, references to its constant companionship appearing in her letters, journals, *Mrs Muttoe and the Top Storey* and *The Usurpers*, the patterns of the work are still set by the original authors however much linguistic or artistic skill was needed to translate them into English. Of Muir's two final prose works, the first was as much rooted in the need to earn a living as the translations had been. It came from a commitment entered into by Edwin Muir before his death in 1959. Kirsty Allen believes that 'Muir's own voice and vision are never far beneath the surface psychologising, politicising and philosophising of her fiction' (Allen, 1996 xi); I have shown in earlier chapters the way in which Muir's narrative voice also analyses constantly in her non-fiction. In these two late works, Muir's 'own voice and vision' is naturally central to *Belonging*, but, however unexpectedly, her 'own voice' is also prevalent in *Living with Ballads*. Written in fulfilment of Edwin's contract, it is grounded in Muir's own childhood and her prejudices about Scotland as well as providing the commissioned study of ballads. The second work, *Belonging*, provides summary and culmination of her life with Edwin. *Living with Ballads* also contains summary and culmination but of her intellectual and emotional beliefs and preconceptions rather than of her life with Edwin. Both are as much part of her creative achievement as her earlier published fiction and non-fiction works.

## Living with Ballads

Edwin had been given a grant by the Bollingen Foundation in 1956 to write a book on ballads but had only made some notes by the time he died. The Foundation continued the grant to Willa Muir, providing a financial and emotional lifeline. Whatever book Edwin might have written, it would not have been this one. Peter Butter writes that 'it was to be the death and absence of Edwin that released her flow of creativity' and thinks that the book shows 'her close kinship in mind to Edwin . . . . Her book, like the one he would have written, is an enquiry into human nature and its needs, not just into the past and art' (Butter, 1990 69-70). But he acknowledges that unlike Edwin who might have concentrated on the supernatural, 'the bridge between the individual, the race and ultimate reality', Willa Muir's 'emphasis was more on psychology — the bridge between conscious and unconscious' (Butter, 1990 70). Given the differences in approach and content between Willa Muir's *Belonging* and Edwin Muir's *Autobiography* (1954) and his desire 'to recreate imaginatively the whole world of the ballads' (EM to Kathleen Raine, 28 Feb. 1956; Butter, 1974 179), it seems unlikely that Edwin's book would have been anything like Muir's book. Willa Muir's discussion of the ballads ranges through the oral tradition, children's singing games, discussion of specific ballads and of Scottish history (religious and cultural), the conscious and the unconscious and matriarchy and patriarchy. It has both a broad sweep in its structure and the most specific of analyses in its discussion. Its approach is rooted in the personal and is informed by Muir's feminism.

It was reviewed at the time by William Montgomery in *Scottish Studies*; he noted that Muir 'chose the psychological approach' and thinks the 'book has many flashes of insight that illuminate the background' (Montogomery 221-22) but he questions Muir's emphasis on Calvinism: 'between Catholocism and Calvinism there are resemblances that Mrs. Muir does not mention . . . . There must have been a Catholic fear of social and ecclesiastical disapproval long before Calvinists felt that fear. But why did this aspect of Calvinism have such a profound effect on the Ballads, when the same aspect of Catholocism did not?' (Montgomery 224). He concludes that the book 'takes its place naturally in this process of revaluation . . . . Human nature is the subject of this book' (Montogomery 224). Muir's papers in St Andrews contain a typescript of a radio discussion of *Living with Ballads* for Arts Review, BBC Radio (Scotland), 18 March 1965. Robert Kemp both draws attention to Muir's own pre-war publishing history (and its disappearance) and specifically connects the book with Edwin Muir:

> [H]ow good it was to see this book from Willa Muir because those of us
> who remember some of her own excellent writings know that there's a

generation who think of her perhaps only as the devoted wife of Edwin Muir, and here is something on a subject on which we know Edwin Muir was working — which comes out with her own stamp. (typescript; St Andrews)

But the panel also expresses some doubts about Muir's pessimism over whether the ballads can continue into the present as a living form, with Alexander Scott thinking that Muir 'doesn't do justice in [sic] the way the ballad has developed and changed and I see no reason why it shouldn't go on developing and changing'. The 'Introductory' of *Living with Ballads* begins with a chapter on 'Children's Singing Games'; Forsyth Hardy draws attention in his concluding remarks to the personal element within the book itself, and the contribution this makes to its opening pages:

I thought that Willa Muir writes with remarkable warmth of her own days as a schoolgirl and expresses the meaning of these playground songs in a quite delightful and charming way — and that she takes space and time to do that gives the early passages of the book a very special appeal and character. (typescript; St Andrews)

Ruth Perry, professor of literature at Massachusetts' Institute of Technology, who uses *Living with Ballads* in one of her courses, gives a more recent comment on this section; Perry admires 'the way she introduces the oral tradition through singing games and then talks so intelligently and sensitively about how those games function psychologically for the girls who play them' (Perry; email to Aileen Christianson; 23 Sept. 2005).

Muir claims value for children's singing games, 'transmitted orally from generation to generation of schoolgirls . . . . an inheritance from the same kind of people who made and sang the Scottish Ballads' (*Living* 13); she positions herself as part of this 'living experience . . . . [w]e were both singers and audiences in our singing games' and part of the 'elementary Board School for working-class children, where education in the three R's was provided free' (13). This was the school where she had learned Scots from the age of nine to twelve, using this knowledge later to criticise Douglas Young's poor Scots in his translation of Aristophanes (Anna J. Mill, 29 Jan. 1963; St Andrews). Her description of the segregated school playgrounds provides a metaphor for her own need to move outwards from any environment that she finds constrained:

It was a drab, gabled grey stone building on the outskirts of the town, with two playgrounds, a larger one of beaten earth for the boys and a smaller one, partly concreted, for the girls and infants. The boys' playground was left open on two sides, but the girls' playground was walled round except for the gate we went out and in by, which opened on a country road. There were as many girls as boys in the school, and since our playground cramped us, we used to run out through the gate in fine weather and play on the road. The year was 1901, and there were no motor cars; nothing came down our road except the occasional farm-cart or tradesman's van. Out there we had an open horizon looking over fields; we could and did turn our backs on the school, especially in our singing games. // Inside the school our education was wholly utilitarian. (13)

The boys may have had a playground open on two sides with implicit encouragement to range further than the girls, but the walled surrounds of the girls' playground, meant to contain them, simply led them to flow into the outer world of the country road. There they played their games of movement and exchange in which they were both 'singer and audience' in their participation. Muir left the school when she won a bursary to Montrose Academy, setting her on the path of middle class education and intellectual attainment at university but, looking back, she felt 'lucky to have learned them when I did. Only the working-class girls in our town kept that tradition alive, and only in the school playtime . . . . The girls sang them no longer when they went out to work' (14).

Her analysis of the repetitiveness of the singing games is grounded in her understanding of the unconscious:

The foundations were being laid for a bridge between unconscious feelings and conscious personalities; there was not yet much traffic to cross the bridge and the territory beyond it was largely unexplored, but the lines of communication were being kept open. // Yet although we neither queried nor analysed our feelings, we were aware of a profound satisfaction that made us play the games again and again, day after day. What we understood in this underworld of fluid feelings that merged easily into each other was just enough to make rational explanations superfluous, enough, anyhow, to keep us pleased and happy. (20)

Muir continues this preoccupation with 'the underworld of fluid feeling' in her chapter on 'Ballad Background I. The Underworld of Feeling'. The chapter begins with a discussion of imagination:

Imagination takes its rise in the underworld of feeling, which, like the sea, has tides and currents and is continually in motion. Imagined actions may form there and vanish again, trends of feeling may be discernible, but there are no concepts in that world, no categories; one might almost say no boundaries. In such a flowing medium a sense of personal identity must be difficult to come by. One has to emerge into some degree of consciousness to find that, and then chart oneself by reference to other people. Images must also have some relation to consciousness if they are to take coherent shape and be recognizable. In the underworld of feeling there is a sense of power, of rhythmic flow, of movement, of living energy, but only when it issues into consciousness, however dim, can all that energy find itself a name and a purpose. (53)

This can be related back directly to the world of Elizabeth Shand's feelings and reactions to the tumultuous passion of the sea (*Imagined Corners* 69, 116), Muir using her ideas on imagination as an underpinning to the psychology of her young, passionate heroine in her 1931 novel.

When Muir moves to a consideration of 'Material' and the position of magic in the ballads, she relates this to the possibility of a liminal world at certain times of the year: 'cracks in Time, as it were, through which the uncanny powers could come. That the dividing or boundary line between the one dispensation and another could let in other-worldly dangers was a widespread ancient belief . . . . [O]n the boundary line itself law was abrogated and the forces of chaos, of misrule, struggled to assert themselves' (127). Muir presents these as part of the archaic world, one of many perceived dangerous boundaries between the conscious and unconscious, but the metaphor itself can also represent the place of the debatable lands of argument in modern criticism, where the new, the indefinable, can enter and become part of our knowledge, however ambiguously.[1] For Muir its power came from the closeness of the unconscious to surface, conscious life and she prefers this evidence of the archaic to the modern post-Calvinist world:

> Scottish civilization was already becoming elaborately and consciously cerebral, thanks to Calvinism, with an excessive respect for cerebration rather than intelligence; the countryside was still deep in the world of archaic feeling, self-conscious only to a limited extent, aware of power and the forces of power, guided not by abstract concepts but by traditional feelings and stories in which passionate feelings, presented in episodes, were embodied. (86)

Her distinction between cerebration and intelligence is important, preserving her right to exercise her own intelligence while condemning the aridity that she, like Edwin, defined as one of the consequences of the controlling influence of Calvinism in the post-Reformation world in Scotland. But at the same time as she argues that the earlier world was richer in instinctive feeling and stories, she also acknowledges earlier embodiments of the patriarchy: '[i]n the older folk-tales there is no happy ending: the patriarchal hero usually advances ruthlessly over the deserted, forgotten figure of the woman' (109-10). The last section 'The Reformation and After' is much concerned with the presence of Calvinism in Scottish culture. Muir asserts earlier in the study that Calvinists reformers were 'totalitarian on principle and by temperament' (139).

When writing on the ballads and Calvinism, she struggles, loathing Calvinism 'so much that I kept losing my sense of proportion and writing pages of brilliant polemic which all had to be torn out as quite irrelevant' (Raine; Feb. 1963; NLS). In the published chapter, she attempts to account for some innate connection between Calvinism and Scotland, however negative she feels Calvinism's effects to be:

> The Confession of Faith drawn up by the Reformers in 1560 describes how 'some are elected to everlasting salvation and others ordained as vessels of wrath without reference to their merits or vices'. The individual has no choice whether he shall be saved or damned, this being solely determined by 'the incomprehensible mercy of God', which is not unlike the arbitrary operations of luck or Fate. The Calvinist creed, that is to say, chimed in with some of the deeper resonances in the imagination of the Ballad audiences. (191)

The drama of the preaching reminded congregations that 'they were participants in a cosmic drama' (191) giving them the same excitement as the best renditions of the old dramas of the ballads. But the intensity of the Scottish response and acceptance, greater in Muir's view than elsewhere, came because it was part of their 'makeup':

> Reforming Calvinists elsewhere must have had the same experience, but outside Geneva they did not compensate themselves by insisting upon the extreme authority, the theocratic absolutism, so fervently demanded by these first Scottish ministers, with a vehemence as narrow and concentrated as the war-passion of ancient Norsemen. That berserk passion seems to have been part of their make-up. (191)

Muir had already attacked in passing the effect of religion in its Presbyterian form on Scottish society in *Mrs Grundy in Scotland*. *Mrs Ritchie*, also written in the nineteen thirties, is a sustained attack on both the patriarchal control of women's options and the life-denying nature of Calvinist belief; it shows graphically the dangers to the individual of Calvinism's emotional force in the character of Annie Ritchie. So Muir could afford, perhaps, to edit out her more violent polemic against Calvinism in *Living with Ballads*, contenting herself with assertions. Metrical psalms were created by the Scottish reformers for their congregations to sing because they 'could not help knowing that everyone sang Ballads . . . . The metrical versions of the Psalms and Paraphrases are a curious tribute to the strength of the Ballad tradition' (197) and, since the ballads were 'a very ancient habit of mankind', the ballad tradition was 'both older and more deeply founded than the Calvinism which tried to repress it' (197).

Willa Muir was writing *Living with Ballads* at the time of the nineteen sixties' folk revival which itself had followed on the great collecting of ballads by Hamish Henderson and others for the School of Scottish Studies in Edinburgh in the nineteen forties and nineteen fifties. Muir cites an article by Henderson in her discussion of 'Young Beichan' (108);[2] she also refers to the technique of Jeannie Robertson[3] (one of the greatest sources for the School's recordings of the traditional ballads) in the context of James Hogg's mother's famous complaint to Walter Scott about the damage done to the oral tradition of the ballad by his printing of them:

> Jeannie Robertson sings the ballad in a way that conveys the full resonance of tradition behind the story . . . . Margaret Laidlaw, Mrs Hogg, said to Sir Walter Scott, when he was preparing his Minstrelsy of the Scottish Border: 'There were never ane o' my sangs prentit till ye prentet them yoursel', an' ye hae spoilt them awthegither. They were made for singing an' no' for reading; but ye hae broken the charm now'. // What she called 'the charm', since it was a mystery she could not put a name to, was the slow impersonal underlying rhythm of traditional feeling, which carries with it vestiges of ancient beliefs and long-forgotten, or half-forgotten, rituals and ceremonies. To allow room and time for these a tragic Ballad must be sung as Jeannie Robertson sings it, in a slow, impersonal, unhurried, unregimented manner. The slowness is essential. (47-48)

Just as Muir admires Robertson's singing technique and all the time that it allows for listeners' reactions, so Ruth Perry admires Muir's formulation that ballads 'tap into "the underworld of feeling" and provide people with materials to exercise their imagination on and a line of connection between the everyday world and the unconscious'. Perry uses Muir's analyses of the '"core of feeling" in a ballad' to start her students thinking about how a ballad works. She sees Muir as dating ballads and examining their historical accuracy ('and all the other issues that ballad scholars discuss') but that Muir 'does it in a way that is so digested, so assimilated, so lived as opposed to merely theoretical. The title of her book is accurate and it is what makes it so special' (Perry; email to AC; 23 Sept. 2005). Lumir Soukup thought it a pity that Muir 'felt morally obliged to write it', the effort given to *Living with Ballads* taking away from the time and energy needed to write *Belonging*, the memoir of Edwin that she was already planning (L. Soukup 31). But the praise by Perry, a modern scholar and teacher, for *Living with Ballads* establishes the work as still having value as part of the study of ballads in the general field of ethnology. The work can be seen as having objective value, rather than being seen either as a work inextricably connected to Muir's other published books through its preoccupations (as I certainly see it) or as a work that comes not from her individual intention but as an inheritance from Edwin, therefore the least individual of her works.

Muir ends the work with an attack on the idea that 'mass-culture' can ever produce anything that can provide 'as much deep satisfaction as Ballads have done':

> Mass-culture, unless its meaning changes radically, remains a preposterous statistic produced by the categorizing intellect. The kind of culture presented by the cinema or by television, the latter of which especially is closely related to clock-time and the focused eye of consciousness, is also unlike Ballad culture. Whether mankind will again shape a popular culture that provides as much deep satisfaction as Ballads have done I cannot tell; I can only hope so. (260)

This essentially negative rejection of mass-culture means that the work remains a discussion of the past, however much it is called *Living with Ballads*. Her analysis is made personal by the anecdotes of the children's singing games and of her first hearing of a ballad 'on a late summer evening of 1906, when a ploughman sang it to me' (35). I also read it as a late modernist text opposing the old, slower worlds of feeling to the fast modern world in a way that Muir touches on in *Imagined Corners* (IC 7) and Nan Shepherd explores explicitly in *A Pass in the Grampians* (1933) in the character of Dorabel / Bella, learning ballads in childhood, returning in adulthood to her childhood surrounds as a modern singer and practitioner of all that was 'fast'. Muir is explicit about the contrast between fast / slow, modern / the past, conscious / unconscious in the earlier discussion of Jeannie Robertson's singing in *Living with Ballads*:

> Feelings can be embodied in imagined actions swiftly enough, as in dreams or reveries, but the feelings themselves may have taken nearly a lifetime to grow. One cannot travel fast through this underworld of feeling and be fully aware of it, just as one cannot travel in a fast car through a fast landscape and be as fully aware of it as one would be on foot. Clock-time with its counted minutes, its stress on speed, is for the conscious self, not for the underworld of feeling where the imagination takes its rise. Ballads belong to this imaginative underworld and the traditional rhythms of feeling behind their tunes and words need a longer wave-length than dancing songs, work songs, or gay entertainments. (48)

It is these worlds of feeling, of past and presents that she explores so successfully in relation to her own and Edwin's life in *Belonging*.

# Belonging

Muir began planning *Belonging A Memoir* (1968)[4] early in the nineteen sixties; George Mackay Brown, the Orkney poet whom she knew from his attendance at Newbattle, wrote to her in 1964, hoping it was coming along well (20 Feb. 1964; St Andrews). William Knox misleadingly describes it as 'a marvellous autobiography' (Knox, 2006 226). It was always intended to be her memoir of Edwin and to interpret it as her own autobiography is to misunderstand her purpose. But she did intend it to be a memoir of her life with Edwin, exploring that shared life in a way that Edwin himself had been incapable of doing in *An Autobiography* (1954). *Belonging* begins with their first 'unlikely' meeting in Glasgow in September 1918 when Willa was a lecturer in London and Edwin was a 'costing-clerk in a Renfrew shipbuilding firm' (*Belonging* 11). Unlikely as their friends thought it that the marriage (which followed nine months later in June 1919) would last, Muir records in the first paragraph of *Belonging* that, when Edwin died in January 1959, she realised that she had assumed they would die together, 'hand in hand. I could not believe it possible for me to be alive and for him to be dead. It did not make sense. We belonged together' (11). The rest of the memoir is Muir's narrative of their life together, an assertion of her belief in the idea of 'Belonging to the Universe' (14) and that they 'belonged' together. Muir also refers to this idea in *Living with Ballads*, initially being written at the same time as *Belonging*:

> You belong to the Universe, and you must 'dree your weird' with courage.
> // This sense of 'belonging', in some way, to the Universe and to power-
> ful human groups like a family or tribe, is a characteristic of any old-time
> community. From the Ballads one can legitimately infer that the Scots,
> especially in rural districts, felt this sense of community. They 'belonged'
> also to the places they happened to live in. (*Living* 190)

In *Belonging* Muir links it with Edwin even before she has met him. Muir finds a paragraph headed 'Love and Innocence' (Moore 210) in Edwin's *We Moderns* (published 1918, under the pseudonym of Edward Moore) which reminds her of her childhood feeling of being floated 'out and up into . . . the Universe' (*Belonging* 14). She notes that Edwin even contradicted Nietzsche (in the paragraph headed 'Love and its Object'), arguing that 'only lovers can generate such wealth of life that it overflows, enriching their friends, their enemies, all the world' (Moore 211), and Muir wonders if this 'sense of overflowing feeling' was 'essentially the same' as her own feelings of 'Belonging to the Universe' (14-15). Shortly after this thought, Edwin is introduced to her. At their second meeting in December 1918, they talk about his origins in Orkney and hers in Shetland, and where they felt they belonged. Edwin told her about his displacement from Orkney to Glasgow and the 'shocks he suffered' (18), while Muir spoke of her first shock being in relation to language, 'my first words were in the Norse dialect of Shetland' and, age two, she remembers being mocked outside in the Montrose street by older girls squealing 'in delighted mockery' at her dialect (19). Clearly a formative as well as an early memory, she had described it to Lochhead in 1933: '*Not* born in Shetland, but in Montrose, of Shetland parents. The first words I spoke were Shetland, and I can still remember being surrounded by a group of Montrose girls who roared and laughed at my outlandish speech' (NLS; see Appendix I). She records her reflections in the train after the meeting with Edwin that her interest in language dated from that moment 'when my intelligence came to the rescue of my hurt feelings and told me that I could learn to "belong" by speaking Montrose' (20). She could speak 'Shetland, Montrose and the kind of English used at the small private school in Bridge Street' by the time she was four (20). Her thoughts about her early trilingual skills are placed retrospectively. She concludes the first chapter: 'About the great shock in my adult life, the 1914 war, which knocked me to pieces for a time, I did not think at all'; her thoughts 'lingered comfortably within the lesser ambience of personal displacements' and 'compared with [Edwin] I had been let off lightly' (20). Muir thus positions herself equally with Edwin from the first chapter of *Belonging*. The 'great shock of her adult life', the first world war, remains unexplored; she writes about it in her published fiction, directly in *Mrs Ritchie* but with only the slightest of hints at the end of *Imagined Corners*.

In 1938 Edwin was working on *The Story and the Fable* (1940) while Willa was working on *Mrs Muttoe*. He wrote to Sydney Schiff about it:

> I am taking notes for something like a description of myself, done in
> general outline, not in detail, not as a story, but as an attempt to find out
> what a human being is in this extraordinary age which depersonalises
> everything. Whether it will be a success or a failure, I can't say; it may
> be that I have found at last a form that suits me; it may be that I haven't
> found a form at all, but merely a collection of fragments. I have begun
> to note myself, anyway, and I find that in doing that I am noting other
> people too, and the world around me. That is bound to have some value:
> the problem is to discover what you are, and then what your relation is
> to other people: I am starting from that, and it takes me in ever so many
> directions, inwards and outwards, backwards and forwards: into dreams
> on the one hand, and social observation on the other; into the past by
> a single line, and over the present by countless lines. At any rate I am
> learning in the process, whatever the artistic result may be. (17 May 1938;
> Schiff papers; Butter, 1974 100)

Willa and Edwin Muir, Marienbad.

*The Story and the Fable* became the first section of Edwin's *An Autobiography* (1954) and the process he describes above was continued there. Willa herself is far less central in his story than he in hers, however much she might have been ever present in his daily life; the index lists her only thirteen times under her maiden name of Anderson, although he does write '[m]y marriage was the most fortunate event in my life' (*Autobiography*, 1954; 1993 147). In *Belonging*'s index, Muir concentrates on listing references to Edwin's works as he is so central to the narrative. It was when he was preoccupied in 1952 with extending *The Story and the Fable* in Newbattle that he so annoyed and depressed Muir by failing to read her typescript of *The Usurpers* and by admitting that he would leave out from his autobiography the painful episode in their marriage when he told her about his intention to leave her and return to Gerda in Germany. Muir heads the entry in her journal recording their long discussion about this '*Why I am to be described as a mess*', taking her pain into herself. She describes her anguished feelings on the shores of Lake Garda in *Belonging* (82-84). As he had acknowledged to her, Edwin makes no reference to the episode in *An Autobiography*. This difference illustrates Willa Muir's central positioning of her self and feelings in *Belonging* and Edwin Muir's intense concentration on aspects of himself rather than on a narrative of his life. However important Muir was in his life, he writes the kind of autobiography which foregrounds intellectual and artistic development over any exploration of his emotional life with his wife. There is a clear contrast between Edwin's *An Autobiography* with its interest in the symbolism and allegory rather than the detail of his life and Muir's *Belonging*, grounded as it is in the details of their lives together as well as in her interest in psychology and her own feminist perceptions of a patriarchal world. Sabine Vanacker, writing about Gertrude Stein, H. D. and Dorothy Richardson, notes that those modernist women writers 'managed to make autobiography into the never-finishing performance of the female self, and not the definitive, significant male life-history' (Vanacker 198). Edwin's *An Autobiography* is too interested in the story and the fable behind his own 'male life-history' for it to be 'definitive' as a life history, with its attention to the inner, the poetic and philosophical. Muir's memoir of Edwin in *Belonging* resists any reading of it as 'definitive, significant male life-history' by placing herself firmly in the story, ensuring that she too, even though it is not her autobiography, produces a 'never-finishing performance of the female self' where her constructed self acts both as narrator and narrated.

Lumir Soukup discusses the differences between the Muirs' life-writing in his short memoir, 'Belonging'. He calls Willa Muir's *Belonging* 'her memoirs'. He believes their 'autobiographies' should be read together as they are 'complementary'

(L. Soukup 30). His comparative judgment on their works trusts Muir's accuracy over Edwin's:

> From our countless encounters after many events experienced together, I can vouch for Willa's recollections as the more accurate. She was more down-to-earth, a factual, relevant observer; a recorder, whereas Edwin was concerned with atmosphere and the impressions made on him. Occasionally . . . he did not see or remember certain things, because he had withdrawn into a dream and a search for formulation. He was an interpreter. To give just one example, Willa's operation and recovery as described in *Belonging* (p207) and in *An Autobiography* (pp248-49), one almost wonders whether they were writing about the same event. Knowing Willa, I believe her unsentimental account. (L. Soukup 30)

Despite the passage in *Belonging* (describing 'the frozen landscape' that Muir was lost in before she opened her eyes) being expressively and bleakly poetic, Soukup's preference is still based on Willa the 'recorder', whereas Edwin achieves the artistically superior role of 'interpreter'. Soukup thought 'Edwin's additional chapters', written while at Newbattle Abbey, were 'uneven', lacking 'firmness of thought and judgment' (L. Soukup 30), and thought it 'likely because he felt that his real writing was poetry' (L. Soukup 31). Thus both Edwin's successful early chapters and (in Soukup's view) less successful later ones, are described and justified in relation to Edwin's artistic role as a poet, and Willa's success is related to her 'accuracy', even though Soukup concludes that '*Belonging* is her long poem, the Story written in prose' and dedicated to Edwin (L. Soukup 32). Sherry Simon in *Gender in Translation* thinks Muir 'a talented writer'. She defines *Belonging* as Muir's 'memoirs', seeing them as 'a remarkable demonstration of the fluidity of her style and the acuity of her perceptions' (Simon 1996 76). Simon's reference to Muir's 'fluidity of her style' implies artistic capacity but Muir herself writes defensively in her journal of her attitude to style: 'In writing a book I attend far more to the construction, the sequence of incidents, the feeling conveyed, than to the style, although I am not aware of neglecting the style' (14 April 1952; journal; 1951-1953). This description seems to corroborate Soukup's view of her as a 'recorder' even though this list of what she pays attention to in her writing (at that time *The Usurpers*) implies artistic choices. Muir herself, in an opposition between Scottish and English baking, categorises *Belonging* as 'very like a Scotch bun . . . because it has a bit of everything in it, not classified into layers like a respectable English cake' (Tom Scott; 22 March 1968; NLS). This opposition implies solidity and completion, with Muir for once taking Scottish as positive and dismissing the respectability of an English cake's layering.

Most commentators on Muir's work take *Belonging* as 'straight' memoir, using parts of it to give biographical information or to discuss Muir's feminism. Robb certainly uses the passage about the Muirs' respective studies in Hampstead as straightforward information about her position which indicates 'an occasional twinge of resentment without which she would not have been human' (Robb 149). As I have already mentioned in 'Fragments of a writing life', this passage is closely paralleled in *Mrs Muttoe and the Top Storey* (*Mrs Muttoe* 15). What Muir does in *Belonging* is to show the contrasts between their two studies in ways that more than hint at gendered divisions, with Edwin in the role of austere, privileged poet whose study's peace and separation is sacrosanct while Willa's work space is constantly intruded on by the household:

> In his study at the top of the house which contained only a table, a chair, an ink-pot and a fine view over roofs and tree-tops, Edwin now and then produced a poem. The bareness of his study was how he liked it; my memory may have exaggerated that, but slightly. Ten poems, some composed in Crowborough and some in Hampstead, were published in 1934 by Dent, with the title: *Variations on a Time Theme*. My study on the ground floor was neither so bare nor so secluded. Here I was intruded upon at all hours by household staff, the weekly washerwoman, any casual caller ready for a gossip, and Gavin whenever he came home from school . . . . Toys, picture-books and hoards of Gavin's were in my study, an upright piano, a wicker wash-basket for laundry, a sewing-machine, a small sofa for visitors and goodness knows what else. I envied Edwin's power of sitting down immediately after breakfast to concentrate in solitude on what he wanted to do. // Yet there was always a press of work, and so I reverted to a student habit of mine, working at furious speed late at night into the small hours, after the vibrations of the day had died down . . . . I cannot tell now how I managed to finish a second novel, but it does not surprise me that I lost control of it in the second half. (162-63)

Edwin was also working on novel reviewing for *The Listener* from January 1933 ('an article of about 1500 words about once a fortnight, dealing usually with three novels' (Butter, 1966 130)) which provided their most regular income ('small, but assured' (Butter, 1966 130)) for several years, as well as any contribution he made to their translating of Sholem Asch (see 122), Kafka's *The Great Wall of China* and 'another Broch' (*Belonging* 162); Muir acknowledges all of this work immediately before the study passage, but still manages to imply in the passage itself that all that Edwin had to do in his study was write his poems, concentrating 'in solitude'. She, meanwhile, at the centre of their domestic space is 'intruded upon at all hours', busily entertaining visitors ready for gossip, mothering, housekeeping (in an organising rather than a doing sense) as well as translating and completing her second novel, *Mrs Ritchie*. Muir ensures that a reader's sympathy should be with her not Edwin, providing an example of what Sidonie Smith calls 'both the process and the product of assigning meaning to a series of experiences . . . by means of emphasis, juxtaposition, commentary, omission' (S. Smith 45).

This trope of female / male writing conditions is not an unusual one. Virginia Woolf's *A Room of One's Own* (1929) may be the most famous and extended of the contemporary explorations of the female lack of private writing space and its effect on a woman's chances for literary productivity, with its conclusion that 'it is necessary to have five hundred a year and a room with a lock on the door if you are to write fiction or poetry' (Woolf, 1929 103). But in 1934 Winifred Holtby makes a comparison between two unrelated Victorian writers who, in their respective houses in Chelsea and Manchester, were enacting the same trope as the Muirs in Hampstead eighty years later:

> While Carlyle was shutting himself up in his sound-proof room, and
> sacrificing his wife to his dyspeptic or creative agonies, Mrs. Gaskell was
> writing her novels at the end of a dining-room table, among a constant
> whirl of children, servants, draughts and callers. Carlyle's achievement,
> considered by purely intellectual standards, was the more impressive; but
> the author of *Mary Barton* and *North and South* had an alert intelligence
> and imagination which, had they been adequately respected, might have
> raised her literary work from competence to greatness. (Holtby 104)

This employs the identical feminist suggestion to Muir that the intrusion of domestic concerns undermines any possibility of 'greatness' although Muir also questions her own competence because of the demands of her surroundings. Undoubtedly accurate in its analysis and implied criticism of the privileged position of the male, Holtby does not take account of the capacity of some writers (such as Jane Austen) to produce works of 'greatness' in the midst of domestic activity. It works best as an interesting trope in the history of feminist analysis of male / female relations, rather than as an explanation or excuse for the 'success' or otherwise of particular kinds of literary production.

While I would not assert that all Muir's work constitutes autobiography (and would think it a reductive assertion to make), certainly Muir's works, all of which interknit her own experiences and concerns to some extent, might be interpreted in this way if Sidonie Smith's widest definition was adopted: 'Since all gesture and rhetoric is revealing of the subject, autobiography can be defined as any written or verbal communication' (S. Smith 19). To some degree Muir certainly follows this idea, every piece of written work (published or not) including some reflection on her self and experience. Elphinstone, while understanding the complexity of Muir's relationship to 'autobiography' and that *Belonging* is not Muir's autobiography, nevertheless uses the concept of autobiography to underwrite her own analysis of Muir's works:

> Willa Muir's autobiography is an elusive text; ostensibly it was never actually written, but that need be no deterrent to making it the starting point of this examination of self, gender and society in her work. On the contrary, the location of autobiography as a hidden subtext, both in the novels and in the late works *Belonging* and *Living with Ballads*, is exemplary of Muir's analysis of marginality and identity'. (Elphinstone 400)

Muir's works are also exemplary of Sidonie Smith's view that the autobiographer joins 'together facets of remembered experience — descriptive, impressionistic, dramatic, analytic', constructing 'a narrative' as she works on 'self-interpretation' (S. Smith 45). What underlies Smith's analysis of the genre is the clear point that autobiography or memoirs are necessarily artistic constructions using memory (which is itself selective and creative), that non-fiction texts are as much constructs using literary skills as fictional texts are. No more than history can memoirs or autobiography be taken as 'truth' and any attempt to use *Belonging* as narrative 'truth' about the Muirs has to be accompanied by awareness of Muir's creative capacities in interpretation and use of her material. For me, *Belonging* represents a pulling together of all Muir's concerns: Edwin, gender, the patriarchy, Scotland, the unconscious. It is a final writing of Edwin, herself and their joint story, re-mining her past work whether published or unpublished, using her experiences and her interpretations of past life with Edwin, to construct her memoir of him in *Belonging*, ensuring that she is not only present as the narrating 'I' but also as a fully developed presence as the narrated 'I' accompanying Edwin's 'he'.

Throughout this study of Willa Muir I have used *Belonging* in counterpoint to her other works, as source of both information and commentary. Butter calls it 'an intelligent and honest account of her life with Edwin' accepting her 'truth' with no apparent awareness of the 'art' that goes into the book. He also describes her writing it when 'in her mid seventies and living again with a poet in Kathleen Raine's house in Chelsea' (Butter, 1990 70), as though Muir needs a poet to inspire her best writing. But, as befits a memoir written by the Willa Muir who appears in her letters and her journals as an intelligent, analytic feminist who is yet simultaneously overly insecure about herself, *Belonging* is an opinionated and heartfelt interpretation of Edwin and Willa Muir's lives together as she remembers and interprets them. Taken on its own, separate from her other works, it is a moving reconstruction of two lives in the twentieth century and an illuminating analysis by a particular feminist of those two lives, of Scotland, Europe and that century. In the end, I read it as both informative and creative, and as Muir's last great work.

## Notes

1. Cf. Maggie Humm, *Border Traffic: Strategies of Contemporary Women Writers* (Manchester: Manchester University Press, 1991) and Aileen Christianson, 2002, 'Gender and nation: debatable lands and passable boundaries'.

2. For further discussion of the ballad, see Hamish Henderson, 'The Ballad and Popular Tradition to 1660' (1988); Henderson cites *Living with Ballads* in his secondary texts (1:284).

3. Jeannie Robertson (1908-75), traditional singer; among my memories of being a student in Aberdeen in the nineteen sixties are Jeannie Robertson's wonderful singing of north east ballads at the folk club and visiting her at her home. On one of my visits, she read my future in tea leaves left in the cup; sadly, I have no memory of what she read the future as being.

4. The National Library of Scotland has a proof copy of *Belonging* with a publication date of 1967 on the title page. Muir notes on it: 'Specially procured for Gavin and Dorothy (Proof not finally corrected — Another photograph to be squeezed in: Edwin & I outside Prague University with a crowd of students just after he was made Ph.D.)' The added photograph appears opp. 65 in the final 1968 copy, next to a reproduction of Muir's official, Prague 1945 identity card (see 150 and 168).

# Conclusion

This study of Muir's work has, on the whole, proceeded in an orderly fashion through discussion of her works, chapter by chapter. Muir's assertion of herself in her life-writing has been apparent throughout, used in commentary and in extension of my analyses of her published works. Nan Shepherd, her fellow north east novelist, with only three novels and one collection of poems published between 1928 and 1934 and *The Living Mountain* in 1977, and less personal papers available, seems more purely modernist than Muir precisely because the texts of her novels can be taken separately from her retiring self. But separating Muir's texts from their author is much more difficult. I have used one solution by writing two specific chapters about her two published novels as texts almost independent of their author. In the other chapters, even while separating the unpublished from published works, her other works blend into a mix which crosses boundaries between published and unpublished life-writing, and published polemic and memoir. Writing always from the belief system she had worked out in her youth and twenties, Muir intrudes into nearly all her texts through the voices of her controlling narrators or strong authorial point of view. Her letters and journals exhibit the combination of assertion and insecurity that was apparently an inextricable part of her being. This passionate writer of journals and letters, seeking to define her life and self through analysis of dreams and events alike, transmogrifies in her fiction into the cool, analytic narrators while the passion is shown by the characters in her novels. The discipline of publication ensures that her fiction explores complexities and ambiguities in female / male relations and society; her non-fiction adds historical context for gender binaries and explorations of Scotland while it analyses the current existence of the patriarchy and the need for change.

Muir's writings are exemplary in showing the struggle for twentieth century women to escape the traditional gender constrictions (building on the work of Victorian feminists) and the attempt to move into a world of more equal gender relations, the world that Muir always believed would come. In all of Muir's works, published and unpublished, she foregrounds her ideology. She writes, from the earliest to the last works, with a kind of honest puzzlement that the world's divisions are both gendered and unfair. Her late writing connects back to her earliest by harking back to her childhood, pointing up her early resentment of the hierarchy of oppositions between girls and boys, then men and women. It is her interpretation of gender that has troubled some critics when it is seen as essentialist (whether in works or letters: 'I *will* not be abstracted out of my thick, emotional, feminine life' (Raine; 29 March 1960; NLS)). Her lack of obvious address of the issue of Scottishness is another tendency that was questioned by her contemporaries. Finally there is a noticeable disconnect between her lifelong personal insecurities and her bold, sometimes brash, assertion of her personality in life and in her published explorations of gender imbalances and assertions of women's strengths.

I have referred in the previous chapters to Muir as performer, that performance of the woman writer enacted by modernist women life-writers seeking 'to "perform" themselves as a strong female presence in front of an audience of reader-listeners' (Vanacker 179). I base this particularly on Muir's letters and journals but all of her works exhibit a self consciousness of effect that indicates awareness of performance. Despite her dislike of Calvinism and the Presbyterian churches in Scotland, she identifies the power of the performative in Presbyterian preaching: 'The preachers, moreover, proclaimed the doctrine dramatically, staging performances in the pulpit which excited the congregations and reminded them that they were participants in a cosmic drama' (*Living with Ballads* 191). It is clear that the dramas described in her letters and journals were fuelled by her capacity for the dramatic in her life. I refer in 'Life and context' to the difficulty some men and women found in her character. A different perspective is given in 1980 by George N. Scott in his affectionate short memoir (gained when he was 'a youngster on holiday in St Andrews before the war'):

> She was a constant source of entertainment, she lived to talk, to tease, to act out the meaning of being a social animal to the last flicker of an eyelid. She personified the joie de vivre . . . . Dark haired, her features aquiline, with soft blue grey eyes arresting and persuasive as the look of the Ancient Mariner, and lips ever ready to form some provocative witticism at the expense of the present company or some current cult or fashion . . . . And while she revelled in the effect of her performance like an actress who has the audience at her mercy, Edwin would watch with a contented smile playing about his lips. (Scott 38)

The attractiveness of this picture, even while acknowledging that 'her wit at times verg[ed] on the unkind' (Scott 42), counterbalances the performance of mood swings and insecurity that Muir gives in her life-writing. But it also makes clear how much performance was ingrained in her life.

Muir lists some characteristics of Scotland in the middle of her notes on 'Culture as a style of life':

(In Scotland — Saturday night drunks, whisky
high tea / football
presbyterian Church
'but and ben' & box beds
reels / porridge
common stairs
Robert Burns
Scots Law
belief in the Devil &c&c). (notebook; ca. 1953; St Andrews)

Like a succinct poem calling up Scotland, this list of assumptions about what characterises Scotland perhaps harks back to the past of Scotland; even in 1953 '"but and ben" & box beds' were hardly common. It is not clear whether she intends them as a list of a past Scotland or simply a note of what resonates for her about Scotland. But it is the case that much of her adult life is lived outwith Scotland, and that her reactions to it are influenced by assumptions that the Scotland she knows is narrow and oppressive and best left behind. Despite her assertion of Scottishness to Gunn, 'being Scottish, my approach to any universal problem is bound to be by way of Scottish characters' (Pick, introduction ix), her reactions when living in Scotland tend to be negative. What Edwin writes to Sydney Schiff in 1924, when the Muirs had returned to Montrose from their first batch of travels in mainland Europe, seems representative of Muir's views as well:

Scotland has been a sad disappointment to us after all the longing we
had for it, so shut in, unresponsive, acridly resolved not to open out and
live. For our own sake, we shall not live here for long . . . . We love the
landscape here, and the lingering twilights, not the people. (2 Aug. 1924;
Butter, 1974 41)

Later in the nineteen fifties, Muir expresses the same kind of feeling in her journal: 'the whole of Scotland is a locked area for me, and I had better keep out of it' (26 Sept. 1955; journal; Sept.-Nov. 1955). Just as Elizabeth in *Imagined Corners* can only imagine surviving if she leaves Scotland, so the Muirs themselves always ended up leaving Scotland with relief after periods spent living there.

There is an extent to which Muir's connection to Scotland is ambiguous from the moment she is made to feel an outsider at the age of two on the streets of Montrose because she speaks in Shetland, not Montrose, Scots. She recalls 'not fitting into Angus tradition' and feeling 'critical, resentful, unsure' because her parents are displaced persons in Angus, emigrants from Shetland (n.d.; journal; 1947-Jan. 1948); in one of her last letters she writes of her reluctance to give up her furniture and books because that felt like 'final homelessness' (Raine; 27 June 1969; see Appendix I). Her ingrained sense of insecurity about herself is more than a female inscription of insecurity taken from the surrounding society's attitudes. It may be grounded in her early sense of the family of having been displaced from Shetland to become outsiders in Montrose, doubtless compounded by the financial insecurity that followed her father's death when she was nine. Muir does not address directly why she and Edwin were so peripatetic; these oblique hints perhaps allow an interpretation that she felt an outsider from very young because of her family background. She then married a man who had lost several of his family when he was still young after a traumatic move from Orkney to Glasgow and who felt even more of an island outsider in mainland Scotland. Muir, first leaving Scotland after university, never apparently settled into an adult feeling of secure Scottishness. This definition of herself as someone whose roots are peripheral to mainland Scotland, just as her gender is defined as peripheral to the male, may provide some explanation as to why, despite occasional hints of nationalist feeling, she rarely publishes or writes privately expressions of Scottish identification or nationalism of the kind that others friends of the nineteen twenties and nineteen thirties espoused (from Hugh MacDiarmid to Helen Cruickshank). Her letter to Cruickshank about the PEN conference in Hungary is an extremely rare expression of the need for a separate assertion of Scotland:

> Our personal difficulties as Scottish delegates must be added to this. From
> the very start we were treated as members of the English delegation, not as
> independent representatives . . . . From all this I would add that a Congress
> in Scotland will be the best and most immediate method of driving the
> fact home to the smaller nations of Europe. The Congress invitation was
> given in the name of *Scotland*, and a thoroughly Scottish Congress in 1934
> would educate a vast mass of opinion throughout Europe. (26 May 1932;
> Butter, 1974 74-75; see also 'Life and context')

It is symptomatic, perhaps, that Muir only felt a need to assert Scottishness when she is away from Scotland in a situation when Scotland is being subsumed ignorantly into 'England'.

Rachel Blau DuPlessis writes of women writers having to 'negotiate with divided loyalties and doubled consciousness, both within and without a social and cultural agreement' (40). This idea of double marginality stems from W. E. B.

DuBois's 'peculiar sensation, the double-consciousness, this sense of always look-ing at one's self through the eyes of others, of measuring one's soul by the tape of the world that looks on in amused contempt and pity' (*The Souls of Black Folk*; cited DuPlessis 208). The idea has been much used in Scottish feminist writing, from Joy Hendry's 'double knot in the peeny' through Alice Brown's 'double democratic deficit' to my own discussion of Scotswomen's feelings of 'a double otherness, a double marginality' (Hendry 291; Brown 204; Christianson, 2002 68, 70). Muir is part of this world of double marginality; all her works address the peripheralisation of women while her letter to Cruickshank addresses the ques-tion of Scotland as a small nation on the periphery of power. But her own sense of marginality comes apparently from her feeling an outsider whose parents are displaced Shetlanders as well as from her femaleness on the edge of the patriarchy of Scotland, reminding us that double marginality itself is an ambiguous feeling that alters in complex ways within the individual.

Muir's feminism is certain and established even though her political action is confined to her student days (in debating or membership of the Suffrage Society) when, according to George Scott, she took part in 'holding up a train in Leuchars station before the first war' (Scott 40), presumably as part of her suffrage activi-ties. Muir's writing style, straightforward, clear, judicious, implies a detachment, an objectivity, yet she never apparently lost her sense of imbalance in the world. Attaching herself to Edwin, to the life of the intelligent freelance writer (but not to the aridities of the 'categorizing intellect' (*Living with Ballads* 260)), helped assuage this sense but could not stop her circling and returning to the same con-cerns all her writing life. She asserts in conclusion to 'Moving in Circles': 'It's my business to think in circles, the wider the better. I'm a woman' (*Listener*, 22 Sept. 1938 603) and her late poem, 'Not for Me', is still making clear her choice of the natural, the flowing and the circular over categorical intellectualisms:

> Not the intellectual-isms,
> categorical, sundering,
> splitting personalities,
> splitting hairs.
>
> For me the curves of an embracing arm,
> or the flowing contours of moving animals
> the joyous freakish shapes of moths and flowers
> on this well-rounded planet. (*Laconincs*; see Appendix IV)

However much she might seem intellectual herself in her education, curiosity and cultural interests, she cannot resist in this poem the binary that opposes warmth to cold, nature to intellect.

Marion Lochhead concludes the first article about Muir and her work with a thoroughly positive response and an entirely valid judgement of Muir: 'It is possible that we have in her one of the best Scots novelists of our time. Both in her rich background of culture and her own immense vitality, she is one of the most fascinating of the women writers of to-day' (*The Bulletin*, 29 March 1933 19; see Appendix I). Muir's 'rich background of culture' can be seen in her poetry as much as in all her other works while her vitality underpins all her life-writing. She writes in the nineteen sixties that she and her female schoolmates had been 'both singers and audience in our singing games' (*Living with Ballads* 13). This expresses the way that Muir is simultaneously singer and audience in her own works, the narrating 'I' and narrated 'I' in her life-writing, with her construction of herself complicated by an awareness of the movement of self between conscious and unconscious. She places in all her writing elements of her own life, interrogating the idea that fiction is separable from the author's life. A prolific life-writer, her constant urge to self-criticism apparently stems from both her self-consciousness and self-awareness. Muir's presence and authority in her life-writing, the intellectual curiosity of her non-fiction works and the imaginative power of her fiction, all these contribute to the sense of a writing life well lived.

This book has been a study of all of Willa Muir's writing; its intention has been to consider her works in the most rounded way possible in order to broaden appreciation and understanding of her fiction and her non-fiction published works while extending analysis to include consideration of her unpublished works and her life-writing in letters and journals. It has been a charting of the intertwining of Muir's life and work, always 'moving in circles', placing both the woman and the work within the framework of her time and world. It is also an assertion of her rightful position in any discussion of modernism and renaissancism and of twentieth century Scottish writing and culture.

# Appendix I

## Willa Muir to Marion Lochhead, 3 March 1933.

Hampstead 1280

7 Downshire Hill,
London. N.W.3
3d March 1933.

Dear M. C. Lochhead:

Every woman her own biographer — wouldn't that bring out some highly-coloured histories! You tempt me, you know, to give my imagination full rein, and to lead you to believe that never was there a woman so cultured, so clever, so handsome, so beloved as myself. Well, well! The facts are very sober, on the other hand, and almost incredibly heavy reading. I don't envy you your job of compiling an article about me. Incidentally, I must apologise for keeping you waiting: you are quite right, I am very busy and also very desperate, for I cannot, no I cannot get my novel finished, and until it is finished I shall be scarcely human; so that is why I did not answer your letter. Your postcard, however, reads like an S.O.S. and so I sit down to fling you a few scraps of information in my present sub-human manner.

*Born 1890. Not* born in Shetland, but in Montrose, of Shetland parents. The first words I spoke were Shetland, and I can still remember being surrounded by a group of Montrose girls who roared and laughed at my outlandish speech.

*1900*   Removed from private school to Board School.

*1902*   Bursary to Montrose Academy.

*1907*   Bursary to St Andrews University.

*October 1910*   M.A. degree, First class Hons Classics.

*1911-14* classical mistress in county Durham

*1914-15* assistant to Prof. of Humanity, St Andrews.

1916-17 – Lecturer, Mansfield Training Centre for Continuation school teachers, Canning Town & Tavistock square, London.

*1919*   married Edwin Muir: set up house in Guilford St, London.

*1920 –* for about eight months headmistress of Debenham & Freebody's Continuation School, London.

*1921*   vanished abroad with Edwin Muir:
*Prague* eight months (once bankrupt)
*Dresden & Hellerau, Germany* eighteen months.
(Helping A. S. Neill with his International School.)
*Italy* six months: Forte dei Marmi, seacoast near Carrara.

Salzburg & Vienna *Austria* six months — bankrupt again, and took refuge with Neill on a Sonntagberg mountain where he had shifted to, after Communist government established in Saxony.

Here we began translating, because a New York publisher asked us to, and as we had no money at all we could not say "no". We have translated ever since.

*1924*   came to England and tried living in a cottage in Penn. Damp cottage — no go.

*1925*   commissioned to translate that bugbear, Jew Suss. Went to St Tropez, France, on the strength of it, and translated the book there.

*1926-7* Living in Mentone, France.

*1927*   My son, Gavin, due to arrive, so we came to England.

*1927 — up to date*: still in England. Living first in Surrey, then in the depths of Sussex; recently moved to London.

How do we live? Translating from the German, reading German books for publishers, doing anything that turns up.

How do we want to live? On the proceeds of our own creative work.

Apparently quite impossible.

My own publications — apart from the translations — are very few.
*Women, an Enquiry* [sic]— An essay published by the Hogarth Press in 1924 [sic].
*Imagined Corners.* A novel published by Secker, 1931.

But I am finishing *Mrs Ritchie* of which I have some hopes. It is — or will be — much better than my first novel. However, I think my best piece of work is Gavin — a large, well-made, healthy clever boy!

I have become terribly interested in the motive power of *symbolism* in all our thoughts & actions, & this, I think, is to some extent worked out in "Mrs Ritchie". There is much work that I could still do in this direction.

And, finally, when we translate a book, we divide it in two: after we have finished, Edwin goes over my half ruthlessly, and I go over his half ruthlessly, and the combined effort is put together. We have no hesitation in cutting each other's versions to pieces in the interests of the final product.

*Photographs.* I have none of which I am not ashamed, except snapshots. Perhaps some day I will be photographed satisfactorily. The difficulty lies in the fact that I have naturally a grave, heavy horse-like face, but that it is a mobile face when I am speaking and creates the illusion of good looks, which no photograph ever confirms! Consequently I dislike photographs of myself, and I don't want to send you one.[1]

I really do know something about Latin & Greek,

Ditto ditto about German.

I know a little about education & psychology.

I have a smattering of music and can play the ocarina and make a loud noise in a chorus.

I am a very bad housekeeper, but a good cook.

I smoke and drink and in my youth I played cards a lot.

I like fun and high spirits, and I like a serious argument, but in between these two extremes I am not very competent socially.

Altogether; I do not see how you are to write that article at all!

Perhaps it could be summarised by describing me as half a "stickit" scholar,[2] with scholarly & intellectual leanings, and half a temperamental woman: if I were whole-heartedly one or the other life would be much easier for me. I drive too many incompatible horses in my team. As a scholar, a writer, a psychologist, I have a conscience: but when I feel daft I have no conscience at all. The only hopeful thing about me is that I am more civilised now than I was at twenty, and with increasing age I may become completely civilised.

Yours sincerely

Willa Muir.

[Willa Muir to Marion Lochhead, 3 March 1933; MS: NLS 26190.95; pbd. in part: McCulloch, 2004 212-13. Marion Lochhead (1902-85), poet, social historian, apparently did not know Muir at this time, although they later became friends. Like her friend Helen Cruickshank, she was a founder member of Scottish PEN.]

1. Lochhead's article (see 196) is illustrated in column two by a photograph of Muir with the caption: 'Willa Muir is the wife and collaborator of Edwin Muir, and they have a son, Gavin. He, however, has not yet contributed to the literary partnership, being just six years old'. The photograph was apparently taken especially as its reproduction as an illustration to Catriona Soukup's 'Willa in Wartime', *Chapman* 71 (1992-93) 21, identifies it as 'Studio photograph of Willa Muir taken during the mid-1930s (photo courtesy Irene Abenheimer / Ethel Ross [Edwin's nieces])'. For the photograph, see frontispiece.

2. Stickit: shut out, prevented from advancement into a position for which they are qualified.

# WOMEN'S INTERESTS

*Scottish Women Writers of To-day*

# WILLA MUIR AND HER WORK
### Translator, Novelist and Poet

*By MARION C. LOCHHEAD*

IT is fitting that, in a country that has always had a decent pride in learning, so many of our women writers of to-day are scholars, with their creative work solidly based on an intellectual heritage. Among them Willa Muir takes high place. Indeed the full force of her intelligence is not yet felt, for even her best work, so far, hardly does her justice.

Mention of her name would probably draw from most people the response: 'Willa Muir? Oh, yes! She translated "Jew Süss", didn't she?' That was certainly no small achievement; but it is as an original writer that Mrs Muir chiefly counts, and as such she must be estimated.

### Lass o' Pairts

Her parents were natives of Shetland, but she herself was born in Montrose — though as a child, she spoke the Shetland dialect, to the huge amusement of her schoolfellows. She was a 'lass o' pairts', and after her schooldays in Montrose went, with a bursary, to St Andrews University, where in three years she took her degree with a First in Classics. A tolerable record.

For the next nine years she held various appointments: held a scholarship, was classical mistress in County Durham, was classical lecturer in her University, then a research scholar, and a lecturer in London. In 1920 she married her distinguished fellow-Scot and fellow-writer, Edwin Muir, and they set up house in London.

For some months she was headmistress of Debenham and Freebody's Continuation School. Then, in 1921, she and her husband went abroad for about six years. They have lived in many parts of Europe, both expert linguists. Prague, Dresden, Austria and France all held them for a while. Part of their time was spent with their friend, A. S. Neill, the famous 'dominie', whom they helped in his international school.

## Literary Partners

During a brief return to London Mr and Mrs Muir were commissioned to translate 'Jew Süss', and on the strength of it went to Mentone, where most of that joint task was done. In 1927 they returned to England, where their son Gavin was born. At first they lived in Surrey, later in Sussex; they are now London-Scots, settled in Hampstead. Last year they officially represented the Scottish P.E.N. at the International Congress in Budapest, and by their valiant championship placed their fellow-members deeply in their debt.

Translation and reading of German books make their bread-and-butter; the ambition of both is their own creative work. Apart from German translation Mrs Muir has done a few songs from the Auvergnat into terse Lowland Scots. Here is one, 'The Wee Man' (Lou Pitchiout Omé):—

*I dinna want a wee man, a wee man,*
*I winna ha'e a wee man, he wadna dae*
*ava!*
*If I set him at the table, the table, the*
*table,*
*The cock wad come and peck at him,*
*and peck him clean awa'!*
*If I set him in the garden, the garden,*
*the garden,*
*The pig wad come and grumph at him,*
*and grumph him clean awa!*
*If I set him on the hillside, the hillside,*
*the hillside,*
*The stanes wad fa' upon him, and knock*
*him clean awa'!*
*If I set him at the water-side, the water-*
*side, the water-side,*
*The tide wad rise and catch at him, and*
*wash him clean awa'!*
*O, I dinna want a wee man, a wee man,*
*a wee man.*
*I winna ha'e a wee man, he wadna dae*
*ava'!*

## Solo Performance

Off her own bat, as it were, Mrs Muir has published an essay 'Women: An Enquiry' (1924) [sic], and a novel, 'Imagined Corners' (1931). She is at the moment finishing another novel, 'Mrs Ritchie', which she thinks will be an advance on anything she has yet done. But — 'My best piece of work is Gavin', she declares.

Scholar and linguist, expert in education and psychology, a lover of music, 'a bad housekeeper, but a good cook' (to quote herself), Willa Muir is a figure of unusual strength and vitality. And strength and vitality are the first qualities discovered in her novel.

'Imagined Corners' describes, vividly, a Scots provincial town, dealing chiefly with one family, the Shands. It is neither steeped in the sentimentality of the Kailyard, nor is it a protest in the manner of 'The House with the Green Shutters'. The characters are alive and credible, and they develop in the course of the action. Especially the younger Elizabeth, who is indeed only coming to her maturity when the book ends.

As a creative artist Mrs Muir is only just coming to her full powers. Whether she will cultivate her real poetic gift, or develop as a novelist, with a subtle use of 'symbolism' (which is her own hope) is an alluring question. It is possible that we have in her one of the best Scots novelists of our time. Both in her rich background of culture and her own immense vitality, she is one of the most fascinating of the women writers of to-day.

[Marion C. Lochhead, 'Willa Muir and her Work: Translator, Novelist and Poet', *The Bulletin and Scots Pictorial* (29 March 1933) 19]

Two of Willa Muir's late letters to Kathleen Raine.


Church Farm / Over / Cambridgeshire                    27 June 1969

My dearest Kathleen: I am now hurling a hand grenade at you. When I leave
here (end of Sept or beginning of Oct.) I am going to St Andrews, Fife to live
with Lovey Scott. I have resisted her pleas for at least a year, but she burst
upon me recently and argued and cajoled and swore there was a plane service
from Heathrow to Leuchars, and bribed me in addition with offering to get
me a kitten (!) — and, in short, I gave in and said: yes, all right. The obstacle
to my finding a lodging in the South has just been my books and bits of furniture which I did not want to dispose of (final homelessness) and which Lovey
is ready and eager to take in. I think by that time I shall be able for the journey
— I have now days of relative *betterness* although, my dear, I am not able yet to
go on a visit, much as I should love to come to you. (And to surprise Popsy.)
Well, I feel as if in October I shall be going to see the Wizard, the wonderful
Wizard of Oz — next stage (and I hope the last) on my Pilgrim's Progress.

My other item of news is that Gavin should be in Ely today — for how long
he did not say on the letter announcing that he was coming. I suppose I shall
see him and Dorothy sometime this weekend: there is no communication
yet —
— I do get bored here. The patients are all bed-ridden except me and the old
lady of 98 who cannot hear, will not use a stick, tries to walk on her own, fails,
and demands constant attention — Not my cup of tea, at all, but I must put
up with it. My physiotherapist is good & the part-time village women are very
nice people. But — !

Jiřina Haukova wrote, wanting to know why you never came to Prague —
really, I think, fishing for an invitation. Much love, Willa —

Church Farm / Over / Cambs.                                         2 July 1969

Dear Kathleen —The post comes here at breakfast time, when I am at my most vulnerable, so your letter this morning made me cry my eyes out. Hard facts are dispiriting, but do not vanish.

H.F.1 You are going to Ireland in September. (Could you give me the date of your leaving?)

H.F.2. I cannot go to St Andrews in September because Lovey Scott won't be there till the end of September, which is why we arranged for me to go as soon thereafter as I can. She is starting and running a tea-shop in Falkland for the thousands of visitors to Falkland Palace who can't get a cup of tea anywhere in the town.

H.F.3. This place, Church Farm, has two poodles who would eat Popsy up if she came here. Well, since you rule out a Cat Home — (I don't.) I believe Nellie le Grey would take Popsy, perhaps Popsy and me, until we went to Heathrow together, with the help (I hope) of Spike. All this has to be found out — perhaps Nellie won't take us, perhaps Lovey has changed her plans, perhaps anything. But if you wish tell me *when* you leave for Ireland, I shall see to it somehow.

Thank you for keeping Popsy so long. She has had a good life and I ought not to be so afflicted at the thought of putting her down, but I *am* afflicted.
O, Hard Fact 4: Lovey has no garden.
H-F-5- (nothing to do with Popsy) Dorothy is booked to have a hysterectomy, — womb removed — I don't think my soft-hearted Gavin is likely to divorce in the meantime, anyhow.

I am not so bad as long as I stick to my walking frame; without it I am still restricted to short little totters. But I am told I *look* better.
I hope this letter is coherent, for I am not very! / Willa.


[Willa Muir to Kathleen Raine, 27 June and 2 July 1969; MS: NLS 19703.208 and 209. Kathleen Raine (1908-2003, poet.]

# Appendix II
## Clock-a-doodle-doo

They were all wag-at-the-wa' clocks, but of every conceivable size and shape, and they covered three walls of the room, which had a fourth wall of clear glass as if it were an enormous show-case. Every day a Woman opened a little side-door and came in to wind up any weights that had run down. She always came in just when the sunlight, having fingered its way round half the room, touching clock after clock, had withdrawn for a siesta on the floorboards before creeping back to finger the clocks on the other half of the walls. She handled the weights lovingly as if she liked feeling them, and the clocks were excited and glad to see her, so that they whirred and chimed in unison no less than twelve strokes, the maximum effort of which they were capable. A great deal of their tick-talking and clock-clacking was concerned with her and her doings, yet she never showed the least interest in their mechanism, except for the weights, and the clocks, who were proud of the cog-wheels inside their heads, especially when daylight failed and they could not see each other, were puzzled by her indifference. In the dark they lived only in their cog-wheels and so the shadow that hid each clock from its neighbour was also a shadow of fear, for if a wheel were to fail in the night or a spindle break the damaged clock could not ever show a face to the world but was as if annihilated. In the dark, therefore, they were resentful of the Woman's indifference, but they did not discuss her except to accuse her of stupidity, for they were eager to forget their fear by speculating on the nature of cog-wheels and propounding theories for their repair. Every night the discussion waxed, in liveliness until the defiance of the clocks culminated in striking midnight, after which they relapsed contentedly into the hum-drum routine of the small hours where little effort was needed.

On moonlight nights, however, the liveliness continued as long as the moonshine lasted. And on these occasions they speculated about the moon, arguing that it must be a super-clock, permanently lit-up and delivered from the fear of darkness, not to speak of its power to [47] move freely, if erratically, across the wall of the sky. One very grandfatherly clock, reputed to be the oldest inhabitant, sought in vain to discourage what he called the heresy of revering the moon; the other clocks were tired of hearing his admonitions to honour the punctual sun, which was, he said, the Author of their Being: 'He is like ourselves, only greater. He too vanishes from sight in the darkness. He too is regular in his movements—does he not visit us daily, each in turn, to watch over our welfare and to remind us that we belong to the great cosmic rhythm of Time? Your moon is no clock-face, your moon spins round until only its edge is visible, your moon is merely the sun's pendulum.'

'Bah!' said the young, impatient clocks, and they said it loudly ten times so that the wheezing, grandfatherly clock was quite inaudible. 'Of course the moon is a clock-face. Can we not see the signs upon it although they are difficult to read?'

'Use your cog-wheels, old fool, use your cog-wheels,' added a very Clever Clock, who claimed to have twice as many cog-wheels as any of the others. 'It's face-values you're trying to foist on us, face-value wrapped up in pious sentimentality. If the sun takes the trouble to visit us it's because he thinks it worth his while. And as for you,' he addressed the young clocks, 'it's face-values you're serving too, the whole clacking of you, when you say that you admire the moon *although* you can't read its face! Admire it rather *because* it is illegible, because its meaning lies hidden in its private cog-wheels, because it is an intricate and baffling piece of mechanism, unlike your hum-drum, bourgeois sun.'

The moon shone straight in upon the Clever Clock. 'Ah! I am lit-up too!' he cried. 'Now I shall tell you the truth. The numbers on our faces are only a device to keep us marking time, to prevent us from inquiring into the nature of reality ——'

He had to break off to strike Eleven, and this made him furious; besides, in spite of his multifarious cog-wheels, his voice was not the loudest in the room. A much simpler-looking clock on his right had a fuller, more resonant chime, and the Clever Clock, aware of his superior intricacy, kicked his pendulum petulantly as far as it would go.

'I appeal to my friends on the left,' he exclaimed, as soon as the echoes had died away. 'What is this so-called Time to which we [48] are bound in slavery? Can anyone define it? Is it anything but an ideological figment?'

These words impressed the young clocks. And when the Clever Clock went on to point out that the Truth of things lay inside their own heads, and was to be discovered only by the study of their own cog-wheels, they were interested. But when the Clever Clock said that a knowledge of the springs of their own conduct would enable each of them to detach himself from routine and become an independent moon, they were elated.

'Let us make a beginning — any beginning!' they cried.
'Good,' said the Clever Clock, 'Watch me.'

He shrugged and twisted himself until he had dislocated the numbers on his face, so that they were all in the wrong places.

'That is the first step towards illegibility,' he announced, 'the first step on the road to freedom. *A nous la liberté!*' And he struck Twelve on a high, tinny note of exulatation, with both his hands pointing to the number One. 'Now I shall withdraw into myself and meditate on my cog-wheels,' he said. 'I have already made several important discoveries ——'

'Do tell us,' buzzed the clocks. But at that moment the moon fled behind a cloud-bank and the clocks began to be a little fearful at the return of darkness. The Clever Clock felt their fear creeping into him, and muttered 'Fools!' so savagely that the clocks did not dare to address him again that night.

Now the Clever Clock had really discovered something. By listening very intently to himself he had discovered that his cog-wheels were interlocking and moved each other. But which of them was the *primum mobile*? He groaned in private over the difficulty of his task. 'If I could only be quit of this nonsense of striking the hours!' he reflected. 'What I want is Pure Horological Thought . . . . [Muir's ellipses]' He fell into a kind of trance, murmuring to himself: 'I am I. I am my cog-wheels.' This so refreshed his self-conceit that on the morning after, when the other clocks looked uneasily at his face, wondering what the Woman would say, he tick-tocked and clack-clacked more arrogantly than ever. 'She won't dare to say anything. She is a mere servant of the cog-wheels. Does she not handle our weights simply and solely to minister to the cog-wheels?' he declared, and was proved right, too, for the Woman did not look at his face at all. [49] He was a clock who could run for months at a time without her, and she disregarded him. 'In any case,' said the Clever Clock, after she had gone, 'she is stupid. And so are most of you — all of you. Marking time is all you're fit for. Not one of you is capable of becoming a free agent, except myself. However, when I am a moon I shall be lit-up for ever, and I shall be famous when you are all on the scrap-heap.'

'No, no!' cried several young clocks, so young that they were almost watches. 'We want to be lit-up too!'

'How can you take him seriously?' growled the grandfatherly clock.

The Clever Clock interrupted him. 'We must free our terminology from the materialism of content, if we are to discover the laws of Pure Horological Thought,' he said rapidly, impressing his audience once more.

At that moment the finger of the sun touched him, giving him a warm, tickling sensation which was so pleasant that, even while reminding himself how much he despised sensation, he forgot momentarily to continue talking. As the sun slid over him the carved detail on his case stood out clearly, and one could see what a very fine clock he had been meant to be. Twelve little wooden figures stood in niches around the clock-case, and an angel with a little trumpet was perched on the very top. There could be no doubt that his intricate machinery had been planned to set these figures in motion, but something must have gone wrong, for they were gathering dust, and looked a little forlorn. And the Clever Clock, pondering his cog-wheels, had never even suspected that what they really needed was the adjustment of a minute pinion to set the little figures dancing. There was a tiny screw loose in the Clever Clock, but he was too busy boasting and studying Pure Horological Thought to observe anything of the kind.

He felt restless again when the finger of the sun left him. The Daily Dope! he muttered to himself, sneering at the travelling beam of light. And he shrugged himself so hard that his numbers fell into confusion; one of them even came off and tinkled on to the floor. That delighted the Clever Clock.

'Now I am well on the way to become unintelligible,' he said. 'I an unique among clocks!'

'But you are still marking Time,' retorted the grandfatherly [50] clock, for at that moment the Clever Clock had to strike Two along with all the others. This so exasperated him that with a violent kick he dislodged the balancing weight from his pendulum.

'Now I am Really Unique,' he gasped, somewhat out of breath, since his pendulum was clacking wildly. 'Now I can swing from one extreme to the other as much as I like! There is no other clock like me in the whole universe. Clack-clack! Clack-clack! CLACK! Not one of you can do this! Clack-clack-clack-clack!!'

'Oo-oo-oh!' cried the young clocks, feeling excited. 'What marvellous high-kicking!'

And that night, when he was lit-up, the Clever Clock set all the others to shrugging and kicking in imitation of him, crying at top-speed:

'This is — clackety-clack — this is the Horological Renaissance!'

When the Woman came in the next day her foot struck against a little pile of discarded numbers and a pendulum balance. Also, she could hear the Clever Clock clack-clacking at furious speed. She reached up and took him from the wall and blew the dust off the little wooden figures.

'Watch me!' said the Clever Clock to the admiring young clocks. 'Now I move from the wall as I promised you. This Woman is the servant of my will.'

And he went out in her arms and the door shut behind them.

['Clock-a-doodle-do', *The Modern Scot* 5 (June 1934) 46-50 (original page numbers are inserted above); repbd: Moira Burgess (ed.), *The Other Voice* (Edinburgh: Polygon, 1987) 168-72]

# Appendix III

## *Mrs Muttoe and the Top Storey*

[The concluding nightmare, 267-84]

The soaring edifice of the Money fabric loomed high before Alison Muttoe. Somewhere within it she would find a cook. She peered at it, staring up at its many pinnacles.

It was like a faint pencil silhouette on grey paper rather than a solid structure. Yet while she peered at it something very curious must have happened, for she became aware that she was clinging to its outer surfaces like a fly on a window-pane. Her nose was pressed against a hard, glassy substance through which she could see bewildering activities going on in the interior. Small human structures, with windowed top-storeys and jointed arm-cranes, were swarming on Meccano-like legs through an endless perspective of corridors and offices apparently made of the same transparent, resilient substance against which her nose was pressed. She could distinguish a succession of upper storeys receding above her as far as the eye could see, and three — or was it four? — floors beneath her the building descended into what looked like a vast pit.

The arena of this pit was covered with a mass of moving humans, divided into sections by straight lines radiating like spokes of a wheel from some far-off central point. The curved side of the pit rose smooth and glassy above the moving masses, unscalable except for extremely short ladders that hung down here and there. Alison noted these ladders only because the humans at the circumference of the pit were continually climbing on the backs of their fellows in an effort to catch hold of a rung and gain a footing on one of them. Then she saw that each floor had its ladders dangling at the outer wall of the fabric, though none of these were so short as the ladders hanging down into the pit. There was a ladder immediately before her own face. Apparently she was stuck midway between two floor-levels, and that was why the perspectives looked so baffling. Dear me, a human in the pit had actually managed to scramble on to a ladder. The massed crowd beneath him gaped upwards, watching him as he scuttled up it as fast as he could, until he climbed over the edge of the next floor-level, where he merged in the smaller crowds that thronged there. But why should there be little ladders leading from floor to floor when there were so many lift-shafts, or what looked like lift-shafts, away in the interior of the fabric?

Alison strained her eyes to make out whether the lifts were really lifts. Each office had a pair of lift-doors opening on to its own section; surely these must be lift-shafts? As she peered at them, she made out the inscriptions above the nearest pair of lift-doors; one was marked "Goods Ascending", and the other, "Profits Descending". Unlike the framework of the fabric, these lift-shafts and doors were made of solid-looking metal; one could not see what they enclosed. Suddenly a bell whirred on the level beneath her, and a small group of humans ran across the floor to the door marked "Goods". Yes, it was a lift; the door rolled back to display an ordinary lift-compartment filled with boxes and packages of various sizes. The humans began to drag these out and wrap them up in extra packing paper. It seemed to be a kind of competitive game, since each man used a different colour of paper and tried to wrap as many packages as possible in it, working as fast as he could. One of them succeeded in grabbing nearly half the packages, whipping his blue paper round bales and boxes at incredible speed, while the green, the orange, the purple and the red parcels multiplied much more slowly. When the goods were all wrapped in the various colours they were bundled back into the lift; the door closed and the lift moved noiselessly upwards, heralded by a whirring bell on the next floor level. Peering through the transparent roof above her, Alison watched the group of humans waiting up there for the coloured goods; what could they intend to do with them? Again the lift doors rolled back, again the humans seized the packages and dragged them out, but this time they merely branded the various parcels and boxes with rubber stamps, again apparently striving against each other, before bundling everything back into the ascending lift. What happened to the cargo on the higher levels Alison could not make out; her attention, in any case was distracted by a descending lift that stopped on the floor above her almost as soon as the branded goods were despatched. There was a uniformed official inside this lift-compartment; he handed out what looked like small bags of coin and a largish block of some transparent substance, — probably the same substance of which the entire fabric was constructed, thought Alison, since it was apparently hard enough to be dumped on the floor below and chipped with a hatchet. What was left of it after each human had had his whack went back into the lift and down to the floor below, where the same process was repeated. The energetic human who wielded the blue packing papers had managed to chip off a large chunk of the stuff; he hugged it in his arms and with a gleeful air leaped up on to the nearest ladder, which happened to be the ladder in front of Alison. His feet seemed to be advancing over her body, although he obviously did not see her at all, and she could not help flinching. Arrived on the next floor, he deposited his chunk of precious transparency in a strong box of some kind, and rubbed his hands in satisfaction.

At this moment, Alison became aware that someone from below was trying to dislodge her from her place on the outer skin of the fabric, and that a female voice was calling up irritably: "Let me pass, please!"

"Can't you go round me?" she asked back, since she was afraid of loosing her footing if she moved. "Can't you let me pass?" repeated the voice. "Don't you see that my husband has just gone up? You *must* let me pass."

"Oh, all right," said Alison, cautiously beginning to edge sideways across the glassy slope, "if you insist." A female crawled up alongside and stopped to take breath, remarking: "Are you going up or coming down?"

"I really don't know," said Alison.
"Well, you'd better make up your mind," said the female, "instead of blocking the way like that."

She began to climb again, and Alison said: "Hi! What's up there? Where are you going?"

"I'm going up to the thousand-a-year level, my good woman," said the female. Her feet were already scrabbling on the slope above Alison's head. At the risk of falling off and breaking her neck, Alison braced her hands against the glassy fabric and gazed straight upwards. Like the roof above her, a broad balcony ran right round the outside of the Money fabric, on the same level as the next floor. The female climber was just hoisting herself on to it through a trap-door.

"There must be a balcony at each floor level," thought Alison, "and I'd better get down to the one below me; it isn't very safe here on the slope."

She was so preoccupied with the problem of keeping her footing as she toed her way down that she had no attention to spare for the interior activities of the fabric itself. Little by little she lowered herself until the next balcony stretched beneath her. Rectangular buildings, like nests of boxes, filled the space below her, but she saw a narrow lane between two of them, slithered safely down it, and stood up.

This balcony was very broad, broader than the one above had seemed to be. It was as broad as a street, indeed it was very like a one-sided street, with a plain wall bounding its outer verge. Small motor-cars whizzed along it, and small-brightly-painted houses clustered against the wall of the fabric like the cells of a honeycomb.

Alison strolled along past them, noticing a large street sign in decorative letters: "The Social Round".

She met nothing but women. None of these females apparently did any shopping, thought Alison, wondering a little at the absence of shops. Presently, however, she came to a pair of lift-doors between two houses; each was marked "Service", and each had a row of labelled push-buttons beside it. The buttons of the right-hand lift said Grocer, Butcher, Baker, Dairy, Laundry, and so on, while those of the left-hand lift announced Cook, Housemaid, Cook-general. Apparently one pressed the appropriate button and the Money fabric delivered what one needed.

Alison pressed the one marked Cook. There was some delay before the lift-door opened, and it disclosed instead of a cook a female official in uniform who said snappily: "Sorry, shortage of cooks at the moment; try again later." The service lift clanged shut again.

Hearing an angry murmur behind her Alison turned round to see a group of females, each opening and shutting a large handbag.

"They're sending all the cooks up higher, that's what it is," said one of them. "We have no luck on this level."

"What level is this?"

"This is the five-hundred-a-year level, of course," said the female. "Don't you know where your husband works, or your father?"

"I don't think my husband's in the fabric at all," said Alison. "At least I hope he isn't."

"The woman's a fool," said the voice. All the females turned their backs on Alison and stalked away.

The floor beneath her feet jarred a little, and she perceived that she was standing on a trap-door through which someone was trying to emerge. Hastily she stepped aside, and since the emerging female seemed to find a difficulty in hoisting herself up, she bent down and gave her a helping hand.

"Ta muchly," said the newcomer, dusting herself. "That wasn't half a climb, I can tell you. I never thought I'd make it. Where's my old man got to?"

"What's it like down below?"

"Coo, I'm going to have one of them baby cars . . . . There ain't many cars down below, if that's what you want to know, dearie."

"No, it's a cook I want," said Alison. "I suppose I can get down through this trap-door?" She began to lower herself.

"One good turn deserves another," said the jolly newcomer. "I'll hold it open for you, though what you want to go down there for beats me."

Again Alison slithered and toed her way down the glassy slope. To right and left of her, some distance away, she could see the flat dark bands of the service lift-shafts, striping the surface of the fabric like metal ribbons. These bands of metal apparently ran right up to the top of the colossal structure. What kind of service did one get on the higher floors? Butler, valet, lady's maid, governess, said Alison to herself; cocktails, of course, and early morning tea. Cooks must be sent all the way up from the basement, or near it; the further down she slid, the closer she would get to the source of supply.

The next balcony was even broader than the one she had just quitted, yet it was more crowded. There were indeed fewer cars, and these mostly aged-looking, but there was a profusion of bicycles and perambulators. The houses were smaller and less brightly-coloured, the balcony floor more littered, the women shabbier. Most of them were laden with marketing-bags and baskets. Alison hurried to the nearest Service lift to see what the new push-buttons said. "Tea, sugar, flour, lard," she read, "soap, washing-powder, dog biscuits . . . " Among the left-hand items, which resembled those on a restaurant menu, at the very bottom of the list, next to "Cup of coffee 2d and 4d" she discovered: "Mother's Help", "Charwoman", and in extremely small letters, "Cook-general."

"Cup of coffee first," she thought and pressed the coffee-button. A loud-speaker somewhere above her said: "Put in the money, then press button B."

"But I haven't any money," said Alison to herself. She must have spoken aloud, for a passer-by said reprovingly: "Pay as you go, like all respectable people."

Ignoring this comment, Alison pressed the Cook-general button and stood waiting. A slot appeared beside the button, showing a metal tag which said: Out of Order.

No cooks on this level either? Alison began to shake the lift-doors, as if they belonged to a penny-in-a-slot machine which had refused to function.

"Got the wrong change back?" said a kindly voice behind her.

"No," said Alison, turning round to see a female with a shopping-bag, "no, I was wanting a cook-general, and it says 'Out of Order'."

"Been out of order a long time, that has," said the kindly shopper. "Where have you been not to know that?"

"I've just come down to this balcony."

"Come down in the world, eh? Well, you've a lot to learn yet."

Alison caught her by the shopping-bag as she turned away and said: "Do tell me, please, what level is this."

"Two-hundred-and-fifty pound a year," answered the female with visible pride.

"And what's below this?"

Briefly, as if the subject was distasteful, came the answer:

"Hundred and fifty".

"And below that?"

"Below that's not worth mentioning," said the shopper, suddenly ceasing to be at all kindly.

"Thank you," said Alison, "I think I'll go down and see for myself. Where's the trap-door?"

"If you're going to let yourself down to *that* level, you'd better not ask *me* to be a party to it," said the other indignantly.

Alison appealed to another female, who was pushing a perambulator with two children in it: "Where's the nearest trap-door, can you tell me?"

"The nearest way up, you mean, surely?"

"No, I want to go down, not up."

"You want to go down?" repeated the female, looking frightened.

"What's so odd about that?" asked Alison. "I want to see for myself what it looks like down there. Besides, I want a cook."

"Your husband hasn't gone down, I suppose?"

"No, not so far as I know."

"Slumming, are you? There's an air service for slummers, but I don't know if it stops at this floor."

"No, I'm not exactly slumming: I just want to see for myself. Can you tell me where there's a trap-door?"

"If your husband had gone down, you wouldn't need to ask; a trap-door would open under your feet, where you didn't expect it," said the female in a half-whisper. "There's trap-doors all over the place . . . Shsh, we never talk about these things in front of the kiddies."

"Oh, I'm sorry," said Alison. "But how can I find one of these contraptions?"

"Try pressing button B without putting in the money," said the female in a low scared voice, pushing her perambulator quickly away from Alison.

"That's easy," said Alison to herself, returning to the Service lift. Just at that moment a light van, painted red, white and blue, with a loud-speaker on it, came roaring past. Alison tried to catch what it was saying, for she was eager to learn whatever there was to know about life on the balconies of the Money fabric. "Eat more fruit," roared the van. "Drink More Milk. Beer is Best. Buy British." With another screech, which, as far as she could make out, recommended an increased consumption of herring, the van curved out of sight and hearing.

"That's the hearty van," said a young passer-by, with a cheerful grin. "Here's the sob-sisters coming."

A funereal-looking van now came gliding past, running much more smoothly and slowly than the other.

". . . . Night Starvation," the loud speaker was saying, in a mellifluous, persuasive voice. "That's why she was looking so tired and washed-out. But in less than six months' time her friends were remarking that Mary was the most popular girl at the club dances. She never," said the loud-speaker impressively, "Lacked a Partner. And soon she was a Happy Bride." At this point, the loud-speaker gave a deprecating little cough and went off on another tack: "Do your friends begin to avoid you? Do you wonder why you aren't invited to parties? Halitosis . . . "

"Dear me," thought Alison, "the people at this level seem to be well looked-after."

She faced the Service lift again and studied the left-hand items. Bacon and Two Eggs, 1/4d. With a curious flicker the 4 turned into a 5, while she was looking at it. The tail of her eye caught another flicker, lower down: was it Glass of Milk that had changed price, or Fruit Salad? Certainly, Cup of Coffee, which had been 2d or 4d, was now 3d or 6d. "Eat More Fruit", said Alison to herself, "Drink More Milk . . . Well, then."

She pressed both the Fruit Salad button and the Glass of Milk button.

Above her head, the mechanical voice reiterated: "Put in the money, then press button B. Put in the money, then press button B."

Button B? There were two buttons, one on either side. Extending both arms Alison put a firm forefinger first on one and then on the other.

A shrill buzz came from the loud-speaker above her head, and the left-hand door began to roll back slowly. Alison just had time to see a Glass of Milk and a plate of Fruit Salad set on a small table inside the lift, when the buzz changed to a siren wail, and the loud-speaker began to shriek: "Thief! Thief! Thief!" The lift door clanged shut. A police whistle blew. Beside Alison a large trap-door suddenly opened, and without looking over her shoulder, since she felt waves of hostility converging on her and heard the sound of running feet, she hastily let herself down through it.

There was no foot-hold. She was falling straight down a shaft of the same transparent material as the Money fabric, passing the next balcony so quickly that it seemed only a vague blur through the glassy wall; she was falling down, down, down . . .

A large policeman at the foot of the shaft caught her and swung her to her feet, so that the shock of her landing was somewhat broken. She felt bruised and shaken, but intact.

"First Offence," said the policeman curtly. "Out you go, and don't do it again."

A revolving door pushed Alison out on to a deserted sidewalk.

It was a blank, dreary passage-way, running between two high, glassy walls, with the floor of the first balcony, Alison guessed, for a roof. It was startlingly empty; it contained nothing to occupy the attention, not even an advertising poster; in itself it was entirely featureless, an apparently infinite extension of monotony. But, for compensation, the transparent walls enclosing it allowed one to watch scenes of the most varied interest; on one side lay the vast pit in the basement of the Money fabric, on the other side a perspective of fields and woods, with distant mountains visible on the horizon.

Forgetting the policeman, forgetting the cell from which revolving doors had newly thrust her out, Alison paused to gaze at the entrancing view of the countryside. In the nearer fields she could see human figures at work, — hoeing turnips, she fancied. Ripening wheat waved behind them against a back-ground of beech-trees, and in the foreground some hay-cocks stood on a green aftermath of young clover . . . Between the hedge-rows dividing the hay-cocks and the turnips from the wheat, she could see flat rectangular objects moving along at intervals, black, maroon, fawn — why, these were the tops of motor-cars! A road must run there, a real country road! And was that not a large red bus lumbering along in their wake? A London double-decker! . . . .Well if one could ride into the heart of a summer afternoon among fields and woods, on a regular London bus, there was no need to feel trapped, was there?

Alison's spirits began to mount. After all, she had come down of her own free will, to see what was to be seen in the basement of the Money fabric. There must be some way of escape from the monotonous, blank passage . . . At intervals, on both sides, revolving doors were set. True, in a little cell behind each of them a policeman was on guard. But there must be *some* way out large enough for a bus; a smooth road spiralling down from balcony to balcony, most likely, for the convenience of the inhabitants who wanted to drive into the country-side. Sooner or later she was bound to find it.

Meanwhile, she had better see what was happening in the pit. She crossed to the inner wall, the wall of fabric, and peered through it . . . As far as her eyes could see, the vast arena was crammed with humans engaged in the most diverse activities. It was difficult at first to distinguish individuals, there was such a whirling of wheels and flashing of shuttles and dipping of large frames, such a swinging of hammers and shunting to and fro of trucks; it made her eyeballs ache to look at so much bewildering movement . . . It was a relief to follow the straight lines which ran undeviatingly, like the spokes of a giant wheel, towards the obscure interior and divided the humans into sections . . . But these straight lines were blurring with movement — or was it her own eyes that were blurring? No; the straight lines were moving conveyor-belts.

Alison gazed, in fascination, at the nearest of these belts. The mechanical fingers of workers were busy all along it, putting things on, snatching things off; an interminable procession of articles went sliding towards the interior, by tens, by twenties, by hundreds, by thousands . . . Match-sticks undipped, match-sticks dipped, boxes of matches, wrapped packets of match-boxes, parcels of packets of boxes of matches . . . Where were they all going to? Where did the match-sticks come from? . . . Oh, the trucks! They rolled around unceasingly, at right angles to the conveyor belts; trucks with logs supplying trucks with planks, with billets of wood, with bundles of sticks, sticks cut, split, chopped and fed to the conveyor belt, match-sticks undipped, match-sticks dipped, boxes of matches, wrapped packets of match-boxes . . .

She shut her eyes for a moment and leaned her head against the smooth, cold wall. This was like a nightmare. How could they stand it, the workers who waited tensely beside the belt, snatching things off, putting things on, for ever and ever, amen?

And there were females among them . . . Or had she imagined the females? On the upper levels the females were nearly all outside the Money fabric, on the adjoining balconies. Surely, if there were females on the floor of this pit, any of them would gladly exchange her job for a cook's place in the Muttoes' house? . . .

Alison opened her eyes again, pressed her nose against the glassy wall, and stared as steadily as she could at the scene within. Biscuits, tooth-brushes, bars of soap, hats; by twenties, by hundreds, by thousands . . . bicycle-bells, door-handles, cigarettes . . .

"Don't look at the belts, you idiot," she told herself. "Look at the workers instead."

Yes, there were females among them! Why, in the middle of each section there were whole families! Humans of both sexes sat there, at several removes from the conveyor belts, shaping, filling, stitching, glueing and pasting things together, while among them crawled, squatted, whimpered and squabbled small dirty children. Did they never get out of the Money fabric? Did they spend all their lives in the pit? Could the Centre do nothing about it?

"I must find a way out," said Alison to herself, looking forward and then back along the monotonous passage, but the smooth surface of the inner wall curved out of sight in both directions without any sign of an exit.

She crossed to the nearest policeman's cell and tapped on the glass of the revolving door. The policeman was sitting at a high narrow desk; he merely turned his head and invited her with a jerk of the thumb to enter.

"Well?" he said.

"How does one get out into the open country? Why, you've got an exit door here," said Alison.

"Show your contract," said the policeman.

"What contract?"

"Work contract. What are you going to work at? Farm labour, domestic service, strawberry picking?"

"Supposing I just wanted to take some children for a country ramble?"

"Any Money on you?"

"No. But supposing I just wanted to go for a walk?"

"No admission," said the policeman.

"But there must be some way out of the Money fabric, isn't there?"

"Not that I know of," said the policeman.

"But I saw a bus on the road out there."

"Well, that's not outside the Money fabric. Pay as you go, you know."

"Is the countryside part of the Money fabric too?"

"Look for yourself," said the policeman. "See that roof?"

Alison craned her neck. Above the fields and the clouds she saw a far-off translucent glassy film glittering faintly against the sky.

"That can't be a roof; it's too high up," she said.

"The sky's the limit," said the policeman.

"But what keeps it up?"

"Top pinnacles of the Money fabric; what do you think? Here, where do you come from, asking these questions?"

"I don't know," said Alison, feeling more and more bewildered. "Is there *no* way of getting out of the Money fabric?"

"Unless you get off the Earth, there's none that I know of," said the policeman.

"Are all the mountains inside the Money fabric? What about Everest?"

"Look here, you're wasting my time. What do you want?"

"Where's the bus exit? How do the cars get out?"

"Straight on, past the Labour Exchange."

"To the right or the left?"

"Right *or* left, doesn't matter. You won't get very far without Money."

"I shall appeal to the Centre," said Alison.

The effect of these words was remarkable. The policeman's face crimsoned and seemed to swell; he was blowing violently on a whistle and at the same time playing the fingers of one hand on a row of push-buttons set in his desk. The cell darkened because a posse of policemen appeared on either side, blocking all the light that had filtered through the glassy walls. Almost before Alison could turn round in surprise, one of these policemen came in from the passage and clicked a pair of handcuffs on her wrists.

"Central Agent," said the cell policeman, saluting.

"What's the charge, street-walking?" asked the other.

"I'm not a street-walker," cried Alison.

"Revolutionary activities," said the policeman.

"I don't belong to any Party," cried Alison, trying to wrench her hands apart. "I won't have my hands like this. I'm a woman, and I'm concerned with the welfare of humanity. I want loving-kindness to have fair play. I appeal to the Centre —."

"Gag her," said the second policeman.

"I won't be gagged."

She was being smothered by something, as if a hood had been put over her head; she struck out with her bound hands and kicked with her feet; her heart was hammering and she was sweating with fear. But she managed to push the smothering hood off her face and opened her eyes. She could see nothing. She was lying flat on her back. How had they got her down? She struck out again with one hand, which was unaccountably free, and the blow landed in the soft mass of the eiderdown which she had just flung from her face.

Alison pinched the eiderdown, to make sure that she was in her bed, and ran her fingers over the surface of her bedclothes. The blanket and the sheet were rucked and twisted, exactly as if she had been fighting a pair of constables, and her heart was still pounding. "This is what happens when you abandon the top storey altogether," she said to herself, trying to feel brave. And then, without any relevance, she cried aloud passionately: "Is there no escape? Oh God, is there no escape?"

"What is it, darling?" came Dick Muttoe's sleepy voice from the next bed. "What's the matter?"

"I've had a nightmare. I didn't mean to wake you up. I'm *so* sorry —"

Dick's hand groped towards her and she caught it and clung to it.


[All ellipses in the text are Muir's.]

# Appendix IV

## A selection of Willa Muir's poetry

### To Edwin, absent

A roof I have in Prague, four walls, a floor,
a bed, a desk, an easy-chair, much more
than simple need demands, more than my due;
yet I am homeless, homeless, lacking you.

The trees are friendly still, though bare  and blown,
neighbours are kind, I breathe a friendly air;
and yet I fit no pattern, left alone;
my home is in your bosom, only there.

[23 Oct. 1947; written at end of Muir's journal; Nov. 1946-June 1947; MS: St Andrews 38466/5/2]

When I'm depressed I stack
a pillow at my back,
a rubber bag at my feet,
to give me heat,
and a book to soothe my mind.
I do not feel inclined
for the nudgins and finickins
of Charles Dickens.
At Gogol
I boggle,
with Dosto
I'd be lost O.

I say shucks!
to Aldous Hux,
& look at Laurence
with abhaurence.
I might give a boost
to Marcel Proust,
or start a-tippling
at Kipling.

[Undated poem; written on the inside cover of Muir's journal; 1947-Jan 1948; MS: St Andrews 38466/5/3]

*From*: Willa
*Date*: Sunday
*B.F.* to B.T.
*on* Reg. Close
*Put Away* at once.

Subject The MisRepresentative

### Rondeau

Unhappy Reg! by stale moralities
encircled as within a thorny hedge,
from behind which his enemies he spies,
    (unhappy Reg!)
men lacking principle or loyal pledge
advancing to attack him in disguise.
He has but moral thorns to turn the edge
of their keen ridicule, yet he will rise
from his close-stool and stab where he can stretch
with printed half-truth and still sharper lies.
    Unhappy wretch!

[Written by Muir on printed memo paper (printed words at top italicised), filed with a printed prospectus for the British Institute, Prague, dated December 1948; MS: St Andrews 38466/5/4]

## Address to Edwin

I hope that old age makes me merely comic,
a funny, fat old woman with false teeth,
that click or treacherously clack together,
and bosom bursting from a straining sheath,
vast hips and creaking knees and hobbling feet
enveloped in a merciful skirt and cloak,
a shameless old grey head, and mounted on it
some foolish trifle of a hat or bonnet
or even — God be good to us — a toque!

I was not born to be a comic figure,
but life has changed me into one at last.
I hope, my love, you will not find me tedious
although my double chins are doubling fast,
I hope you'll go on laughing at my foibles,
and till I die find merriment in me;
but when I'm dead among the elementals
I hope you will forget the accidentals
remembering rather what I meant to be.

[10 April 1947; journal; 1947-Jan. 1948; MS: St Andrews 38466/5/2; pbd:
Mudge 2]


What is the matter, baby mine?
Why do you burble like Gertrude Stein?
I've been with the British Council, my dear,
A year is a year is a year is a year,
And so I have simply ceased to cohere.

Whatever I say goes up in a vapour,
And so I scribble on bits of paper,
With burnt-out matches instead of a pen,
numbering all from one to ten,
then spike them on files and do it again.

[10 May 1947; journal; 1947-Jan 1948; MS: St Andrews 38466/5/3]

**Ephemeridae / Very Private,**[1]
*For my dear Edwin. / from Willa, with love.*


You may think PERCY BYSSHE
A cold, abstract fish,
But I think SHELLEY hot
Compared with ELIOT.

CHRISTOPHER GREIVE
keeps HUGH MCDIARMID up his sleeve,
but HUGH MCDIARMID
growing frisky
finds a mermaid
in the whisky.

NORMAN MCCAIG
prancing like a staig,
keeps on good terms
    wi' a' the callants
though he winna
    write Lallans.

EDWIN MUIR
In that farm-cart of His
carries a cure
for ELIOT'S artifice.
He reclaims the waste land
as he creaks along;
on either hand
grow flowers of song.


[MS: NLS 19703.40, 44, 46. 'You may think . . . ELIOT', pbd: Scott 38;
Freeman 166; 'EDWIN MUIR', pbd: Scott 38]

**Ephemeridae** (2) Scots dramatists and novelists[2]
*for Edwin, with love*


N. BRYSSON MORRISON
is a gowk if there was ever one,
for instead of being a
            ranter and roarer
she writes good novels
            and so the Scots ignore her.

[MS: NLS 19703.52; pbd: Anderson and Christianson 11]


**Requiem**

And so let the loud tongue fall dumb.
Cease to mock time with forced, unseemly jests;
Compose the aching limbs, protuberant bum,
Still more protuberant belly and slack breasts.
Lay them all down, relax the vertebrae,
And sleep, old wife, after your too long day.

[Willa Muir, 'Poems', *Bottehge Oscure* 24 (Rome, 1959) 101]


**Laconics**

### 1. Nightmare and Reality

Sobbing, I beat upon your door;
you did not open.
Sobbing louder, I called your name;
you did not answer.
Sobbing still louder, howling, shrieking,
I woke myself out of the nightmare
into this blank silence.

They tell me you are dead.
This, then is what 'dead' means,
this terrifying silence,

this void.
Incredible and real.

### 4. In the Modern World

My true Love lies alone,
a has-been,
picked clean
bone by bone.

I am still his.
What has been, is.

Yet this murderous world around me,
Warring, does so confound me
I can be glad
my true Love lies dead.

### 5. [no title]

Where have you come from, shred of a daughter,
daughter I longed for and never bore?
Here you are in my dream
blown by what wind?

a shred, a wraith that cries in a piping voice:
'Don't leave me behind!'

## Jingles

### 3. [no title]

When imagination boggles
We put on goggles;
so our intellectuals
all wear spectacles.

The question is; does what they see
make any sense to you and me?

## 6. [no title]

Cliché, that's France's own and master-word,
second only to her other product: Merde.


## 7. Not Even Cupboard Love

Having emptied the dish
that I filled with fish
my cat makes at a run
for the sun, the sun,
as if chasing some prey
in an Ibsen play.
She hoists her tail
and leaves me un-friended
a lone Abigail till the day is ended.


## Verses

### 2. Not for Me

Not the organ cactus.
categorical with its straight lines,
prickly with refutations
making too heady sap.

Not the urban towers
categorical with their ruthless right-angles,
cutting the living air into sections of nothing,
channelling its flow into false certainties.

Not the intellectual-isms,
categorical, sundering,
splitting personalities,
splitting hairs.

For me the curves of an embracing arm,
or the flowing contours of moving animals
the joyous freakish shapes of moths and flowers
on this well-rounded planet.

[W. J. A. Muir, *Laconics Jingles & other Verses* (London: Enitharmon Press, 1969); 'Where have you come from', also pbd: Butter, 1993 93; Freeman 166]

Notes

1. Printed by hand onto Newbattle College notepaper and sewn together into a little book by Muir  for Edwin, 1951 or 1952.

2. Another little hand made book for Edwin, dated 5 Sept. 1953.

# Bibliography of Willa Muir's writings

## Novels

*Imagined Corners* (London: Martin Secker, 1931) (first pbd. June 1931; second printing Aug. 1931; republished Edinburgh: Canongate Classics, 1987).

*Mrs Ritchie* (London: Martin Secker, 1933).

Both available in Kirsty Allen (ed.), *Imagined Selves*, Canongate Omnibus (Edinburgh: Canongate Classics, 1996).

## Non-fiction

*Women: An Inquiry* (London: Hogarth Press, 1925).

*Mrs Grundy in Scotland* (London: George Routledge & Sons, 1936).

Both available in Kirsty Allen (ed.), *Imagined Selves*, Canongate Omnibus (Edinburgh: Canongate Classics, 1996).

*Living with Ballads* (London: Hogarth Press, 1965).

*Belonging* (London: Hogarth Press, 1968) (Willa Muir's memoir of Edwin Muir).

## Short story

'Clock-a-doodle-doo', *The Modern Scot* 5:1-2 (June 1934) 46-50; also pbd. in Moira Burgess (ed.), *The Other Voice* (Edinburgh: Polygon, 1987) 168-72;  see Appendix II.

## Poetry

'Poems', *Bottehge Oscure* 24 (Rome, 1959) 99-101.

*Laconics Jingles & other Verses* (London: privately pbd. for the author by the Enitharmon Press, 1969).

Butter, Peter, 'Some Poems by Willa Muir', *Chapman* 74-75 (1993) 93-96.

### Articles and reviews

'Women in Scotland', *Left Review* 2 (1935-36) 768-70; available in Kirsty Allen (ed.), *Imagined Selves*, Canongate Omnibus (Edinburgh: Canongate Classics, 1996).

'Have you the "Whipper-Tooties"?', Listener 20 (21 July 1938) 122. BBC Scotland talk, 12 July 1938, on John Jamieson's *Dictionary of the Scottish Language*.

'Moving in Circles', *Listener* 20 (22 September 1938) 602-3.

'Translating from the German', part II (part I by Edwin Muir) in Reuben A. Brower (ed.), *On Translation* (Cambridge, Mass.: Harvard U. Press, 1959) 94-96.

### Willa Muir's publications in *The Modern Scot*

'The New Education', review of A. S. Neill's *The Problem Parent* in *The Modern Scot* 3:1 (Apr. 1932) 74-75.

'The Proposal. Chapter from a Novel by Hermann Broch', *The Modern Scot* 3:2 (Aug. 1932) 98-103. (note: 'From *The Sleep Walkers* . . . translated by Edwin and Willa Muir' (98).) (Broch's chapter is followed by Edwin Muir, 'Hermann Broch' 3:2 103-10, introducing Broch and *The Sleepwalkers*.)

'Chapter from a Novel', *The Modern Scot* 3:3 (Oct. 1932) 198-201 (chap. 11 of *Mrs Ritchie*).

'Aphorisms by Franz Kafka (Translated from the German by Willa and Edwin Muir)', *The Modern Scot* 3:3 (Oct. 1932) 202-08 (with a brief introduction by Edwin Muir (202)).

'A Passing Cloud by Hermann Broch', 'Translated by Willa Muir', *The Modern Scot*, 4:4 (Jan. 1934) 304-12.

'Clock-a-doodle-doo', *The Modern Scot* 5:1-2 (June 1934) 46-50; also pbd. in Moira Burgess (ed.), *The Other Voice* (Edinburgh: Polygon, 1987) 168-72; see Appendix I.

'*Mrs Grundy Comes to Scotland*', *The Modern Scot* 6:4 (Jan. 1936) 289-96 (chap. 2).

## Fragments

"Elizabeth" and "A Portrait of Emily Stobo", *Chapman* 71 (1992-93).

'Why I am to be described as a mess', extract from Muir's journal, Patricia R. Mudge, 'A Quorum of Willas' *Chapman* 71 (1992-93) 4-6.

## Broadcasts

'Have you the "Whipper-Tooties"?', BBC Scotland, 12 July 1938, on John Jamieson's *Dictionary of the Scottish Language*, *Listener* 20 (21 July 1938) 122.

'On Susan Ferrier', BBC Scotland, 14 November 1954 (typescript St. Andrews MS 38466/2/1).

'Reminiscences'. 'In Search of Edwin Muir', BBC Scotland, 26 February 1963; recollections with others ('Mrs Muir's Reminiscences', typescript St. Andrews MS 38466/2/5).

## Unpublished works

*Mrs Muttoe and the Top Storey* (1938-40) (typescript, St. Andrews, MS 38466/1/2).

*The Usurpers* (1951-52) (typescript, St. Andrews, MS 38466/2/9 and 10).

'The Fur Coat' (n.d. [1948?]); written on reverse of Muir's Journal, Jan. 1848, St. Andrews MS 38466/5/3).

'This Lop-sided World' (two typescripts, 99 and 82 pp., ca. 1960-61; by Anicula, pseud. Muir; St Andrews MS 38466/2/7 and 8).

## Letters, journals and notebooks

St Andrews University Library

MS 38466/1-8. Notebooks, including journals, miscellaneous papers, typescripts and letters.

MS 38466/5/1. Marmaduke journal, 1927 (with some later entries).

MS 38466/5/2. Prague journal, November 1946-June 1947.

MS 38466/5/3. 'Dirty work', Prague journal, 1947-Jan. 1948.

MS 38466/5/4. 'The Putsch, and after' journal, Jan.-May 1948.

MS 38466/5/5. Journal, Jan. 1951-Sept. 1953.

MS 38466/5/6. Journal, Sept.-Nov. 1955.

MS 38466/6/3. Notebook, 'Clock-a-doodle-doo' and miscellaneous poems.

MS 38466/6/9. Notebook, ca. 1953, 'An Old Wife's Grumble' (in Scots), notes on culture and poems in Scots.

MS 38466/6/17. Notebook, list of the Muirs' books in Swaffham [1963].

MS 38466/8. Letters; these are listed alphabetically and include Muir's letters to Edwin Muir (1958) and Edwin Muir's letters to her (1957-58); letters from George Mackay Brown, George Bruce (including a typescript of the radio discussion of *Living with Ballads*), Hermann Broch, Valerie Eliot, Archie Hind, Eleanor Hind, Hogarth Press, Robert Lowell, John MacMurray, Anna J. Mill, Gavin Muir, A. S. Neill, Kathleen Raine, May Sarton, Tom Scott, Janet Adam Smith and many others, including Sir James Donaldson's recommendation letter.

### National Library of Scotland (NLS)

MS 19703. This includes Willa Muir's letters to Kathleen Raine, Tom Scott, Janet Adam Smith; and Gavin Muir's and 'JAC' Cowie's letters to Kathleen Raine after Muir's death.

MS 19674. This includes letters from Stanley Cursitor (a testimonial for Muir, 23 Aug. 1940), T. S. Eliot, Douglas Young.

MS 26194.98. WM to F. Marian McNeill, 26 Jan. 1926.

MS 26190.95. WM to Marion Lochhead, 3 March 1933.

MS 19703.39 and 47. Willa Muir's Ephemeridae for Edwin.

MS 19670. Letters to Muir.

MS 19675-91. Notes and drafts for *Living with Ballads*.

MS 19692-98. Drafts and typescripts of *Belonging*.

MS 19699. Notes on psychology and literature (1959).

**British Library (BL)**

Sydney and Violet Schiff papers, Add MS 52920.

**Miscellaneous sources of biographical information**

University of St Andrews Court Minutes (1911, 1912, 1914).

University of St Andrews Calendar (1912/13), Class Slips (1907-12), Matriculation Register (1907-8).

*College Echoes*, XXII-XXIII (1908/9-1911/12).

**Translations by Willa Muir** (in chronological order within each author's list)

Anon., *5 Songs from the Auvergnat done into modern Scots* (Warlingham: Samson Press, 1931).

'A Passing Cloud by Hermann Broch', *The Modern Scot* 4:4 (Jan. 1934) 304-12.

Carossa, Hans. *A Roumanian Diary*, Agnes Neill Scott (pseud. WM) (trans.) (London: Martin Secker, 1929).
   *A Childhood*, Agnes Neill Scott (pseud. WM) (trans.) (London: Martin Secker, 1930).
   *Boyhood and Youth*, Agnes Neill Scott (pseud. WM) (London: Martin Secker, 1931).
   *Doctor Gion*, Agnes Neill Scott (pseud. WM) (trans.) (London: Martin Secker, 1933).

Hofmannsthal, Hugo von. *The Difficult Man* in Michael Hamburger (ed.), *Selected Writings of Hugo von Hofmannsthal* 3:633-823.

Kafka, Franz. 'First Sorrow', *European Quarterly* 1 (1934) 46-49. 'Selections from Diaries and Notebooks', *Orion* 1 (1945) 104-15.

Winsloe, Christa (Baroness Hatvany). *The Child Manuela*, Agnes Neill Scott (pseud. WM) (trans.) (London: Chapman and Hall, 1933); repbd. in the Virago series, Lesbian Landmarks (London: Virago, 1994).
   *Life Begins*, Agnes Neill Scott (pseud. WM) (trans.) (Chapman and Hall, 1935).

**Translations by Willa and Edwin Muir** (in chronological order within each author's list)

Asch / Ash, Sholem. *Three Cities*, Willa and Edwin Muir (trans.) (London: Victor Gollancz, 1933).
  *Salvation*, Willa and Edwin Muir (trans.) (London:Victor Gollancz:1934).
  *Mottke the Thief*, Edwin and Willa Muir (trans.) (London: Victor Gollancz, 1935).
  *The Calf of Paper*, Edwin and Willa Muir (trans.) (London: Victor Gollancz, 1936); pbd. in U.S. as *The War Goes On*, Willa and Edwin Muir (trans.) (New York: Putnam's Sons, 1936) (see 122).

Broch, Hermann. 'The Proposal. Chapter from a Novel by Hermann Broch', Edwin and Willa Muir (trans.) *The Modern Scot* 3:2 (Aug. 1932) 98-103. (From *The Sleepwalkers*).
  *The Sleepwalkers: A Trilogy* (*The Romantic, The Anarchist, The Realist*), Willa and Edwin Muir (trans.) (London: Martin Secker, 1932).
  *The Unknown Quantity*, Willa and Edwin Muir (trans.) (London: Collins, 1935).

Burckhardt, Carl Jacob. *Richelieu and His Age: His Rise to Power*, abridged by Edwin and Willa Muir (trans.) (London: Allen & Unwin, 1940).

Feuchtwanger, Lion. *Jew Süss*, Willa and Edwin Muir (trans.) (London: Martin Secker, 1926); pbd. in US as *Power*, Willa and Edwin Muir (trans.) (New York: Viking Press, 1926).
  *The Ugly Duchess*, Willa and Edwin Muir (trans.) (London: Martin Secker, 1927).
  *Two Anglo-Saxon Plays: The Oil Islands; Warren Hastings*, Willa and Edwin Muir (trans.) (London: Martin Secker, 1929).
  *Success: Three Years in the Life of a Province*, Willa and Edwin Muir (trans.) (London: Martin Secker, 1930).
  *The False Nero*, Edwin and Willa Muir (trans.) (London: Hutchinson and Co, 1937). pbd. in US as *The Pretender* (New York, 1937)

Glaeser, Ernst. *Class 1902*, Willa and Edwin Muir (trans.) (London: Martin Secker, 1929).

Hauptmann, Gerhart. *Der Weisse Heiland, Indipohdi, The White Saviour, A Winter Ballad in Hauptmann, Dramatic Works*, vol IX [VIII Butter 66]
  *The Island of the Great Mother*, Willa and Edwin Muir (trans.) (London: Martin Secker, 1925).

Heuser, Kurt. *The Inner Journey*, Willa and Edwin Muir (trans.) (London: Secker, 1932).

Kafka, Franz. *America*, Willa and Edwin Muir (trans.) (London: Routledge & Sons, 1938).
'Aphorisms by Franz Kafka (Translated from the German by Willa and Edwin Muir)', brief introduction by Edwin Muir (202) *The Modern Scot* 3:3 (Oct. 1932) 202-08.
*The Castle*, Willa and Edwin Muir (trans.), with introductory note by E. Muir v-xii (London: Martin Secker, 1930).
*The Great Wall of China and Other Pieces*, Willa and Edwin Muir (trans.) (London: Martin Secker, 1930).
*The Trial*, Willa and Edwin Muir (trans.), with introductory note by Edwin Muir vii-xvi (London: Victor Gollancz, 1937).

Kühnelt-Leddihn, Erik M. von. *Night Over the East*, adapted by Edwin and Willa Muir (trans.) (London: Sheed & Ward, 1936).

Lothar, Ernst. *Little Friend*, Willa and Edwin Muir (trans.) (London: Martin Secker, 1933).
*The Mills of God*, Willa and Edwin Muir (trans.) (London: Martin Secker, 1935)

Mann, Heinrich. *The Hill of Lies*, Edwin and Willa Muir (trans.) (London: Jarrold Ltd., 1934).

Neumann, Robert. *The Queen's Doctor: Being the Strange Story of the Rise and Fall of Struensee, Dictator, Lover and Doctor of Medicine*, Edwin and Willa Muir (trans.), (London: Victor Gollancz, 1936).
*A Woman Screamed*, Willa and Edwin Muir (trans.) (London: Cassell and Co., 1938).

Paléologue, Georges Maurice. *The Enigmatic Czar: The Life of Alexander I of Russia*, Edwin and Willa Muir (trans.) (London: Hamish Hamilton, 1938).

Renn, Ludwig (pseud., Arnold Friedrich Vieth von Golssenau). *War*, Willa and Edwin Muir (trans.) (London: Martin Secker, 1929).
*After War*, Willa and Edwin Muir (trans.) (London: Martin Secker, 1931).

Rheinhardt, E. A. *The Life of Eleanora Duce*, Willa and Edwin Muir (trans.) (London: Martin Secker, 1930).

## Reviews of Willa Muir's work

Review (anon.), 'The Future of Women', including *Women: an Inquiry*, *Times Literary Supplement* (26 Nov. 1925) 790.

Review (anon.) of *Imagined Corners*, *Glasgow Herald* (2 July 1931) 4.

Review (anon.) of *Imagined Corners*, *Times Literary Supplement* (2 July 1931) 526

Review (anon.) of *Imagined Corners*, *The Modern Scot* 2:2 (July 1931) 171-73.

Review (anon.) of 5 *Songs from the Auvergnat*, trans. Willa Muir, *The Modern Scot* 2:3 (Oct. 1931) 251.

Review (anon.) of *Mrs Ritchie*, *The Modern Scot* 4:2 (July 1933) 157-58; available in McCulloch, 2004 94.

Review (anon.) of *Mrs Ritchie*, *Times* (7 July 1933) 20.

Review (anon.) of *Mrs Ritchie*, *Times Literary Supplement* (13 July 1933) 478.

Review (anon.) of *Mrs Ritchie*, *Scotsman* (13 July 1933) 2.

Review (anon.) of *Mrs Ritchie*, *Listener* 10 (16 Aug. 1933) 260.

Review (anon.) of *Mrs Grundy in Scotland*, *Manchester Evening News* (9 May 1936).

Review by Catherine Carswell, *Mrs Grundy in Scotland*, Spectator 156 (22 May 1936) 946.

Review by George Scott Moncrieff, *Mrs Grundy in Scotland*, 'Counterblasts to Knox', *New Statesman* (27 June 1936) 1040.

Review by William Montgomerie, *Living with Ballads*, *Scottish Studies: The Journal of the School of Scottish Studies* 9 (1965) 221-24.

Review by Elizabeth Jennings, 'A poet's love. Belonging. A Memoir', *Times*, 13 Jan. 1968 21.


## Obituaries

'Death of Scottish woman writer and translator', *Glasgow Herald* (27 May 1970) 5.

# Bibliography of Other Sources

Alberti, Johanna. *Beyond Suffrage: Feminists in War and Peace 1914-1928* (London: Macmillan, 1989).

Alberti, Johanna. 'Striking Rock: The Letters of Ray Strachey to Her Family, 1929-1935' in Broughton and Anderson (eds.), *Women's Lives / Women's Times. New Essays on Auto/Biography* (Albany, NY: State University of New York Press, 1997) 73-93.

Allen, Kirsty A. 'Introduction' in Willa Muir, *Imagined Selves* (Edinburgh: Canongate, 1996) v-xiii.

Allen, Kirsty A. *The Life and Work of Willa Muir, 1890-1955* (St Andrews: University of St Andrews PHD, 1997).

Anderson, Carol, and Aileen Christianson (eds.). *Scottish Women's Fiction, 1920s to 1960s: Journeys into Being* (East Linton: Tuckwell Press, 2000).

Anderson, Carol (ed.). *Opening the Doors: The Achievement of Catherine Carswell* (Ramsay Head Press: Edinburgh, 2001).

Anon. review. 'The Italian Futurists. Nightmare Exhibition at the Sackville Gallery', *Pall Mall Gazette* (1 March 1912) 5.

Anon. review. 'The Futurists', *Times* (1 March 1912) 11.

Baker, Houston A. *Modernism and the Harlem Renaissance* (Chicago: Chicago University Press, 1987).

Barker, George. 'Coming to London – IV' *The London Magazine* 3.1 (Jan. 1956) 49-54.

Barthes, Roland. 'The Death of the Author' in Stephen Heath (trans.), *Image Music Text* (London: Fontana, 1977) 142-48.

Benjamin, Walter. 'Franz Kafka On the Tenth Anniversary of His Death' in W. Benjamin, Hannah Arendt (ed.), *Illuminations* (London: Fontana, 1992) 108-35.

Benjamin, Walter. 'Max Brod's Book on Kafka' in W. Benjamin, Hannah Arendt (ed.), *Illuminations* (London: Fontana, 1992) 136-43.

Benjamin, Walter. 'The Task of the Translator' in W. Benjamin, Hannah Arendt (ed.), *Illuminations* (London: Fontana, 1992) 70-82.

Bold, Alan. *MacDiarmid: Christopher Murray Grieve; A Critical Biography* (London: John Murray, 1988).

Bold, Alan (ed.). *The Letters of Hugh MacDiarmid* (London: Hamish Hamilton, 1984).

Boone, Joseph Allen, *Libidinal Currents: Sexuality and the Shaping of Modernism* (Chicago: University of Chicago Press, 1998).

Brod, Max. 'Epilogue' to Franz Kafka, Willa and Edwin Muir (trans.), *The Trial* ([1937]; London: Minerva, 1992) 252-55.

Broughton, Trev L., and Linda Anderson (eds.). *Women's Lives / Women's Times. New Essays on Auto/Biography* (Albany, NY: State University of New York Press, 1997).

Brown, Alice. 'Women and Politics in Scotland' in E. Breitenbach and F. Mackay (eds.), *Women and Contemporary Scottish Politics: An Anthology* (Edinburgh: Polygon, 2001) 197-212.

Brown, George Douglas, Dorothy Porter (ed.). *The House with the Green Shutters* (1901; Penguin books; Harmondsworth, 1985).

Brown, Mary Ellen. 'Old Singing Women and the Canons of Scottish Balladry and Song' in Gifford and McMillan (eds.), *A History of Scottish Women's Writing* (Edinburgh: Edinburgh University Press, 1997) 44-57.

Burns, Robert. 'Holy Willie's Prayer' in James Kinsley (ed.), *Burns: Poems and Songs* (Oxford: Oxford University Press, 1969) 56-59.

Butter, P. H. *Edwin Muir: Man and Poet* (Edinburgh: Oliver and Boyd, 1966).

Butter, P. H. (ed.). *Selected Letters of Edwin Muir* (London: Hogarth Press, 1974).

Butter, P. H. 'Willa Muir: Writer' in C. J. M. Shields and D. S. Robb (eds.), *Edwin Muir Centenary Assessments* (Aberdeen: A.S.L.S., 1990) 58-74.

Caird, Janet. 'Cakes Not Turned. Willa Muir's Published Novels', *Chapman* 71 (Winter 1992-93) 12-18.

Campbell, Ian. *Kailyard: A New Assessment* (Edinburgh: Ramsay Head Press, 1981).

Carswell, Catherine. 'The Grundy Woman'. *Spectator* 156 (22 May 1936) 946.

Carswell, Catherine, John Carswell (ed.). *Lying Awake* (1950; Edinburgh: Canongate, 1997).

Carswell, Catherine and Donald (eds.). *The Scots Week-End and Caledonian Vade-Mecum for Host, Guest and Wayfarer* (London: George Routledge & Sons, 1936).

Carswell, John. *Lives and Letters: A. R. Orage, Beatrice Hastings, Katherine Mansfield, John Middleton Murray, S. S. Koteliansky: 1906-57* (London: Faber and Faber, 1978).

Carter, Gillian. *Domestic Geography: A study of Nan Shepherd's Geographical Politics* (Perth: University of Western Australia PHD, 2003).

Christianson, Aileen. 'Dreaming Realities: Willa Muir's *Imagined Corners*' in Anderson and Christianson (eds.), *Scottish Women's Fiction, 1920s to 1960s* (2000) 84-96.

Christianson, Aileen. 'Gender and nation: debatable lands and passable boundaries' in G. Norquay and G. Smyth (eds.), *Across the Margins* (Manchester; MUP, 2002) 67-82.

Cixous, Hélène. 'Sorties' in Elaine Marks and Isabelle de Courtivron (eds.), Ann Liddle (trans.), *New French Feminisms An Anthology* (Hemel Hempstead: Harvester Wheatsheaf, 1981) 90-98.

Craig, Cairns (ed.). *The History of Scottish Literature* (Aberdeen: Aberdeen University Press, 1987), vol. 4.

Craig, Cairns. 'Twentieth Century Scottish Literature: An Introduction' in Craig (ed.), *The History of Scottish Literature* (1987) 4:1-8.

Crawford, Robert. *Devolving English Literature* (1992; Edinburgh: Edinburgh University Press, 2000).

Davenport-Hines, Richard. *A Night at the Majestic: Proust and the Great Modernist Dinner Party of 1922.* (London: Faber and Faber, 2006).

Dekoven, Marianne. 'Modernism and Gender' in Levenson (ed.), *The Cambridge Companion to Modernism* 174-93.

Dickson, Beth. 'Foundations of the Modern Scottish Novel' in Craig (ed.), *The History of Scottish Literature* (1987) 4:49-60.

Dickson, Beth. '"An ordinary little girl": Willa Muir's *Mrs Ritchie*' in Anderson and Christianson (eds.), *Scottish Women's Fiction, 1920s to 1960s* (2000) 97-106.

Dodd, Kathryn. 'Cultural Politics and Women's Historical Writing. The Case of Ray Strachey's *The Cause*', *Women's Studies International Forum*, 13:1/2 (1990) 129-37.

Drew, Elizabeth A. *The Modern Novel: Some Aspects of Contemporary Fiction* (London: Jonathan Cape, 1926).

DuPlessis, Rachel Blau. *Writing Beyond the Ending: Narrative Strategies of Twentieth-Century Women Writers* (Bloomington: Indiana University Press, 1985).

Eliot, T. S. 'The Waste Land' and 'Notes on the Waste Land' in *Complete Poems and Plays* (London: Faber and Faber, 1969) 59-80.

Elphinstone, Margaret. 'Willa Muir: Crossing the Genres' in Gifford and McMillan (eds.), *A History of Scottish Women's Writing* (Edinburgh: Edinburgh University Press, 1997) 400-15.

Ewan, Elizabeth, Sue Innes, Rose Pipes and Siân Reynolds (eds.). *The Biographical Dictionary of Scottish Women* (Edinburgh: Edinburgh University Press, 2006).

France, Peter (ed.). *The Oxford Guide to Literature in Translation* (Oxford: Oxford University Press, 2000).

Frazer, J. G. *The Golden Bough: A Study in Magic and Religion* [abridged edition] (London: MacMillan, 1922).

Freeman, Alan. *Imagined Worlds: Fiction by Scottish Women 1900-1935* (Frankfurt am Main: Peter Lang, 2005).

Galison, Peter. *Einstein's Clocks, Poincaré's Maps* (London: Hodder and Stoughton, Sceptre, 2003).

Gaskill, Howard. 'Edwin Muir in Hellerau', *Scottish Literary Journal* 11 (May 1984) 45-44.

Gibbons, Luke. *Transformations in Irish Culture* (Cork: Cork University Press 1996).

Gifford, Douglas, and Dorothy McMillan (eds.). *A History of Scottish Women's Writing* (Edinburgh: Edinburgh University Press, 1997).

Grieve, C. M. 'Neil Munro', *The Modern Scot* 1:4 (Jan. 1931) 20-24.

Gunn, Neil M., J. B. Pick (ed.). *Selected Letters* (Edinburgh: Polygon, 1987).

Hamilton, Cicely. 'The Backwash of Feminism', *Time and Tide* 3:36 (8 Sept. 1922) 853.

Hart, Francis Russell, and J. B. Pick. *Neil M. Gunn. A Highland Life* (London: John Murray, 1981).

Harvey, Sir Paul (ed.). *The Oxford Companion to English Literature* (Oxford: Clarendon Press, 1934).

Henderson, Hamish. 'The Ballad and Popular Tradition to 1660' in R. D. S. Jack (ed.), *The History of Scottish Literature* (Aberdeen: Aberdeen University Press, 1988) 1:263-84.

Hendry, Joy. 'Twentieth-century Women's Writing: The Nest of Singing Birds' in Craig (ed.), *The History of Scottish Literature* (1987) 4:291-309.

Holtby, Winifred. *Women and a Changing Civilisation* (London: John Lane, 1934) (part of 'The Twentieth Century Library').

Huberman, Elizabeth. 'The Broch / Muir Correspondence: Teaching Each Other', *Modern Austrian Literature*, 22:2 (1989) 45-57.

Huberman, Elizabeth. 'Translating Broch's *The Sleepwalkers* — Ordeal and Reward' in C. J. M. MacLachlan and D. S. Robb (eds.), *Edwin Muir Centenary Assessments* (Aberdeen: ASLS, 2000) 47-57.

Innes, Sue. *Love and Work: Feminism, Family and Ideas of Equality and Citizenship, Britain 1900-1939* (Edinburgh: University of Edinburgh PHD thesis, 1998).

Joannou, Maroula. *Beyond Suffrage: Feminists in War and Peace 1914-1928* (London: Macmillan, 1989).

Joannou, Maroula. '*Ladies, Please Don't Smash These Windows*': Women's Writing, Feminist Consciousness and Social Change 1918-38* (Oxford and Providence, R. I.: Berg, 1995).

Kerrigan, Catherine. 'MacDiarmid's Early Poetry' in Craig (ed.), *The History of Scottish Literature* (1987) 4:75-85.

Knox, William W. J. *Lives of Scottish Women: Women and Scottish Society, 1800-1980* (Edinburgh: Edinburgh University Press, 2006).

Lawrence, D. H. *Women in Love* (London: Martin Secker, 1921; Harmondsworth: Penguin, 1980).

Levenson, Michael (ed.). *The Cambridge Companion to Modernism* (Cambridge: Cambridge University Press, 1999).

Lewis, Wyndham. *The Apes of God* (1930; London: Grayson & Grayson, first cheap edition, 1931).

Leydecker, Karl. 'Fiction: Nineteenth and Twentieth Century' in P. France (ed), *Oxford Guide to Literature in English Translation* (Oxford: Oxford University Press) 331-36.

Lochhead, Marion C. 'Willa Muir and her Work: Translator, Novelist and Poet', *The Bulletin and Scots Pictorial* (29 March 1933) 19.

Lumsden, Alison. '"To Get Leave to Live": Negotiating Regional Identity in the Literature of North-East Scotland' in Ian Brown (ed.), *Modern Transformations: New Identities (from 1918)*, *The Edinburgh History of Scottish Literature* (Edinburgh: Edinburgh University Press, 2007) 3: 95–105.

McCue, Kirsteen. 'Women and Song 1750-1850' in Gifford and McMillan (eds.), *A History of Scottish Women's Writing* (Edinburgh: Edinburgh University Press, 1997) 44-57.

McCulloch, Margery. 'Inter-War Criticism' in Craig (ed.), *The History of Scottish Literature* (1987) 4:119-33.

McCulloch, Margery. *Edwin Muir* (Edinburgh: Edinburgh University Press, 1993).

McCulloch, Margery Palmer. '"Oh Scotland, oh my country!" Catherine Carswell and the Scottish Renaissance' in Anderson (ed.), *Opening the Doors: The Achievement of Catherine Carswell* (2001) 36-50.

McCulloch, Margery Palmer. *Modernism and Nationalism: Literature and Society in Scotland 1918-1939. Source Documents for the Scottish Renaissance* (Glasgow: Association for Scottish Literary Studies, 2004).

McCulloch, Margery Palmer. 'Edwin and Willa Muir: Scottish, European and Gender Journeys, 1918-1969' in Ian Brown (ed.), *Modern Transformations: New Identities (from 1918)*, *The Edinburgh History of Scottish Literature* (Edinburgh: Edinburgh University Press, 2007) 3:84-94.

Mackenzie, Agnes Mure. *The Process of Literature: An Essay Towards Some Reconsiderations* (London: Allen & Unwin, 1929).

McMillan, Dorothy Porter. 'Heroines and Writers' in Caroline Gonda (ed.), *Tea and Leg-Irons: New Feminist Readings from Scotland* (London: Open Letters, 1992) 17-30.

Manning, Susan. '"Belonging with Edwin": Writing the History of Scottish Women's Writers', *Scottish Literary Journal*, supplement 48 (Spring 1998) 1-9.

Miller, J. E. *Rebel Women: Feminism, Modernism and the Edwardian Novel* (London: Virago, 1994).

Mitchell, Hannah, Geoffrey Mitchell (ed.). *The Hard Way Up: The Autobiography of Hannah Mitchell, Suffragette and Rebel* (London: Faber & Faber, 1968).

Mitchison, Naomi, Isobel Murray (ed.). 'Beyond This Limit' *in Beyond This Limit: Selected Shorter Fiction* (1935; Edinburgh: Scottish Academic Press, 1986) 1-81.

Moon, Lorna, Glenda Norquay (ed.). *The Collected Works of Lorna Moon* (Edinburgh: Black and White Publishing, 2002).

'Moore, Edward' (pseud. Edwin Muir). *We Moderns: Enigmas and Guesses* (London: Allen and Unwin, 1918).

Morrison, Nancy Brysson. *True Minds: The Marriage of Thomas and Jane Welsh Carlyle,* (London: J. M. Dent & Co., 1974).

Mudge, Patricia R. 'A Quorum of Willas', *Chapman* 71 (1992-93) 1-7.

Muir, Edwin. *An Autobiography* (London: Hogarth Press, 1954)

Muir, Edwin (with a personal memoir by George Mackay Brown and an introduction by Peter Butter). *An Autobiography* (Edinburgh: Canongate, 1993).

Muir, Edwin. 'Bolshevism and Calvinism', *European Quarterly* 1 (1934) 3-11.

Muir, Edwin. *John Knox: Portrait of a Calvinist* (London: Jonathan Cape, 1929).

Muir, Edwin (with a preface by T. S. Eliot). *Selected Poems* (London: Faber and Faber, 1966).

Muir, Edwin. *The Story & the Fable: An Autobiography* (London: George G. Harrap & Co., 1940).

Muir, Edwin. 'Translating from the German', part I (part II by Willa Muir) in Reuben A. Brower (ed.), *On Translation* (Cambridge, Mass.: Harvard U. Press, 1959) 94-96.

Murray, Isobel 'Novelists of the Renaissance' in Craig (ed.), *The History of Scottish Literature* (1987) 4:103-17.

Murray, Nicholas. *Kafka* (London: Little, Brown, 2004).

Nicholson, Virginia. *Among the Bohemians: Experiments in Living 1900-1939* (2002; London: Penguin, 2003).

Normand, Tom. *The Modern Scot: Modernism and Nationalism in Scottish Art 1928–1955* (Aldershot: Ashgate, 2000).

Perry, Ruth. Email to Aileen Christianson on *Living with Ballads*, 23 September 2005.

Pick, J. B. 'Introduction' to *Imagined Corners* (Edinburgh: Canongate, 1987).

Pilditch, Jan. '"And so my days are full": the letters of Catherine Carswell' in Anderson (ed.), *Opening the Doors: The Achievement of Catherine Carswell* (2001) 51-63.

Riach, Alan. *Representing Scotland in Literature, Popular Culture and Iconography The Masks of a Modern Nation* (Basingstoke: Palgrave Macmillan, 2005).

Robertson, Ritchie. 'Edwin Muir' in Craig (ed.), *The History of Scottish Literature* (1987) 4:135-46.

Robertson, Ritchie. 'Edwin Muir as European Poet' in C. J. M. MacLachlan and D. S. Robb (eds.), *Edwin Muir Centenary Assessments* (Aberdeen: A.S.L.S., 2000) 102-16.

Robb, David S. 'The Published Novels of Willa Muir' in Joachim Schwend and Horst Drescher (eds.), *Studies in Scottish Fiction: Twentieth Century* (Frankfurt am Man: Peter Lang, 1990) 149-61.

Ross, Ethel. Letter to Aileen Christianson, [n.d.] 1999.

Scott, George N. '"Peerie Willa": A Voice of Scotland', *Chapman* 27/28 (1980) 38-43.

Scott, Walter. 'Lochinvar', Robert Crawford and Mick Imlah (eds.), *The New Penguin Book of Scottish Verse* (Harmondsworth: Allen Lane Penguin, 2000) 319-20.

Shepherd, Nan. *A Pass in the Grampians* (1933), repbd. in *The Grampian Quartet* (Edinburgh: Canongate, 1996).

Shepherd, Nan. *The Weatherhouse* (1930), repbd. in *The Grampian Quartet* (Edinburgh: Canongate, 1996).

Simon, Sherry. *Gender in Translation: Cultural Identity and the Politics of Transmission* (London: Routledge, 1996).

Simon, Sherry. 'Gender in Translation' in France, Peter (ed.), *The Oxford Guide to Literature in Translation* (Oxford: Oxford University Press, 2000) 26-33.

Smith, Alison. 'And Women Created Women: Carswell, Shepherd and Muir, and the Self-made Woman', in Christopher Whyte (ed.), *Gendering the Nation: Studies in Modern Scottish Literature* (Edinburgh: Edinburgh University Press, 1995) 25-47.

Smith, G. Gregory. *Scottish Literature: Character and Influence* (London: MacMillan, 1919).

Smith, Sidonie, *A Poetics of Women's Autobiography* (Bloomington: Indiana University Press, 1987).

Soukup, Catriona. 'Willa in Wartime', *Chapman* 71 (1992-93) 20-24.

Soukup, Lumir. 'Belonging', *Chapman* 71 (1992-93) 29-33.

Spark, Muriel. *The Ballad of Peckham Rye* (1960; Harmondsworth: Penguin, 1988).

Speirs, John. *The Scots Literary Tradition* (London: Chatto & Windus, 1940).

Steiner, George. *After Babel: Aspects of Language and Translation.* (London: OUP, 1975).

Steiner, George. 'Introduction', Franz Kafka, Willa and Edwin Muir (trans.), *The Trial* (London: Everyman, 1992) v-xviii.

Strachey, Barbara. 'New Preface', Ray Strachey, *The Cause: A Short History of the Women's Movement in Great Britain* (London: Virago, 1978) 3-4.

Strachey, Ray. *The Cause: A Short History of the Women's Movement in Great Britain* (London: G. Bell and Sons Ltd., 1928).

Sweet, Matthew. *Inventing the Victorians* (London: Faber and Faber, 2001).

Turnell, Martin. 'Virginia Woolf', *Horizon* vol. 6, no. 31 (July 1942):44-56.

Vanacker, Sabine. 'Autobiography and Orality: The Work of Modernist Women Writers' in Broughton and Anderson (eds.), *Women's Lives / Women's Times. New Essays on Auto/Biography* (Albany, NY: State University of New York Press, 1997) 179-202.

Wittig, Kurt. *The Scottish Tradition in Literature* (Edinburgh: Mercat Press, 1978).

Waugh, Evelyn. 'Turning over new leaves', *Vogue* 72 (17 Oct. 1928) 59, 86 (part cited in '90 years of *Vogue* arts', *Vogue* (Dec. 2006) 108).

Wilk, Christopher (ed.). *Modernism: Designing a New World 1914-1939* (London: V & A publications, 2006).

Woolf, Virginia. 'Geraldine and Jane' in *The Common Reader Second Series* (London: Hogarth Press, 1932) 186-201.

Woolf, Virginia. 'Modern Fiction' in *The Common Reader* (London: Hogarth Press, 1925) 184-95; also in Leonard Woolf (ed.), *Collected Essays* (London: Hogarth Press, 1966) 2:103-10.

Woolf, Virginia. *Mr. Bennett and Mrs. Brown* (London: Hogarth Press, 1924).

Woolf, Virginia. *A Room of One's Own* (London: Hogarth Press, 1929; Harmondsworth: Penguin Books, 1945).

# Index

Willa Muir's published writings are listed under their individual titles. Page references for these works, including her journals and letters, are listed where they are being discussed, not where they are only being quoted. There is no single entry for feminism as discussion of this topic permeates the book.

## E

Einstein, Albert 33, 34, 39, 77
Eliot, T. S. 21, 22, 33, 34, 35, 39, 40, 42,
    51, 89, 133, 134, 221
Ellis, Havelock 90
Elphinstone, Margaret 61, 81, 86, 87, 92,
    98, 106, 140, 143, 148, 150, 151,
    153, 184
*Encyclopaedia Britannica* 89
Enfantin, Barthélemy-Prosper 97
Enlightenment 2
'Ephemeridae' 52, 162, 163, 221-22
Ernst, Lothar 16
Essentialism 61, 62, 69, 70, 81, 187
Europe, Europeans 124, 133, 143, 145,
    148
*European Quarterly* 124

## F

Fairlie, Margaret 21
Fawcett, Millicent 56
Ferguson, John 42, 167
Ferrier, Susan 22
Feuchtwanger, Lion 16, 17, 21, 85, 126,
    129, 132, 193, 196, 197
Fitzgerald, Scott 36
*5 Songs from the Auvergnat* 16, 161, 164,
    230
Forster, E. M. 90
Foucault, Michel 146
Frazer, J. G. 33, 34, 35, 39, 40, 63, 89,
    90, 91, 114
Free Church of Scotland 74, 87, 93, 113,
    115
*Freeman* 14, 15, 125, 221
Freeman, Alan 100, 109
Freud, Sigmund 2, 28, 33, 34, 37, 39, 40,
    58, 63, 64, 66, 67, 69, 89, 90, 91,
    113, 154
Fry, Roger 43
'Fur Coat, The' 47
Futurism, Futurists 34, 35, 39, 49

## G

Galison, Peter 77
Galsworthy, John 36, 90
Garda, Lake 15, 129, 180
Gaskell, Elizabeth 183
Germans, Germany 15, 16, 21
    *see also* Willa Muir
Gibbon, Lewis Grassic 20, 44, 45, 51, 52,
    71, 72
Gide, André 159
Gifford Lectures 89
Glasgow 13, 30, 43, 73, 74, 90, 121, 167,
    177, 189
*Glasgow Herald* 4, 17, 41, 42, 43, 74, 85
Glaeser, Ernst 16
Glenesk 8
Grampians 49
Gray, Alexander 41
Greenock 26
Greenwich Mean Time 77, 95
Greer, Germaine 154
Grierson, Flora 22
Grieve, Christopher 16, 19, 21, 31, 41,
    42, 43, 44, 51, 72, 121, 220
    *see also* Hugh MacDiarmid
Grieve, Peggy 16, 31
Grieve, Valda 29, 31, 72, 121
Guinness Poetry Award 25
Gunn, Neil 44, 45, 52, 62, 71, 89, 99,188
Gypsy Hill Teacher Training College 12

## H

H. D. 39, 180
Haldane, Elizabeth 56
Hamburger, Michael 25
Hamilton, Cicely 56, 69
Hamish Hamilton (publishers) 22
Hampstead, London 19, 20, 21, 103,
124, 140, 141, 142, 143, 145, 153,
158, 182, 183, 192, 197
Hardy, Forsyth 25, 171
Hardy, Oliver 21
Hargreaves, Dorothy
    *see* Dorothy Muir

# T

*Time and Tide* 56, 68, 69
*Times Literary Supplement* 68, 99, 104, 120
Townhead Elementary Board School 8
Tranter, Nigel 165
Turnell, Martin 35
'Twa Corbies' 164

# U

Unst, Shetland 4, 8, 30
*Usurpers, The* 3, 22, 25, 66, 86, 123, 129, 130, 140, 147-54, 158, 169, 180, 181

# V

Vanacker, Sabine 180, 187
Victoria, Victorian 33, 36, 43, 48, 49, 50, 52, 65, 69, 72, 73, 74, 75, 76, 77, 80, 107, 112, 183, 186
Vienna 18, 133, 193
Virago (publishers) 44
*Voice of Scotland, The* 29
Vorticism 34, 39

# W

Washington, Booker T. 40
Waugh, Evelyn 35, 242
Wells, H. G. 36
West, Rebecca 36, 46, 55, 69
Wharton, Edith 36, 43
Whistle Binkie 41, 42, 43
White House, Dormansland, Surrey 17
Whitman, Walt 39
Whyte, James 20, 46, 47, 48, 53, 76
Wiessenseel, Hilde 21
Wilson, Edmund and Elena 23
Winsloe, Christa 16
Wittig, Kurt 44
Wolf, Naomi 154
Women's Debating Society 10
Women's Suffrage Society 10, 155, 190

*Women: An Inquiry* 1, 16, 24, 43, 55, 56, 57, 58, 59, 60, 61, 62, 67, 68, 69, 70, 80, 81, 82, 107, 118, 119, 150, 154, 155, 159, 226
Woolf, Leonard 16, 43, 60
Woolf, Virginia 14, 33, 34, 35, 36, 39, 40, 42, 43, 52, 60, 66, 69, 93, 103, 183

# Y

Yeats, W. B. 41
Yorsten, John 8
Young, Douglas 20, 171

Willa Muir, 1933.